# DAIRY DIARY

# FAVOURITE GARDEN BIRDS

ACKNOWLEDGEMENTS

Executive editor    *Nick Rowe*
Editor              *Debbie Robertson*
Designer            *Alyson Kyles*
Production          *Priti Kothary, Mo Adams*

Printed & bound in the UK by
Butler and Tanner Ltd

This book was designed, edited and
produced by Eaglemoss Publications Ltd,
using material first published as the partwork
*The Country Bird Collection*.

Published by
Eaglemoss Consumer Publications Ltd,
Electra House, Electra Way,
Crewe Business Park,
Crewe, Cheshire CW1 6WZ
Telephone 01270 270050
Website www.dairydiary.co.uk

# CONTENTS

# Introduction

Whether you live in a town or the country, birds treat the trees, shrubs and grass in your garden as an extension of the local woodland, hedgerows, parks and pastures – somewhere to roost at night, to nest in spring and to find food. Your neatly-mown lawn is a carpetful of earthworms to a blackbird, song thrush or starling. And if there are a few overgrown areas, so much the better. A clump of nettles or brambles harbours a feast of insects and spiders for blue tits and wrens.

*Greenfinches have thrived ever since they discovered the benefits of feeding from seed-dispensers in gardens.*

## The Garden Faithful

In *Favourite Garden Birds* you'll discover exactly what birds are looking for in a garden. Size is no object – if you have only a small patch, you can still attract a mixed bunch of birds. The regular cast – the robins, great and blue tits, dunnocks, thrushes, blackbirds, house sparrows, chaffinches and starlings – are always firm favourites. But you won't necessarily see precisely the same birds all the time. There is a rapid turnover of individuals from year to year, as young birds appear on the scene and older ones fly away or perish.

## Surprise Cameo Roles

Guest appearances from less familiar birds add to the excitement. The photographs and illustrations in *Favourite Garden Birds* will help you to identify the unexpected arrivals. The birds that may drop in depend, to some extent, on where you live. If your house backs on to woodland, for example, you may well get a great spotted woodpecker or a jay visiting your bird-table occasionally.

Because the castlist changes with the seasons too, there are separate chapters for spring, summer, autumn and winter. You'll see the usual suspects more or less all year round. But many birds roam about during the colder months in search of food and are only too glad to seek temporary refuge in a bird-friendly garden. You never know when you may be charmed by a flock of long-tailed tits pausing to refuel on your peanut-feeder.

*Without a well-stocked bird-table at their disposal, it would probably be touch and go whether these hungry birds could find enough to eat while there is a carpet of snow on the ground.*

## Behind the Scenes

*Favourite Garden Birds* encourages you to look beyond the bird-feeders and see what birds are doing elsewhere. If you watch patiently, you can often work out where they are nesting – their frequent comings and goings give the game away.

You'll soon learn from experience that things are not always as they seem in bird world. The 'friendly' robin, for example, which keeps you company when you're digging, can be a bit of a tyrant to other birds in the garden. And you'll find that 'your' regulars are rarely loyal to your garden alone. More than likely, they are cleaning up at feeding stations all over the neighbourhood.

## Helping Hand

As this book makes clear, welcoming birds to your garden is a rewarding activity. You not only gain pleasure from watching them, but you also have the satisfaction of knowing you have made their lives easier – your help can be the difference between life and death.

Many birds have come to rely on regular garden handouts, especially in frosty weather, when food and water are hard to find. Once you start putting out bird-food and begin to attract a steady stream of

*With his feathers puffed up against the cold and only a few shrivelled blackberries to eat, this chaffinch needs to find a bird-friendly garden fast.*

*Leaving some prickly bushes in your garden may entice a few long-tailed tits to build their feather-lined nests there.*

clients, you should always keep the supplies well topped up. Although few birds find all they eat in one garden, your support is invaluable.

We hope that all the insights and advice you find in *Favourite Garden Birds* will throw a fresh light on the birds that share your garden space with you – and inspire you to take an even keener interest in their fascinating lives.

*You can think yourself lucky if you catch a glimpse of the white rump of a jay as it beats a hasty retreat to nearby woodland, after a flying visit to your garden.*

CHAPTER 1 · SPRING

# The Chaffinch

*In spring, the cock chaffinch is not only one of the prettiest birds in the garden, but also one of the most vocal, repeating his song more than 3000 times a day*

Chaffinches vie with wrens and blackbirds for the title of the most common songbird in Britain. They regularly sing and nest in gardens during the spring and visit bird-tables during the winter.

## BOLDLY DOES IT

It is easy to take the male chaffinch's brilliant spring plumage for granted because he is such a familiar part of the garden and country scene. But the slate-blue helmet over his crown and nape and the chestnut breast are well worth admiring. You can see him best when he selects a prominent perch, puffs out his chest and sings his short song. Then he flies away in just as business-like a manner to find food or collect nesting material.

► *A male chaffinch in full breeding plumage sings from a regular song post within his territory. He starts singing in early February and there is no stopping him until early July.*

## Dowdy female

Among chaffinches, the male gets all the brightly coloured feathers. The slightly smaller hen chaffinch is a sober olive-brown on top and paler on her front. Although plain, she does share his mossy green rump and two conspicuous broad white stripes on each wing. Her subdued colouring serves as good camouflage, especially when she is sitting on her eggs. The cock chaffinch has the lovely singing voice too. The hen's vocal range is limited to simple warning and contact calls.

The eye-catching cock bird and his dowdy hen both revel in the warmth of the sun. When they can snatch time off from territorial and nesting duties, male and female chaffinches like nothing better than to lie on the ground with outstretched wings and indulge in a spell of sun bathing.

# Surviving the Winter

BY THE END OF July, once breeding is over and done with for another year, the irrepressible cock chaffinch pipes down at last. But you still hear the *pink-pink* contact notes and the *chip-chip* flight call uttered by both sexes throughout the year.

Come autumn, the territorial cock chaffinch of summer has adopted a more sociable, quieter lifestyle to help him to get through the lean, dank wintry days ahead. After moulting, chaffinches abandon their territories and become more gregarious. They congregate in loose flocks, often with buntings on open farmland or with blue and great tits in woodland.

The woodland gang may also be joined by another social finch called a brambling, which is a winter visitor to Britain. Some male and female chaffinches, probably those arriving from the Continent to overwinter here, separate into single-sex groups.

### DIFFERENT DIET

Chaffinches spend most of the spring and summer foraging on the ground or in trees for insects. In April, they feast on swarms of honeydew-bloated aphids tapping into young sycamore leaves. But by autumn, flocks have

*male in winter*

*male in spring*

▲ *In a late-summer moult, a cock chaffinch exchanges his bright but worn-out old feathers for a new coat of duller greys and pinks for the winter.*

formed and start scouring woodland, fields, parks and gardens for seeds and grain. As dusk falls, the whole flock goes to roost together, often in evergreen trees, which offer better protection in cold and wet weather.

## Winter feeding

During the colder, shorter winter days, chaffinches are some of the greediest visitors to a bird-table, often eating the food that falls on to the ground underneath. Not agile enough to clamber over peanut-hangers, they will take melon, pumpkin and sunflower seeds from a seed-hopper and crack them with their strong beaks.

Otherwise chaffinches subsist on any grains and seeds they can find around farms and in the countryside. In years when beech trees produce beech mast, chaffinches flock to beech woods to eat the beechnuts out of their rough seed-cases in the leaf litter.

*beech mast*

# The Essence of Spring

HEARING A COCK chaffinch's merry voice ringing out around the garden in early February is one of the first heartwarming signs that the lighter, milder days of spring are not far off.

Then chaffinch flocks split up and male chaffinches go off to establish their territories, in preparation for the breeding season. In his territorial displays a male chaffinch sings his heart out to attract single females and keep rival suitors at bay.

Any unresolved singing contests between jealous males are generally decided by a boisterous scrap. In the old days, such aggressive behaviour was exploited by gamblers who used to organise cock-finch fights.

### IMPRESSING THE BIRDS

In his courtship display, a cock chaffinch picks out a likely partner and perches stiffly in front of her. By this time, the tips of his dull feathers have gradually worn away over the winter to reveal a vibrant slate-blue helmet over his crown and nape and a glowing chestnut breast. He raises the feathers on his crown into a low crest and turns his body slowly from side to side to show off his white shoulder straps and impress her.

### HER CHOICE

After pairing up, the hen chaffinch selects the site for their nest, usually low down in a shrub or in the fork of a tree near her mate's

▲ CLUES ON THE WING
*In flight, the chaffinch's two shoulder patches and wing bars stand out clearly against the dark wing feathers. The white trim to the tail feathers is another tell-tale identification sign.*

## A jolly good singer

A cock chaffinch's song rattles along with vigorous, uninhibited glee. He pelts out the same accelerating series of notes, *chip-chip-chip-chwee-chwee-tissi*, with great gusto, time and time again, usually ending with a flourishing *chooeo* – a final cheerio.

The song has been likened to a bowler running up to the wicket to deliver a ball in a cricket match. The first six notes are the footfalls of his run up and the last one is the ball sailing through the air after it leaves his hand. For the first few days, when a male starts to sing, there is no final *chooeo* to his audience. It is as though he forgets to release the ball on reaching the crease. But he soon gets the hang of it, and then there's no holding him back.

The whole song lasts for just two or three seconds, but may be repeated several times in a session. It is a simple lyric but, no matter how many times he performs his tune, it always sounds fresh and joyful.

❝ 'Tis spring, warm glows the south,
Chaffinch carries moss in his mouth
To filbert hedges all day long,
And charms the poet with
his beautiful song ❞

from *Birds' Nests* by **John Clare** (1793-1864)

favourite singing post. She also takes charge of building the nest. When the male is not singing or on guard duty, he may help her collect some pieces of nesting material but does not get involved in the building work.

## FAMILY MATTERS

Into her cosy cradle, the hen lays four to six greenish-blue eggs with purply-brown blotches. For the two weeks that the hen is incubating the eggs, the cock bird waits on her devotedly.

As soon as the chicks hatch, they start gaping to reveal a carmine and orange lining to their mouth which spurs their parents into feeding them. Both start collecting beakful after beakful of insects to fill the ever-open mouths. On average, a brood can swallow 4000 caterpillars a week. In 14 days, the fledglings look like their mother and are ready to fly the nest.

▲ **WELL-DISGUISED NURSERY**
*A hen chaffinch's muted plumage makes her hard to spot under the dappled shade where she is incubating her eggs. She sits tight through most disturbances near the nest and in the worst storms.*

## Neatest nest

The female chaffinch's nest is an exquisite masterpiece of bird architecture. She weaves a compact cup of moss, dried grass and rootlets, and lines it neatly with hair and feathers. Then she decorates the mossy sides with pieces of lichen, stripped from trees nearby, which she painstakingly fixes in place with hairs and spiders' webs. It takes her a fortnight to complete but by the time she is done, her nest merges almost invisibly into its surroundings.

# The Wren

*Instantly recognised wherever it goes, famous yet able to shun the limelight, the wren's PR is enough to make superstars and royalty green with envy*

The cock wren is a little bird with a big personality and a phenomenally powerful voice. The contrast between his tiny body and the enormous volume of sound he emits when singing his shrill lyrics is stupendous. His wings and tail vibrate with the effort and excitement. When he gets carried away while courting, a male wren will sing even with a beak full of food or nesting material.

### IN GREAT VOICE

A male wren sings almost throughout the year to keep control of his small territory. Neighbouring wrens often engage in hostile banter and settle unresolved disagreements with a bit of rough and tumble on the ground. As soon as the fight is over, the victor flies off singing triumphantly.

▶ *Whenever you see the blur of a tiny rotund bird with stripy brown feathers and a stumpy pert tail dodging in and out of cover you can be sure that it is a wren.*

## Feathered mice

Rather than being shy or secretive, most of the time wrens are simply getting on with their lives unseen. Like mice, they weave through tightly knotted tangles of briars, stems and roots in hedges and bushes looking for food.

'*They make a thicket fancy alone*
*Can creep through with*
*the mouse and wren*'

from *Fifty Faggots* by **Edward Thomas** (1878-1917)

# An Undercover Agent

WHILE THE WREN is one of the smallest birds in Britain, it is also one of the commonest. Incredibly, there are over 8 million breeding here each summer. Yet sightings are rare enough to be memorable because it generally stays hidden away in a nether world of hedges, scrub and brambles. Wrens can colonise a gorse bush growing on sand dunes or a clump of heather on an upland hillside as readily as build a nest in a garden shed.

The wren is commonly found in gardens, especially in suburbia, where it lives in shrubberies and hedges. It is likely to give itself away by spitting out a churring *tserr-tserr* rebuke if you disturb it. You may only notice your tiny cock-tailed neighbour when it darts out in front of you as it whirrs from bush to bush or when you are fetching some logs from a wood stack where it has been busily searching for creepy-crawlies.

## EVERY NOOK AND CRANNY

Thanks to its small size, the wren has cornered a niche market. It can raid the nooks and crannies, which other birds are too big to reach, where lots of spiders, woodlice, centipedes, flies, aphids, caterpillars and beetles live.

In woodland, wrens examine every crack and crevice in the bark on a tree's lower trunk and branches for hidden food but rarely venture very high up into the leafy branches. They also often hang around ditches where the stagnant water attracts plenty of flying insects. It is just as well that the wren is so light and buoyant: it is able to swim if it falls into the water. For

▲ *To flirt with the local females in spring, a cock wren has to break cover. He finds an open perch, puffs out his chest and fires off his musical lyrics at a breathless pace.*

most of the year, the wren can find all the food it needs by skulking among the undergrowth but in winter it may have to seek extra rations from a bird-table.

## Winter woes

For this puffed-up wren cowering in a frosty ditch, life looks pretty bleak. A spell of wintry weather is a dangerous time for all wrens – many die from starvation because the creepy-crawlies they eat are forced into hiding or locked in a sheet of ice. Hypothermia is also a threat; because they are tiny, wrens have a relatively large surface area from which they can lose heat. Small drops in numbers are soon made up by rearing two broods each summer. Even when populations fell by up to 80% during the icy winter of 1962/63, numbers were largely back to normal by 1965.

‘ *Now is the winter of our discontent* ’

from *Richard III, Act 1, Scene 1* by **William Shakespeare** (1564-1616)

# Old-fashioned Family

THERE IS A VICTORIAN-STYLE division of labour in a wren partnership – the cock bird provides the family home but lets his hen bring up the chicks alone. He only gets involved again in response to calls for help after the fledglings have left the nest.

### LATE START

Wrens get around to nesting quite late in the spring, from the second half of April onwards. Mysteriously, it is the cock wren that is the compulsive nest builder. He selects a number of sites in his territory, usually no more than three to four feet off the ground, that offer sound anchorage and privacy for his nests. Thick creeper climbing over houses, trees or fences, ramshackle outbuildings, greenhouses and sheds, dense briar thickets and chinks in stone walls all fit the builder's brief.

It takes the cock bird roughly three days to fashion each weatherproof hollow ball from dried leaves and bracken, dried grass and moss. He leaves an entrance hole towards the top, reinforces its lower rim with grass and, working from inside, adds a porch to keep out raindrops.

#### ▲ ABSENT FATHER
*With a ready-built nest and her mate on territorial patrol, the hen is free to put all her energy into being sole brooder and provider to their hungry chicks. One busy hen was once recorded bringing food to the nest 1117 times in 15 hours of daylight. All her hard work is rewarded when her large brood is fledged and ready to fly the nest in 15 to 17 days.*

#### ◄ PASSIONATE ABOUT NESTING
*The cock wren often constructs five or six unfinished domed structures, known as cock's nests. Then he chases a likely female, trying to impress her with his banner display of raised wings and fluttering flight. An interested female is invited to inspect his nests.*

◄ **EMPTY-NESTING**

*Armed with a tasty morsel, a female wren tries to bribe her hungry fledglings to leave the nest for the first time. Then, as many parents discover, once their brood is out, it is hard to get them to come home at bedtime. Wrens are often heard cajoling their youngsters back to the safe shelter of their old nest to roost at night.*

His nests built, the cock wren goes courting a mate. He escorts his prospective partner to view his nests. If she approves, she lines her favourite with feathers before laying five to seven white eggs, with a light dusting of red specks, in it.

SIMULTANEOUS FAMILIES

Having set up his first mate in a snug nest, the cock wren sets off in search of another hen to occupy one of his other nests and raise a second family. He may use yet another of his vacant nests to roost in at night.

Meanwhile, the first hen settles down to incubate her eggs on her own for 14 or 15 days. The domed nest insulates her and the eggs (and later the chicks) from everything the weather can throw at them, especially when she has to go off to find food. After hatching, the nest is crammed with helpless nestlings, flashing their bright yellow mouths at their mother, noisily demanding food from her all day long.

'*Among the dwellings framed by birds*
*In field or forest with nice care,*
*Is none that with the little Wren's*
*In snugness may compare*'

from *A Wren's Nest* by **William Wordsworth** (1770-1850)

## Cheat's nest

Cock wrens often choose quaint nesting sites. It was one cock wren's lucky day when he spied this thick woollen sock hanging up in a garden shed. By using it to hold one of his nests, he could skip the laborious business of adding a roof and porch to the nest, saving himself time and effort in his hectic building and breeding schedule.

# The King of Birds

THE SCIENTIFIC NAME for the wren is *Troglodytes troglodytes*, meaning cave dweller. It is an ancient title, presumably awarded because little light penetrates into a wren's nest, which is built in shadowy places.

Not surprisingly for an extremely popular bird, the wren has had many local nicknames. In Celtic areas, it was the *Wranny* or *Wran*. Thanks to its short tail it was *Scutty* across the south of England or *Stumpy Toddy* (small, short thing) in the northwest. From old nursery rhymes there came the familiar *Jenny Wren*.

### AN AWESOME REPUTATION

As the star of many legends, the wren has acquired a reputation for being everything from a brave hero and a pilloried traitor to king of the birds and wife of the robin. To the Druids, the wren was a sacred, regal bird that they used as a messenger. In Celtic lore it was prophetic – various portents were construed from the direction of its call. At the same time, it was believed to be a bird of the Underworld with links to the dead.

▲ *A cock wren finds an open perch and stretches up to his full height to keep an eye on what is going on in his domain. At any moment, he might burst into song – and lustily repeat a series of high-pitched warbles with a trilling finale, over and over again – to let others know he is there.*

'*And now and then a twittering wren would light On a thin twig which hardly bore the weight of such delight*'

from *Charmides* by **Oscar Wilde** (1854-1900)

## WRENNING DAYS

Long ago, in pagan times, the wren and the holly tree symbolised winter. Killing a wren and beating a drum on 21 December (the winter solstice) were believed to drive away the dark days and usher in the light.

In Christian times, this solstice ritual was adapted as retribution for the wren's role in the stoning of St Stephen, the first Christian martyr. Its piercing call was believed to have betrayed Stephen when he was hiding from the Roman soldiers in a bush.

On St Stephen's Day (Boxing Day) in parts of Ireland, boys used to go hunting for a wren and stone it to death. Then they would parade its corpse through the village, beating their drums and singing:

*The wren, the wren, king of all birds*
*St Stephen's day was caught in the furze*
*'Though he be little, his honour is great*
*And so, good people, pray*
*give us a treat*

## TREACHEROUS BIRD

Wrens appear to have got their own back for the Boxing Day killings. It is said that the little bird warned the Vikings of advancing Irish soldiers by beating its wings on their shields. It gave the game away again when it alerted Cromwell's army to the Irish troops before the Battle of Kinsale by pecking crumbs off a drum.

## WORN WITH PRIDE

According to a short anonymous Christian verse, the wren's perky tail has God's blessing:

*When Christ was born in Bethlehem*
*There perched beside his crib a wren*
*Who by the little Saviour laid*
*Two feathers close beside His Head.*
*This did he many times until*
*The softest pillow he had made.*
*The Christ Child smiled most lovingly*
*And touched the brown tail tenderly*
*And that in very truth is why*
*The small bird bears his tail so high!*

# Folklore and legend

● It seems the wren was condemned to live in dark undergrowth after it cheated in a contest to elect the king of all the birds. It was decreed that the bird which could fly the highest would win the crown. The cheeky wren hid itself among the feathers of a mighty eagle and hitched a lift into the air. Soaring higher and higher, the eagle looked assured of the title. But just as it was tiring, the wren emerged and flew higher still to claim the crown.

● In legend, the brave wren fetched fire from hell for mankind.

● Many misfortunes were said to befall you if you killed a wren, from breaking a bone to being hit by lightning. Touching a wren on its nest reputedly caused an itchy rash called the Fire of St Lawrence.

● The story goes that one day in the 7th century, St Malo hung up his cloak on a branch as he was pruning vines in a vineyard. When he went back to pick it up he found a wren had laid an egg in the hood. Being a compassionate man, he did not disturb the tiny bird until her brood was reared. The miracle was that it did not rain in the meantime.

● As part of a stained-glass panel in the Zouche Chapel at York Minster, the wren on the left has been stalking that spider in its web since the 15th century.

● Traditionally, a feather of a wren killed on New Year's Day protects a sailor from drowning in a shipwreck.

● In Christian iconography, the wren could take the place of the dove in symbolising the Holy Ghost in the Holy Trinity – ultimate proof of how revered the tiny bird once was.

# Crowded sleep-over

One frosty night in Norfolk, 61 wrens were seen entering a nest-box which measured just 114 x 140 x 146mm (4½ x 5½ x 5¾in). Such communal roosting is a great way of conserving body heat. As small birds, wrens are very susceptible to heat loss, but when they huddle up together their little bodies keep each other warm. It is difficult to imagine how so many tiny birds managed to unpack themselves again in the morning.

# The Blue Tit

*Watching the high jinks of the irrepressible blue tit around the garden, on the bird-table or in the woods, is always a delight*

As the only resident blue-and-yellow bird in the garden, the blue tit is easy to spot as it flutters from bush to tree, visits the bird-table or flies in and out of a nest-box. Blue tits are fearless, entertaining gymnasts too, whether going topsy-turvy on a bird-feeder or dangling from a wispy twig.

It's also worth watching a flock of blue tits work its way through a wood in winter. What appears to be random skipping over the branches of the trees turns out, on closer inspection, to be an eager search for insects hidden in or under the bark.

### TOUGH COOKIES

The blue tit may be small, nimble and cheeky, but it can be a spiky little bird too – more than able to stand up for itself. If challenged or thwarted, a blue tit expresses its displeasure in no uncertain terms. When sitting on eggs, a female blue tit *hisses* bravely at any intruders, and a pair will *churrrr* furiously if their flight path from food source to nest is blocked while feeding their chicks.

▲ *When a blue tit is excited or angry, the bright blue feathers on the crown of its head stand up in a low crest and its tail flicks constantly.*

## Early days

As yet, this fledgling blue tit still has its juvenile plumage, which is greyer and a duller yellow than the colourful feathers of the adults. Its cheeks are also washed with pale yellow rather than white. Young blue tits only moult out to adult plumage and get their blue skull-caps in the autumn.

After leaving the nest in late June, juvenile blue tits are particularly vulnerable during their first few days of independence. At first, the fledglings continue to call for their parents, who go on feeding them on demand for two to three weeks after they leave home. This gives the youngsters time to master flying, find their bearings and get the hang of catching food for themselves. Even so, on average, nine out of ten fledglings that graduate from the nest will almost certainly die before the start of the next breeding season.

# No Leaf Goes Unturned

TRACKING DOWN ENOUGH caterpillars, moths, aphids and tiny spiders to eat occupies most of the blue tit's time, especially in the spring when it has chicks in the nest. Being neat and nimble, a blue tit can go farther out along flimsier twigs than most other birds to seek out insects and spiders lurking in the tiniest crevices.

Before many insects appear on the scene, blue tits will attack catkins and fruit blossom looking for sweet nectar and protein-rich pollen, which can make them unpopular with some fruit growers. Later on, the blue tit partly makes up for any damage it has caused in the spring by catching thousands of caterpillars and other insect pests that might damage the fruit crop. Favourite foods are apple sawfly maggots, apple blossom weevil grubs, codling moth caterpillars and green oak tortrix moth caterpillars.

### WINTER IN THE GARDEN

During the winter, blue tits have to be less choosy about what they eat, and rely on peanuts, seeds and suet put out on bird-tables. The blue tit's feet are capable of gripping the wire mesh of a bird-feeder firmly enough

to hang from it upside down. Strong toes are also useful for steadying peanuts while pecking off bits and for turning over leaves and twigs to uncover insects concealed beneath.

▲ *A blue tit needs to eat up to half its body weight in food each day just to survive. With a nestful of gaping beaks to feed as well, it has to catch every moth it finds.*

## Grub for chicks

To find the 1000 or more caterpillars it takes every day to satisfy their large brood, parent blue tits must have a plentiful source of nutrient-rich food in close proximity to their nest. This is why the hatching of their eggs is usually timed to coincide with the mass hatching of moth caterpillars on oak and apple trees in the spring.

'*Mark the tree where the bluecap, tootle tee, sings a glee**' *

from *Song's Eternity* by **John Clare** (1793-1864)
(* an unaccompanied song)

# One Large Family

RATHER THAN DIVIDE their breeding efforts between two or three broods, blue tits opt to put all their eggs in one basket, as it were, and raise a single family each year. In early April, a male blue tit starts courting his prospective partner with song and dance. He performs a fluttery flying display, rather like a butterfly, to impress the female. If she is interested, she cheeps and squats low, begging him to feed her.

Only when the male has made the grade as a good provider does the female follow him to one of his pre-selected nesting sites. If it meets with her approval, she will get on with building a nest, laying her eggs and sitting on them until they hatch.

### PIPING UP AND DOWN

On hatching, the chicks are tiny, pink and helpless; they have no feathers and their eyes are shut. But straight away, they can feebly raise their heads, open their huge yellow beaks and *peep* weakly to demand food from their parents.

Soon they have to pipe down while the adults are away from the nest, to avoid attracting the interest of predators. Only when they sense a parent bird returning to the nest with food do the chicks start squawking loudly through gaping beaks until they are fed.

*Guardian of his territory*

**▼ QUITE A CLUTCH**
*The female does all the nest-building, forming a mossy cup in a nesting-box, tree-hole or stone wall. When it is ready, she lays one egg a day until her clutch of seven to 15 red-speckled eggs – ten on average – is complete. Only then does she start incubating the eggs, so all the chicks hatch at roughly the same time, about 14 days after laying.*

During the breeding season, normally sociable blue tits become aggressively territorial. To see off intruders, a male blue tit raises his crown feathers, fans his tail, spreads his wings and swears loudly.

'*Lithest, gaudiest Harlequin! Prettiest Tumbler ever seen!*'

from *The Kitten and Falling Leaves* by **William Wordsworth** (1770-1850)

# Safety in numbers

A group of blue tits enjoys a splash in a shallow pool to freshen up their feathers. Except during the breeding season, blue tits are quite sociable. Nest-leavers often form into small flocks for the winter – sometimes mixing with other tits and familiar garden birds, such as chaffinches. Not only is there safety in numbers, but hunting for food in a gang is more efficient too – an insect uncovered but missed by one bird can be grabbed by another.

## ▲ SHORT FLIGHTS

*Designed for agility rather than speed, the blue tit's short, rounded wings are ideal for flitting between branches in woodland and gardens. It has a jerky way of flying, alternately flapping its wings to gain height, then gliding down.*

## ◄ FEED ME! NO, ME! ME!

*On its return to the nest with food, the parent bird is greeted by a clamorous horde of chicks, all demanding to be fed. Their gaping orange mouths are the parent's spur to stuff a caterpillar into one beak, then fly off to find more food.*

## ▲ ONE MONTH ON

*Just 16 to 22 days after hatching, the young blue tits are feathered and ready to leave the nest. Fledglings from the same brood tend to hang out together in small groups during their first winter.*

21

# The Great Tit

*Animated and endearing, the great tit's performances in the dramas of birdlife taking place in gardens every day are more entertaining than most television soap operas*

There is never a dull moment when you are watching a colourful, acrobatic great tit as it patrols a garden or rifles through a wood in spring. One moment it is searching busily for insects on a tree trunk before dashing back to a nearby nesting-box to feed its family; the next it might be throwing its weight around on a bird-table or hanging cheekily from a peanut-feeder.

## THE SOUND TRACK

Great tits are never silent for long. They chatter all the time with regular, rapid bursts of reedy, high-pitched *tsee-tsee* contact notes. Most males have a bewildering vocabulary of about 32 different calls – especially early in the year when they are still warming up their voices.

▶ *Brightly coloured and boldly marked, the great tit is easy to follow as it moves about the garden, looking for food and bossing other small birds about.*

## Bit of a bully

Great tits have a reputation for being aggressive and bullying, especially towards their tiny cousins, the blue tits. On bird-tables, open warfare often breaks out between domineering great tits and other small birds, including blue tits. The great tits usually muscle their way in and emerge with the spoils. (Being bigger is less of an advantage for finding food in the wild: while featherlight blue tits can feed along the flimsiest upper branches, the heavier, less nimble great tits have to stay nearer the ground, where there is stiffer competition.)

Calculating great tits even resort to daylight robbery. In autumn they follow coal and marsh tits through the woods, spying on where they are storing food for the winter. Then they brazenly raid these caches and steal the reserve supplies.

Tailor-made nesting-boxes can resolve rivalry for nest sites: great tits use those with 28mm (1¼in) entrance holes while blue tits use the 25mm (1in) ones.

# Nesting Affairs

MALE GREAT TITS get their nesting territories sorted out early on in the year, often in February. Each male defends his territory by singing and posturing. The head-up or pointing display, in which the male throws back his head and thrusts his chest forward to exaggerate the width of his belly stripe, is most intimidating. Females appear to favour males with a wide belly stripe and, in turn, they seem to make better fathers.

Generally, great tits nest in holes in rotting trees or in nesting-boxes. The male selects several sites, then takes his mate on a tour of inspection. She selects her favourite and demonstrates her approval by shivering her wings.

## MATERNAL ROLE

The female great tit gathers moss and dried grass to cover the base of the hole, then fashions a cup which she lines with hair and wool. Working on her own, it can take up to 20 days to complete. There she lays from five to 12 eggs, producing one every day, before starting to incubate them. She sits on her eggs for 16 days, during which time the male brings her food.

If disturbed while incubating her eggs or brooding her newly-hatched

chicks, the plucky great tit spreads her tail, puffs out her cheeks, hisses loudly and beats her wings against the side of the hole. This makes her sound rather like an angry snake or a swarm of bees, which may frighten a predator away.

▲ *After visiting the nest to feed its chicks, a parent great tit often waits for one of them to eject a faecal sac, a neat package of waste products. Then to avoid drawing attention to the nest, the bird flies some way away before dropping it.*

## In the early days

For almost five weeks, great tits run a five-star parenting service for their chicks, with catering, cleaning and after-care tuition in flying and foraging thrown in. On hatching, the chicks weigh about 1.3g (the merest fraction of an ounce). Immediately, these naked-pink, blind bags of guts start pleading for food with urgent shrill *tsee tsee tsee tsee tsee* calls and huge, gaping beaks. And they go on pestering their hard-pressed parents until they are fledged – and beyond.

After leaving the nest, young great tits have just 10 to 14 days in which to hone their flying skills and learn about where to roost and find food before their parents leave them to fend for themselves.

In June and July, the independent juveniles are particularly vulnerable to cats and other predators, food shortages and bad weather. On top of everything else, they start a full body moult, from which they emerge in more or less adult plumage by the end of October.

# Feeding the Family

GREAT TITS SPEND most of their time peering into tiny crevices in the bark of trees, rummaging about in the leaf litter, examining leaves and exploring bushes for insects, spiders or seeds.

Diversity and flexibility are the key to the great tit's diet. During the late spring and summer it eats mostly insects. Flies, aphids, butterflies and moths and their caterpillars, beetles and earwigs, wasps and bees are all caught in large numbers.

## BREEDING CONDITION

In the three weeks before laying, the female starts eating greedily, putting on weight at an extraordinary rate until she weighs at least half as much again. Over the next ten to 12 days, until her clutch is complete, she will produce almost her own weight in eggs. While she is laying, the female great tit uses a squeaky *zeedle-zeedle-zeedle-zeedle-zee* call to beg her mate to bring her extra rations of food.

## DEMANDING CHICKS

The hatching of great tit chicks in May and June is timed to coincide with a glut of caterpillars – mainly those of the winter moth, mottled umber and cabbage white. Parent great tits could not keep up with the insatiable demands of their broods unless there were a plentiful supply of protein-rich food nearby.

At first, while the hatchlings are tiny and are still being kept warm in the nest by their mother, the male goes on collecting most of the food. He must look for lots of the smallest caterpillars he can find. Over the first week, as the chicks grow, the size of the prey increases.

By the time the nestlings are five days old, both parents are working flat out, ferrying hundreds of small insects to the nest each day. They also fetch grit to aid digestion and snail shells as a source of calcium to help build strong bones.

*male*

*female*

▲ **IMPATIENT FOR BEECH NUTS**
*Great tits normally find a staple of their autumn diet, beech mast, lying in the leaf litter under beech trees.*

> '*Where tomtits, hanging from*
> *the drooping heads*
> *Of giant sunflowers, peck the nutty seeds*'
>
> from *The Garden in September* by **Robert Bridges** (1844-1930)

## Getting to grips with the grub

Larger insects and seeds that the great tit finds on the ground are carried up to a twig in nearby cover before being processed and eaten. There the tit clamps them to the perch, using one foot to hold a caterpillar and both feet to secure a seed such as beech mast. Then it hammers the food item with its bill to remove the hard head of a caterpillar while the chicks are tiny, or to crack a seed case to get at the kernel inside.

Later in the season, when the leaves that the caterpillars are eating contain more tannin, which is poisonous to the nestlings, great tits extract the grubs' guts in this way too.

The great tit's bill is thicker and stronger in winter when it is eating plenty of tough-cased seeds. In the spring, a great tit does lots of bill-wiping, stropping its bill from base to tip along a perch, until it is finer and in better shape for feeding on insects.

The proportion of spiders in the chicks' diet increases steadily for the first six or seven days after hatching too. The great tit chick's first feathers sprout five days after they hatch and spiders are a good source of cystine, a nutrient which is essential for good feather development.

## PARENTAL CONTROL

Parent great tits gauge the hunger of their chicks by how raucously they beg for food and fetch provisions to match the clamour. In this way, the chicks in a large brood, which make more noise, secure the extra rations they need. And the chick begging the loudest is most likely to be fed first.

The adults call most of the shots in deciding when their brood leaves the nest. As soon as the chicks are nearly ready to fly, they start feeding them at the entrance to the nesting-hole or just waving a juicy caterpillar at the opening to tempt the fledglings to take their first flights.

## THE WINTER MENU

When the weather becomes cooler, the days shorter and insects scarcer, great tits gradually switch to eating more seeds and nuts. They also start making more frequent and regular visits to bird-tables and feeders.

## ▲ HUNTING HIGH AND LOW

*No small insect or spider is safe when an alert and agile great tit is on the prowl in a beech tree. It leaves no twig or branch uninspected, no leaf unturned and looks behind every flake of bark and in all the buds to find its prey.*

## Winter flocks

From November to January, great tits travel around together, often in mixed flocks with other tits, nuthatches, treecreepers and goldcrests. Nomadic winter flocks range in size from two to 50 birds. Small groups may unite to form larger flocks; several hundred birds may gather in a beech wood where there is an abundance of beech mast. In winter, the male great tits tend to grab the richer pickings on the ground, leaving the females to scavenge on the bare branches above.

# The Ingenious Tomtit

As one of the most common and best-known birds in woodland, parks, hedgerows and gardens, the great tit needs little introduction. It stands out as the largest member of the tit family – a small bird endowed with great vitality, obvious intelligence and formidable hubris.

Even in the Latin of its scientific name, *Parus major* – where *Parus* means titmouse – the great tit is a Great tit. Tit is an abbreviation of titmouse, or *titmase* as it used to be in Old English, and usually refers to anything small and mouse-like.

### INTERESTING LITTLE BIRDS

With its gaily-coloured plumage, overbearing behaviour and perpetual chattiness, the great tit is hard to ignore. Throughout the 1940s, Len Howard observed the loves and rivalries of the great-tit families in her garden with inspiring patience. Her account of their behaviour in her book, *Birds as Individuals*, portrayed a delightful picture of determined, courageous, chivalrous, often fickle, sometimes caddish little birds. Each one had its own decidedly individual preferences for roosting perches, nest sites, partners and food.

Naturally inquisitive and fast learners, great tits are astoundingly swift at coming up with imaginative solutions to tests specially devised to assess their intelligence.

> ‘*Of the birds with which I am intimately acquainted, Great Tits reach the highest level of intelligence*’

from *Birds as Individuals* by **Len Howard** (1952)

◀ *It's a bird-eat-bird world out there. To survive, a great tit needs to think faster and act more decisively and swiftly than its competitors for food and nest sites.*

## INFORMATION PROCESSORS

It seems that great tits may have something to teach us about crisis management. Observations on the mobbing of predators near the nest, for example, revealed that parent birds were not always willing to put their lives on the line for their chicks.

Males were generally braver than females but just how brave depended on the circumstances. They evidently rated the enemy and flew closer to an owl than to a more dangerous sparrowhawk. A male was more persistent if his mate was nearby or other birds joined him. His challenge was also much stronger the nearer his chicks were to fledging and the later in the breeding season it was.

It is amazing that under pressure a small bird like a great tit is able to process all this input in a flash, make a risk assessment and come up with an appropriate measured response. Never underestimate a great tit!

## The brains of the family

Great tits are constantly demonstrating how clever they are in their everyday lives. In order not to waste time on a fruitless search for food, a great tit taps an acorn with its beak before trying to open it. The sound tells the tit whether the acorn has been hollowed out by a grub and is worth opening.

When frisking a tree for food, the crafty great tit views the underside of the leaves to check for the shadows of caterpillars on top. Many woodland ones are green and well hidden so this is an efficient way of spotting them.

Over 200 years ago, the naturalist Gilbert White watched a great tit pull straws from a thatched roof and snap up the flies it had dislodged. Few birds use tools to help them capture prey, but one canny great tit was seen using a pine needle to winkle out a grub from a crevice in the bark.

In one ingenuity test, great tits quickly worked out how to use their bill and feet to haul up peanuts dangling on a string from a perch.

'*A Tom Tit clinging upside down, Needs nothing more to raise his wonder*'

from *To Play Alone* by **W H Davies** (1871-1940)

## Country names

• The great tit's sheeny black head attracted the most comment in its country names, where it was variously known as Blackcapped Billy, Blackheaded Bob or Blackheaded Tomtit.

• In East Anglia, Joe Ben was a traditional name for the great tit, after Joseph and his brother Benjamin in the Old Testament. There are tenuous links between the two short sounds and the penetrating two syllable call of the great tit.

• The song of the great tit sounds like a saw blade being sharpened, so in many places it was known as a Saw-sharpener, Sawfiler, Saw-whet (*whet* means to sharpen or grind), Sawfitch or Sawfinch. For the same reasons, it was also known as the Carpenter Bird. In some parts of the country, this particular song was said to foretell rain.

• Ox-eye was a common name for the great tit. It may have been so called after the large white patch on the side of its head, which resembles the markings on the cheeks of some cattle. Alternatively, in France, *l'œil de boeuf* was a popular term for a small bird and ox-eye may just be another way of expressing bull's-eye.

• The great tit was also known as a Bee Biter or Bee Eater because it had a predilection for eating bees, especially early in the year when they were still drowsy from their winter slumbers.

• Sometimes people called the great tit Billy Biter after the female's habit of hissing and pecking at the fingers of anyone trying to steal her eggs while she is sitting on them.

• Green Bottle and Bottle Tit are two old names for great tit, comparing the green of its back with green glass.

# The Siskin

*Siskins are highly sociable, brightly coloured, dainty finches that flock to alder trees to feed in the winter but spend their summers nesting in pine trees*

Until about 40 years ago, the siskin was largely confined to the ancient pine forests of Scotland during the breeding season. Now, thanks to the proliferation of conifer plantations and the growing popularity of decorative conifers in gardens, siskins are flourishing and spreading: they are nesting in pine trees in East Anglia, North and Mid Wales, Devon and the New Forest.

### WINTER WATCH

Flocks of siskins have always been more visible over the winter, dodging in and out of birch and larch copses or alder thickets. As fairly recent converts to garden feeding, siskins are the rising stars of the peanut-net gymnastic display team during the winter and in the spring.

▶ *With his black cap, brilliant-yellow breast and greenish back, a courting cock siskin is a dashing dazzler.*

## The lady siskin

The female siskin is a duller, greyer looking bird than the male. She has paler striped underparts and a streakier head and back, without his greenish-yellow wash over his head or his black cap and bib. Her yellow wing bars may be narrower than the male's but they are obvious proof that she is a member of the siskin clan.

‘ *Where with flame-like plumage flutter Golden birds in glaring flock* ’

from *Song of Palms* by **Arthur O'Shaugnessy** (1844-1881)

*female siskin*

# Pilgrim's Progress

ALTHOUGH THE SISKIN'S life revolves around pine trees over the breeding season, for the rest of the year it is more nomadic in its search for food. The charming little siskin is an agile, tree-based finch which rarely visits the ground to feed. By and large, it is a seed-eater, searching for seeds in conifer cones, birch and alder catkins, and on thistle heads or other weeds. They are attracted to gardens by the seeds of ornamental conifers.

A flock of siskins feeds vivaciously, tumbling about the branches to pluck out the seeds and delicately remove their cases to reach the edible kernels inside. The siskin's fine beak is ideally shaped for probing into deep pockets in ripe cones and catkins. During the breeding season a siskin might also catch some insects and spiders to feed to its nestlings.

### WINTER MENU

In late summer, siskins emerge from the coniferous woodlands, where they spent the summer raising families, and start foraging for tree and weed seeds on farmland, along river banks and in copses. Those from the north drift southwards. They often team up

with other finches, such as redpolls and goldfinches, to form flocks that are always on the move and can turn up anywhere at any time.

The siskins that are resident in Britain are often joined by others escaping from much colder winters in northern Europe. Some years there is a larger influx than others: when the trees in Scandinavia take

▲ *Thanks to its extraordinary tumbling skills, an acrobatic siskin can reach every part of each ripe catkin dangling from an alder bough and extract all the seeds.*

a year off from setting seed, many small seed-eating birds, such as the siskin, have to flee across the North Sea to find precious winter rations farther south.

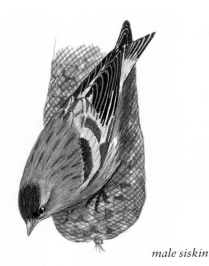

*male siskin*

## Passion for peanuts

In early spring, when provisions in the countryside are running low, small parties of siskins start turning up on garden peanut-hangers. They seem to be especially attracted to red-skinned peanuts in red nylon nets, possibly because these are the easiest to spot and most closely resemble pine cones. The siskins can become quite proprietorial about the nuts and belligerently see off other garden birds.

### ‘The flecks of sunlight shift and crowd so goldenly’

from *A Summer Day* by **Mary Webb** (1881-1927)

# In Pine Form

EACH SPRING, SISKINS disappear into the tree-tops in coniferous woodland and plantations to breed. They start sorting out partners for the coming spring while still travelling around in their flocks during the winter. Then pairs can get on with breeding as soon as they return to their nesting locations.

### PAIRING UP

As the winter flocks start to break up, courtship begins in earnest with some flirtatious chases through the upper branches. The male serenades his mate while circling the tree-top over their nest site, flapping his wings with very exaggerated beats and fanning out his tail to reveal its yellow patches clearly. Sometimes he lands in the tree to show off in front of her, by puffing out his feathers, then drooping and spreading his wings so that she can see his yellow rump and wing patches. He continues his singing long after the female has settled down in the nest to incubate their eggs.

During the breeding season the gregarious siskin becomes less sociable and mildly territorial. Up to six pairs may build relatively close together: not always in the same tree but nearby in a loosely associated colony.

### JOINT EFFORT

The cock and hen siskin collaborate in the building of their nest. They usually position it well out along a branch, at least 4.5 metres (15 feet) above the ground. The nest is compact and often well concealed behind a screen of pine

*female*

*male*

> ' *The green siskin, that lovely little oddity, seeking his food, tit-like, among the pine needles or clinging to pendulous twigs* '
>
> from *Birds in London* by **William Henry Hudson** (1841-1922)

*juvenile*

## Young siskins

Newly-fledged siskins continue to be fed by their parents for several days after leaving the nest. Once their last offspring are independent, the adults undergo a complete moult, emerging in slightly more sober colours which brighten up over the winter.

For the rest of that summer, juvenile siskins look like browner and more heavily-streaked adult females. These young siskins change most of their body feathers in the autumn but retain their wing and tail feathers, which have duller, paler wing bars and tail patches, until the end of the next summer. In his first winter, the young male siskin's black cap is hidden under the pale fringes of his feathers.

During their first full summer, young siskins can still just about be distinguished from older adults by their brown wings and tail and pale yellow wing bars. They moult into full adult colours later that year.

◀ **SUBTLE DIFFERENCE**
*A female siskin also has golden wing
bars like her mate, although hers are
slightly narrower than his.*

▶ **WARMING VIGIL**
*The siskin's bluish-white eggs,
lightly marked with lilac, pink or
brown streaks, are rarely seen: the
nest is tucked away high up in a
pine tree and the female deserts her
post only briefly while she is
incubating the clutch.*

◀ **SPREADING HIS WINGS**
*The male siskin's wings are long and
pointed, with bold yellow bars.
The yellow patches at the end of the
forked tail are also clearly visible.*

needles. They weave the nest cup from slender, flexible
twigs, sprigs of heather, lichen, flakes of bark, moss and
wool, then cosily line it with plenty of soft hair, feathers
and plant down to help keep their chicks warm.

## WORKING TOGETHER

As soon as the nest is completed, the female lays up to
seven, but normally three to five pale blue eggs. These
are often plain but may be streaked with purplish red.
The hen takes charge of incubating her clutch, sitting
patiently on her eggs for 11 to 14 days. During this time,
she depends on the male to bring her food. When the
chicks hatch they are covered in a long, smoky blue-grey
down. The female stays at the nest for a further five to
seven days to keep them warm and protect them from
would-be nest-robbers.

Meanwhile, the male continues foraging for food to
feed his whole family. At first, he regurgitates his finds
straight into the female's beak, which she then proceeds
to feed to her chicks. Later on, both parents have their
work cut out collecting enough caterpillars, aphids and
spiders to satisfy the voracious appetites of their young.
The adults gradually wean their chicks on to a diet of
conifer seeds before they fledge and leave the nest, about
15 days after hatching. In a fine summer, a pair of siskins
often successfully rears two broods.

## Out on a limb

Nesting in pine trees has several
advantages for the siskin: even early in the season,
pine needles shelter the nest from rain and sunshine
and screen it from the prying eyes of hungry predators,
such as squirrels, crows and birds of prey. The siskin's
end-of-the-twig location for the nest, high up in a tree,
makes the vulnerable eggs and nestlings less accessible
to all but the lightest and nimblest of predators.

*male*

# The Yellowhammer

*In spring and summer, country lanes ring to the sound of the cock yellowhammer singing his shrill little song over and over again from the hedge-tops*

Yellowhammers live in open country, mostly on farmland growing cereal crops and oil-seed rape, but also on pastures and meadows, heathland and commons. They always need some hedgerows and gorse or scrub nearby to provide elevated song posts and nest sites.

## YELLOW FLUTTER-BYS

Spring is the best time of year to see and hear yellowhammers as they chase each other up and down the lanes or visit the garden. From afar, a pair of yellowhammers flitting in and out of the hedges can look like a pair of fluttery yellow butterflies.

In spring, a cock yellowhammer displays himself as conspicuously as possible by perching on top of a gorse bush or the highest point in a hedge, even on telegraph poles or telephone wires. Years ago, his cheery song and vibrant colouring earned the cock yellowhammer his nickname of the Hedgerow Canary.

▲ *From the side, a cock yellowhammer in his summer plumage does look a bit like a cross between a canary and a sparrow. Those bright chestnut feathers on his rump are unique to the male yellowhammer.*

▶ *There is less time for singing when a cock yellowhammer is kept busy harvesting beakful after beakful of insects, spiders and millipedes to feed his rapidly growing brood in the nest.*

*male in winter*

## Yellow bunting

The yellowhammer was once better known as the yellow bunting, showing that yellowhammers belong to a group of small songbirds called buntings. Although broadly similar in appearance and habits to finches, buntings are slimmer and more elongated, with longer tails than the average finch. Like most buntings, yellowhammers have short, stout, pointed beaks, capable of husking seeds and grains but also well suited to picking up insects for feeding to their nestlings during the breeding season.

After an autumn moult, both male and female yellowhammers emerge looking duller, with extra dark streaks in their plumage. (Like finches, the females are drabber than the males throughout the year.) Over the course of the winter, the tips of the male's brown feathers gradually wear away so that the cock bird is at his sunniest yellow when courting his mate in spring.

## For the winter

Having fed their nestlings on creepy-crawlies, yellowhammers revert to a vegetarian diet once the breeding season is over. They congregate in flocks, often with finches such as linnets and chaffinches. Groups are seen hopping about on the ground, pecking up stray cereal grains from stubble fields or feeding troughs in farmyards and chicken runs. During the winter, yellowhammers also eat fruits and wild seeds from large grasses and weeds, such as dock.

Although yellowhammers could never really be described as garden birds, during hard winters and early spring they do visit gardens which border on commons and heaths to take small seeds such as hemp, millet and canary mix.

# Singing for his Supper

THE COCK YELLOWHAMMER is famous for repeating his catchphrase, which sounds like '*a-little-bit-of-bread-and-no-cheese*'. He delivers the first seven syllables of his signature tune in a shrill, staccato fashion – *a-little-bit-of-bread-and*. After that he faces a vocally challenging cadence. The second-to-last note is an emphatic higher-pitched *NO*. Then his voice drops straight down to a low, drawn-out *c-h-e-e-s-e*. This final note often tails off, producing a rather wistful effect. Each phrase lasts about three seconds – including the final note that he holds for a full one second – and is repeated at ten-second intervals.

### GETTING IT RIGHT

Male yellowhammers start rehearsing their songs as early as February, as it takes them a while to get up to speed. At first, most cock birds just ask for *a-little-bit-of-bread-and*, leaving out *no-cheese* altogether. It always sounds as though their voices are a bit rusty. In fact, as spring approaches, there are real physiological changes taking

▲ *A jubilant cock yellowhammer repeats his little catchphrase thousands of times each summer. He throws back his head, opens wide his beak and recites his deceptively simple lyrics with great gusto.*

place in a cock bird's larynx (voice box). Only after time and practice does he start to sing fluently.

Even in summer, on overcast days, a lazy cock bird may still not deliver his tricky final notes. But almost as if he knows that his yellow plumage gleams brightest in sunshine, the cock yellowhammer loves singing on a sunny afternoon while other birds are taking a siesta, which makes it all the more notable. His song is also one of the few to be heard in August.

# Family Affairs

YELLOWHAMMERS ENJOY a period of lively courtship which can last for several weeks as a preliminary to the hectic days of nest-building, egg-laying and chick-rearing.

The courting cock yellowhammer sings his heart out but stops when he sees a female entering his territory. Then he flies down to the ground where he ruffles his feathers and starts picking up small sticks and pebbles which he then drops near her perch in a mock feeding ritual.

### PLAYING IT COOL

At first the hen bird plays hard to get, outwitting her suitor by twisting and turning in flight as he chases her along a hedge or from bush to bush. The final stages of pairing take place on the ground, with the male making short runs in front of his prospective mate, fanning his tail, raising his wings and carrying grass stalks in his beak as though he is enticing her to start nest-building.

After the excitement of courtship, the hen yellowhammer gets on with constructing a nest on her own. She usually builds on or near the ground, in gorse and bramble bushes, at the base of a hedge or in a jungle of grass and nettles. There she assembles a large cup of dried grass, stalks, roots and moss, lined with horsehair and finer dried grasses.

Once the hen bird has laid a clutch of eggs, she does most of the incubating, with occasional help from her mate. He spends most of his time singing from the top of the hedge or bush above the nest. If she is disturbed, the female reluctantly leaves the nest,

*male in summer*

### ▲ IN THE AIR

*When flying, a cock yellowhammer's bright chestnut rump and the white edges to his dark tail show up clearly. His flight path is direct but wavers up and down as he regularly closes his wings and coasts for a while.*

> *Five eggs pen-scribbled over lilac shells*
> *Resembling writing, scrawls which fancy reads*
> *As nature's poesy and pastoral spells*
> *They are the yellowhammer's*

from *The Yellowhammer's Nest* by **John Clare** (1793-1864)

## The anonymous young ones

No matter whether it is male or female, a juvenile yellowhammer is a darker, streakier version of its mother: only faintly yellow underneath and with hardly any yellow on its head at all. The youngster's inconspicuous colouring is useful protection while it is still learning the basics of flying and taking care of itself. The bright yellow plumage of the young cock birds starts to show through in their first spring. Then you hear the first-year males warming up their voices and practising their song until they eventually achieve a full run at *a-little-bit-of-bread-and-no-cheese,* just like the experienced males.

*juvenile*

*female*

issuing an abrupt alarm call as she goes, and continues her protest from nearby until the danger is past.

## ACTION STATIONS

The chicks hatch after 12 to 14 days. Although the hatchlings are helpless bundles of grey down, they very soon start flashing their pink-lined mouths to chivvy their parents into finding insects to feed them. The youngsters are ready to leave the nest about 14 days after hatching. Then the parents may go on to raise a second and even a third brood that summer.

Yellowhammer numbers may be falling but studies indicate that its breeding performance – the survival rate from egg to fledging – has got better. The main reason for their decline seems to lie with a lack of winter food, which is where garden feeding comes into its own.

▲ **FURZE THINGS FIRST**
*A pair of yellowhammers have coincidentally arrived back together at their nest in the base of a gorse bush to feed their chicks. The tiny nestlings are ravenous for the grubs and insects their parents have brought for them.*

# Marbled eggs

In late April or early May, as soon as she has finished building her nest, the hen yellowhammer lays her first clutch of the season. Usually there are three to five pale lilac eggs in the nest, each one decorated with original doodlings of darker purple-brown veins and streaks. Long ago, people found these strange patterns absolutely fascinating and they resulted in the yellowhammer being known as the Scribe, Scribbling Lark or Writing Lark.

# The Magpie

*The magpie's striking black-and-white plumage is as unmistakable as its cackling call: once seen or heard, you'll always recognise this attractive bird*

As soon as you see a big black-and-white bird striding across the lawn with a confident swagger, perhaps fighting to keep its streamer-like tail under control in a strong breeze, it has to be a magpie. Yet despite all its self-assurance and savvy, the magpie is still a wary bird, shy of humans. It has good cause: in the 19th and 20th centuries magpies were persecuted by gamekeepers for being nest-robbers.

### SPREADING OUT

Magpies are fairly easy going about where they live as long as there are high thorny hedges or tall trees for nest building and grassland nearby in which to forage. In recent years, they have moved into towns and cities and now frequently visit gardens.

▶ *The magpie's black feathers are usually very glossy, shimmering blue, violet, green or bronze depending on how the sunshine strikes them.*

## Flickering flight

The magpie's wings are very short and its flight can look hesitant and wavy over longer distances, as though it is swimming through the air with bursts of frantic flapping. Usually it stays quite low, where it seems to float rather than fly, skimming over hedges with its tail spread-eagled to catch the breeze. On arrival, it swoops boldly down to the ground or up to a perch, landing with a switch of its tail.

'*But the great and flashing magpie*
*He flies as poets might*'

from *Magpies in Picardy* by **T P Cameron Wilson** (1889-1918)

# The Hungry Magpie

A MAGPIE EATS almost anything, from insects and slugs to household scraps and road-kills. It consumes mainly animal prey during the summer, when creepy-crawlies feature significantly in the chicks' diet. Come the autumn and winter, it starts eating more seeds, acorns and berries.

## ON FOOT

Magpies nearly always forage on the ground, usually on damp grassland or garden lawns. They stride and strut about, often breaking into a run or skipping sideways when they spy a tasty treat or if their long tail gets blown askew by a gust of wind.

The magpie is attracted to feed in pastures where cows and sheep are grazing. It can snap up insects drawn to the droppings and pounce on any grasshoppers disturbed by the hooves. It also picks up caterpillars, beetles, ants and snails or uses its beak to dig for earthworms and leatherjackets.

## CRUEL HARVEST

Recent changes in land use, including fewer hedges and more roads and cars, which make the countryside a much tougher habitat for seed-eating songbirds, have actually made life easier for magpies. Suburbia really suits them too: there is loads of food, in the form of breadcrumbs, fat, nuts and scraps put out for small garden birds, and little predation as most cats dare not tackle them.

## SHARP-EYED PREDATORS

The danger of attracting magpies to the garden is that they are observant and quickly spot where songbirds are nesting. They are notorious for raiding the nests and stealing the eggs and chicks. Not so long ago, magpies used to be demonised by gamekeepers for taking game-bird eggs and chicks, and were killed in large numbers.

▼ *A magpie descends like a vulture on the carcass of a rabbit. You often see magpies squabbling over carrion, especially on the roads around the corpses of road-kill victims. They rarely hunt small mammals but sometimes get blamed for killing the dead ones they find.*

## Hoarding instinct

Magpies are short-term hoarders of food, especially during the autumn and winter. Because they use their stores within a couple of days, magpies can store perishable foods, such as berries and carrion, as well as acorns and nuts. At the storage area it tilts its head, as if to memorise the site, before making a small hole in the ground with its beak. Then it regurgitates the contents of a special food pouch under its tongue into the hole and covers it with grass, twigs or leaves.

*'Glory be to God for dappled things'*

from *Pied Beauty* by **Gerard Manley Hopkins** (1844-89)

# The Lucky Few

EARLY IN THE YEAR, a pair of magpies sets up a territory in which to nest and feed. Both the male and female use noisy, flighty tree-top displays to broadcast and defend their claim and to spy on other magpies in the area. Most incursions are dealt with quite peaceably and the intruder is chased off. If another male does not take the hint and withdraw, a skirmish might break out, with two males grappling with their feet while jabbing at each other with their beaks.

### RIGHT TO BREED

In most regions, only a few of the magpies living there breed each season. Others, mostly the younger ones, are floaters living in local non-breeding flocks. If a male magpie loses his mate, he usually replaces her with indecent haste from this pool.

Noisy ceremonial gatherings of excited non-breeding birds parading in tree-tops constantly test territorial security as the floaters look for an opportunity to take over a weak territory and win a chance to breed. The excitable magpie is notorious for its mechanical chattering alarm call, a persistent grating *chak-chak-chak* noise, which sounds like a wooden football rattle or a bleating goat.

' *Two magpies sought my garden glade,*
*(It brings good luck to look at two!)*
*Tho' not as billing ring-doves woo*
*Do pies discourse of love! They made*
*A grievous chatter in the shade* '

from *For One Man's Pleasure* by **Mary Montgomerie Lamb** (1843-1905)

▲ **KLEPTOMANIAC**
*Living up to its reputation for picking up shiny objects, this keen-eyed magpie has unearthed an old loose metal ring-pull to adorn its nest.*

*juveniles*

## Trials of youth

After fledging in about 27 days, young magpies have very short tails. They stay in their parents' territory for around six weeks while the adult birds continue to feed and protect them by mobbing intruders with daring dives and rattling calls.

Eventually, the juveniles form into a loose non-breeding flock with other young magpies in the area. The youngsters spend their first winter close to where they were reared and often go on to breed in the same vicinity too. Sadly, many die in the early days of independence. Only a third survive the first four months: lack of experience and wariness makes young magpies vulnerable to predators and food shortages.

*Magpies often build their nests in thorny hedges or high up in tall trees to keep their chicks safe from predators. Once built, a nest may be re-used year after year.*

▲ TWIGGY GLOBE

*Magpie nests are large, hard-wearing, spherical constructions, with a well-disguised entrance in the side and a thorny roof to ward off would-be nest-robbers.*

## ERECTING A FORTRESS

A pair of magpies starts assembling a nest by daubing some mud in a fork between two branches to create an anchorage. Then the two birds collect hundreds of twigs – up to 598 sticks have been collected from one nest – which they stack into a rough cup. The magpies line this with mud to create a deep hard bowl, then add a soft lining of hairs, roots and grass and a twiggy awning. It takes them about 40 days to finish the building work. You can see the twiggy domes much better when the trees have lost their leaves in winter.

## MATE GUARDING

Once the nest is complete, magpies often wait for about 11 days before laying any eggs. During this time, the male struts around his partner with his white feathers fluffed out, flirting his wings and tilting his tail towards her while singing a surprisingly soft babbling song. When she is ready to mate she squats down as if begging for food. After mating, the male will not let his mate out of his sight until their eggs are laid, to stop her being mated by another male as well.

## WHEN THE CHICKS ARRIVE

Magpie chicks are blind and helpless when they hatch and must be kept warm by their mother for the first five to ten days of life. Initially, the male brings most of the food for the chicks, which are fed between two and five times an hour.

Four weeks later, the youngsters are ready to leave the nest but need parental attention for a further six weeks. From July to late September, magpies keep a lowish profile while they are moulting their old feathers and regrowing new ones.

## In the nest

The hen magpie lays up to six green-blue eggs heavily mottled with grey or brown blotches. One egg is laid each day, within four hours of dawn, until the clutch is complete. The female does all the incubating for roughly 22 days. While she is sitting on the eggs, she is fed by her partner every hour. She leaves the nest only briefly for a toilet break or to stretch and preen.

# The Thieving Magpie

ONCE UPON A TIME, the magpie was simply known as the pye or pie, after its variegated plumage. The prefix Mag, a nickname for Margaret, was added in the 16th century. The use of a popular girl's name is a sure sign that magpies were familiar, common birds a long time ago.

Other old-fashioned nicknames stem from this Margaret connection: Madge, Maggie, Mag or Margot, Maggot or Magot Pie. In northern England it would have been known as the Pianet, a combination of pie and anet, a nickname for Agnes.

### WICKED WAYS

Steeped in omens and superstitions, the beautiful magpie has an appalling reputation for being a gossip, thief and murderer. Its habit of stealing chicks from nests in broad daylight made the magpie unpopular almost everywhere. In Scotland, the magpie was known as the Devil's Bird.

According to an old superstition, the magpie can be a portent for both good and evil. It all depends on the number of Maggies you see at the same time. In an old counting rhyme, of which there are numerous different versions, if you see a lone magpie it is said to bring bad luck, but catch sight of two together and you can expect to be happy. Apparently, it was only the Chinese who had complete faith in the magpie, believing it to be a bird of utter joy and good fortune, which must never be killed.

*'One for sorrow, two for joy,*
*Three for a girl, four for a boy,*
*Five for silver, six for gold,*
*Seven for a secret never to be told'*

# Lore and legend

- The Romans kept magpies as pets to warn of approaching strangers with their strident calls, as dogs and geese do.

- In Rome, the magpie was sacred to Bacchus, the god of wine, and seen as a token of drunkenness and hedonism.

- A magpie is said to carry a drop of the devil's blood under its tongue. Along with other crows, the magpie went to Christ's Crucifixion but, while the rest wore respectful black, the magpie turned up in jazzy pied plumage.

- Two magpies were said to be the only birds that refused to enter Noah's Ark, choosing to perch on the roof instead and chatter as the world drowned.

- To ward off any misfortune caused by seeing a lone magpie, people would doff their hats or spit three times over their right shoulder. Some used to cross themselves or their thumbs and recite:

*I cross the magpie*
*The magpie crosses me*
*Bad luck to the magpie*
*Good luck to me.*

- In Rossini's (1792-1868) opera, *The Thieving Magpie*, the maid Ninetta is convicted of stealing and saved from the gallows only when a magpie is exposed as the real culprit. The magpies are suggested by raucous musical banter from opposite ends of the orchestra pit.

- A craving for odd foods, especially in pregnancy, is known as *pica* after the Latin for a magpie and its varied diet.

- The word *gazette*, describing a tittle-tattling newspaper, may have come from *gazza*, the Italian for magpie.

- In the Middle Ages some women were called *pies* as their quarrelsome, gossipy behaviour was held to be like a magpie's.

◄ *In late winter or early spring, look and listen out for noisy ceremonial gatherings of magpies, chattering, displaying and chasing each other through the tree-tops, usually to challenge an existing territory.*

## CHATTERING CLASSES

The excitable magpie is notorious for its noisy persistent *chak-chak-chak* alarm call, which sounds rather like a wooden football rattle or a bleating goat. In his poem *Piers the Ploughman*, William Langland (c1332-1400) described the prayers of a rich man as '*the chattering of a pie*'. Thomas Gisborne (1758-1846) also noted in *Walks in a Forest*:

> *From bough to bough the restless magpie roves,*
> *And chatters as she flies.*

The magpie's coarse voice sounded so much like swearing that invoking the name of the pye became an oath. Shakespeare knew it would add extra vehemence to a speech by Shallow in *Henry IV, Part 2, Act V, Scene 1*:

> *By cock and pye, sir, you shall not away tonight.*

> ' *The magpie is a rascal: bold, crafty, full of braggadocio . . . a piebald pirate – but I like him* '

from *Birds of the Grey Wind* by **Edward A Armstrong** (1934)

## The royal magpies

In the royal palace at Sintra, Portugal there is a spectacular blue-and-green tiled room with 136 magpies painted on the ceiling as an enduring record of royal infidelity.

According to one local legend, whenever Queen Philippa saw or heard of her husband, King João I (1385-1433), stealing a kiss from one of the ladies-in-waiting at the royal court, she had another magpie painted overhead. These notorious bauble stealers reminded the king that his wife was aware of his philanderings. Evidently the king protested his innocence because every magpie

carries a rose in its beak, with a label inscribed *Por bem* (for the best). Adding the rose was a contrite king's way of reassuring his wife of his affection for her.

Another version of the story suggests that the king had all the magpies painted, one for each lady-in-waiting. The chattering birds were his way of warning the ladies that palace walls had ears and their gossiping displeased him.

CHAPTER 2 · SUMMER

# The Greenfinch

*It could be that the cock greenfinch is green with envy because, no matter how often it turns up in gardens, other small birds grab all the headlines and it gets scant coverage*

Greenfinches are adaptable all-rounders whose habits have changed in the last hundred years or so. Over this period, they have moved in from the country to the suburbs and come to rely more and more on food put out on bird-tables, especially during the winter. In the latest census of garden birds, the greenfinch came in sixth place, averaging two individuals per garden: no change from previous years either in numbers or ranking.

### LOW PROFILES

Despite regularly feeding and nesting in gardens, greenfinches still get over-looked. It is easy to miss greenies as they blend into a backdrop of foliage and grass in their favourite haunts among hedgerows, churchyards and copses as well as gardens.

▶ *In summer sunshine, a handsome cock greenfinch on a visit to his family in the nest looks as green as a parrot.*

*male in winter*

## Not-so-green finch

During the winter, you may not recognise a cock greenfinch when he visits your bird-table. You may even wonder why he is called a greenfinch at all. This is due to a late-summer moult, when both males and females lose their old, rather tatty feathers and regrow a fresh set of feathers. In the autumn, the brand new feathers on the male's head, back and breast are tipped with russet-brown, which damps down his greenness, leaving him looking a much duller brown colour.

If you suspect that a brownish finch is a greenfinch, always check for the bright yellow signature flashes on the wings and the yellow trim down the edges of the outer tail feathers which are retained all year round. Over the winter, the brown tips of the new feathers get worn away to reveal a bright green coat by springtime, ready for the breeding season.

# Seekers after Seeds

THE THICK-BILLED GREENFINCH is a typical seed-eater. Armed with a large wedge-shaped beak and strong jaw muscles, it can tackle bigger seeds and a wider range of them than most other finches. To the great delight of gardeners and farmers, greenfinches consume vast quantities of common weed seeds in hedges and fields, on verges and around gardens.

As a rule, greenfinches are too heavy to peck seeds directly from seedheads on stems, so they feed mostly on the ground, hopping about rather ponderously under trees or bushes and in stubble. On wasteland and roadsides, seeds of dandelion, thistle, persicaria, burdock, charlock, red spurrey and stately cow parsley form an important part of their diet. On farmland, greenfinches take cereal grains, flax and hemp seeds that have fallen to the ground as well as plenty of weed seeds.

## GETTING CRACKING

In autumn, family parties raid the hedges for blackberries, wild field roses and hawthorns. They open the fleshy casing round the scarlet hips and haws with their strong beaks to extract the seeds, one by one. In the winter, they tackle the large hard seeds of yew and hornbeam.

With practice, greenfinches have also mastered the art of extracting pine seeds from cones. But even their heavy beak is not powerful enough to break into a closed cone. Instead, they have to let the cones ripen and open naturally on a sunny day, then niftily dip a beak into each chamber to extract a seed.

Winter stubbles, ploughed land, cornstacks and waste ground with weeds are in pretty short supply these days. So rather than move out of town in the autumn, greenfinches have gravitated to gardens and rely on bird-table supplies to see them through the winter now.

▼ *The larder is almost empty by the time a female greenfinch is reduced to eating buds in spring. More greenfinches perish in March than at any other time of the year because winter has taken its toll and last year's seeds have been used up.*

## *Garden bounty*

In hard weather, greenfinches visit gardens frequently in search of bird seed mixtures and peanuts. Over 1000 different greenfinches have been recorded passing through a garden during one winter as flocks roam in search of food.

As chunky birds, greenfinches lack the acrobatic skills of the tits and find it difficult to hang on to the sides of a mesh nut or seed-dispenser. A small perch on a peanut-feeder or seeds and nuts strewn on the ground suit them much better.

They are among the pushier guests at a bird-table, guarding the food jealously and fearlessly when other birds come too close.

In gardens, greenfinches craftily eat the red fruits of mezereon and black spurge laurel berries before they are ripe, while the stones are still soft. They also like to find rudbeckia, anchusa and sunflower seeds left on the plant, so leave dead-heading these and other seed bearers until the birds have taken their fill.

# Family Fortunes

AS A RULE, the cock greenfinch is one of the last birds to start singing each spring. He may be slow off the mark but by March he evidently believes that 'faint heart never won fair lady'. He twitters and flutters through his pre-nuptial dance, singing a wheezy song in the air while performing his erratic bat-flight courtship display, circling over the tree-tops with exaggerated slow-motion wing beats.

### SMALL COMMUNITY

Partnerships gradually emerge from the winter flock. In spring, the cock greenfinches become more aggressive to other males in their gang but drop their superiority to the females. They actually start crouching in front of the hens and tentatively stretching out to touch beaks with them.

As soon as a pair of greenfinches has bonded, the cock bird heads off to look for a nest site. Even during the breeding season, greenfinches are sociable birds – several pairs often build close together, forming a small cluster of nests in the same hedge or tree. When her eggs are laid, the hen greenfinch does all the incubating.

### IN THE NEST

On hatching, the chicks are clad in wispy pale down. Their gaping beaks reveal a pink lining and yellowish flanges to their mouths. Both parents cater to their every need. Like other largely vegetarian finches, the chicks are fed insects at first, then weaned on to crushed fresh seeds. A pair of greenfinches usually rears two broods between April and July.

### AFTER THE NEST

About 14 days after hatching, young greenfinches are fledged and ready to take their first nervous flight from the nest. Over the following couple of weeks they gain strength and learn life-skills by trailing everywhere after

*male*

*female*

> ⁶*I listen with delight to the twitterings and silken flutterings of a pair of courting greenfinches just outside my hide*⁹

from *Birds of the Grey Wind* by **Edward A Armstrong** (1946)

▲ **IN GREEN OR BROWN**
*The cock greenfinch is the greener bird of the pair, while his mate wears more muted browner and greyer feathers.*

*female*

## Staying in the background

Here a female greenfinch is busy collecting sheep's fleece. She will weave the crinkly wool fibres into her nest to help hold the moss, twigs and grass together.

If it weren't for the yellow bar on her wing and golden trim to her forked tail it would be hard to tell she is a greenfinch at all. In typical finch style, it is the male which has the jazzier colouring, while his mate is a drabber olive-brown bird.

Until their first autumn moult, all juvenile greenfinches take after their mother by having greyish breast feathers and brownish-olive backs. The youngsters have more streaks than the adult females, which makes them even harder to spot in shadowy cover. On dull days, both females and juveniles can look like female house sparrows but their wing and tail markings give away their true identities.

their parents, constantly begging for food with twittery calls. Eventually, as independent juveniles, they join up in flocks with other young finches.

## WINTER STRATEGY

In August, after moulting, adult and juvenile greenfinches congregate with other seed-eaters – chaffinches, house sparrows, yellowhammers and buntings. Parties range in size from 50 to 300, which may swell to 2000 in midwinter when they are joined by refugees escaping from bitterly cold northern European winters.

Groups of hungry finches forage over fields, along hedges and around gardens during the day and roost together at night. When a flock of greenfinches settles in a churchyard or garden, they usually annexe the evergreen shrubs, such as escallonia and rhododendrons, as the waxy green leaves offer good cover from bad weather and predators.

▲ **SITTING PRETTY**

*Modest brownish-green plumage is good camouflage for the female greenfinch sitting patiently on her eggs for 12 to 14 days. She is well concealed in this currant bush, with only her family signature of yellow wing-flashes gleaming like sunbeams.*

# Nest-builders

The cock greenfinch picks out a well-protected site in a hazel bush, thick hawthorn hedge, tangled wild rose, bramble, ivy or conifer tree. Unusually among finches, the cock greenfinch helps his mate build their bulky nest of twigs, moss and grass and line the shallow cup neatly with hair, willow fluff, thistledown and the odd feather. Once the nest is finished, in late April or early May, the hen greenfinch lays four to six white eggs with variable freckling of dark purplish-red spots. As soon as her clutch is complete, she starts incubating.

# The Song Thrush

*The song thrush is an enthusiastic and dedicated musician – one of the first voices to join in the dawn chorus and the most reluctant to call it a day after sunset*

There are thousands of song thrushes living in gardens, parks and woodland all over the country. Yet, with their brown colouring and speckling, they pass largely unnoticed as they skulk under cover of shrubs and hedges, rooting about for earthworms and snails.

## MEMORABLE SONGS

It is only when a song thrush starts to sing that everyone looks up and wonders where the heavenly music is coming from. In a nearby tree, there's the male song thrush delivering his tune, clearly and fluently. He has a large repertoire of notes and a huge musical range, and delights in making up catchy jingles. The singer usually likes his efforts well enough to repeat each phrase two or three times.

▶ *A song thrush breaks cover and hops or runs across the ground in short bursts, looking for snails, worms and insects. When still, it stands stiffly upright.*

## Trials of youth

Even if it wasn't begging to be fed in chick-like fashion, you could tell that this is a young song thrush by the buff streaks on its back and wings. At this age it is still incapable of fending for itself and will continue to call with a petulant *tcheep* for parental assistance for several weeks after quitting the nest.

Recent surveys comparing the survival rates of different wild birds indicate that, for some reason as yet unclear, young song thrushes are having a tougher time than other fledglings. Adult birds seem to be laying and hatching their eggs, then rearing their broods quite successfully. Even so, fewer than half the juveniles raised in one breeding season live to see their first birthday. One theory under investigation is that, when food is scarce, inexperienced young song thrushes have more trouble than adults in finding enough snails and earthworms to eat.

# Happy Families

HAVING ALREADY established his territory in the previous autumn and winter, a male song thrush starts to sing in earnest in January to attract a partner. Cock song thrushes are most vocal in April and May, and only fall silent in August. Song thrushes do not indulge in an elaborate courtship – most females will have heard the male sing often enough. A few noisy chases and the deal is done.

## BABY BOOMING

Nest-building and incubation are the female song thrush's responsibility. While she is sitting, she is attended by her partner, who always greets her with a nervous twitter when he brings her food. The hatching of the chicks triggers a flurry of activity as both parents work overtime to keep them supplied with food.

If a pair of song thrushes gets its act together early enough in the year, it may rear three broods over the course of a breeding season, which lasts from March to July.

▶ *When spied upon while brooding her young chicks to keep them warm, a song thrush usually stays very still, relying on her markings to keep her hidden.*

'*Star-eyed, strawberry-breasted,*
*Throstle above her nested.*
*Cluster of bugle blue eggs thin,*
*Forms and warms the life within*'

from *The May Magnificat* by **Gerard Manley Hopkins** (1844-1889)

## *Draughtproof cradle*

The female song thrush is the architect, basketweaver and plasterer of the team. She is responsible for building a solid bowl-shaped nest in the shelter of thick foliage in a hedge, bush or dense creeper. First she weaves a cup of twigs, grass and moss, then lines it with a saliva-bound mortar of dung or rotten wood. Before the lining sets hard, she smooths it out with her breast by turning around and around inside the nest and pressing the mortar firmly on to the sides. After the hen has built her spartan nest, she lays four to six blue eggs with black dots, which she incubates for about two weeks.

When the eggs hatch, the chicks are blind and naked, with a skimpy covering of golden down. At first all they can do is open their beaks feebly, revealing a yellow lining to their mouths which sends the parents into feeding overdrive. Well-fed nestlings are fledged and out of the nest in about 14 days.

# Saving the Song Thrush

ALTHOUGH STILL A common and widespread bird, the song thrush's dramatic slump in numbers over the past 30 years has set alarm bells ringing among conservationists.

As yet, no-one fully understands why the song thrush has been in such serious decline in recent years. It is already protected from deliberate persecution under the European Community Bird Directive and the Wildlife and Countryside Act 1981, but its ongoing struggle suggests that further monitoring and control of changes in farming methods and countryside management is needed.

## KEEPING TRACK

Many song thrushes do lead secretive lives, foraging for food in dense undergrowth, woodland, hedgerows and shrubberies. Researchers radio-tag them to find out where and how they prefer to live. Farmers may then be encouraged to adapt their working practices to give the song thrush a better chance of survival.

## THRUSH-FRIENDLY GARDENS

Increasingly, gardens and parks offer sanctuary to song thrushes. Berry-bearing trees and shrubs, such as ivy, rowan, cotoneaster, pyracantha, holly and hawthorn make them more welcoming. Thick hedges and bushes encourage the song thrush to nest there as well. In winter, bird food is more readily accessible to the song thrush if it is scattered on the ground rather than on a raised bird-table.

▶ **UNDERWING COLOUR**
*If you see a blush of pale orange under the wings as a speckled brown bird flies over, you can be sure it is a song thrush.*

▶ **MISSING VOICE**
*Sadly, these days, much less is seen and heard of the brown speckled bird whose sweet song used to ring out from the tree-tops at dusk each evening in gardens all over the country.*

## Changes to the landscape

The resculpting of the traditional 'green and pleasant' English countryside over the past 30 years in the name of greater farming efficiency has left the song thrush beleaguered.

● Up to 6200 miles of hedges have been uprooted since 1990 to create larger fields, destroying nesting sites for the song thrush.

● The drainage of damp land and the destruction of ditches make it more difficult for thrushes to find enough food.

● The loss of natural grassland and meadows has cut the song thrush's foraging grounds.

● Smaller field margins and fewer fields left fallow over the winter have also hit the thrush by depriving the birds of precious seeds and grubs.

## Hunting the thrush

● The tradition of shooting and netting song birds in Europe hasn't helped the thrush either. Song thrush may no longer be a delicacy on British menus, but in France and Italy hunting thrushes is still a popular autumn sport. Flocks of migrating birds are slaughtered each year. On the last Sunday of October, in the Italian town of Montalcino, in Tuscany, the ancient Feast of the Thrush is a musical pageant to celebrate the end of the hunting season. Colourfully dressed townsfolk dance through the streets to the town's 13th-century fortress, where a feast of local dishes is laid out, with thrushes taking pride of place.

● Less flamboyantly, the 9 million domestic cats in Britain take their share of song thrushes, especially helpless young birds.

● The song thrush has other enemies too, ranging from birds of prey and foxes to nest-raiding magpies. Even greedy blackbirds bully it and steal its food.

## Winter rations

With song thrushes struggling to find enough to eat at the best of times, winter feeding is even more of a lottery. When a blanket of snow drives snails to take cover and earthworms to dig deep, a forlorn song thrush is grateful for any food it can find. A windfall apple is a temporary feast; a regular sprinkling of bacon rind and grated cheese on the lawn would be better.

▼ **NATURAL SNAIL EXTERMINATOR**
*By killing so many insects and snails, the widespread use of pesticides on farms and in gardens has robbed the song thrush of its favourite foods. Going easy on the slug pellets could entice more thrushes back into the garden to operate their own form of natural pest control.*

# The Poets' Muse

THE JOYFUL SONG of the thrush has inspired many poets to wax lyrical on the optimism of a new dawn, spring and romance or the anguish of nostalgia and homesickness.

When hankering to be in England for springtime Robert Browning (1812-89) vividly remembered how the song thrush is inclined to repeat each phrase of its song two or three times. As he famously described in *Home-Thoughts, from Abroad*:

> *That's the wise thrush; he sings*
> *each song twice over,*
> *Lest you should think he never*
> *could recapture*
> *The first fine careless rapture!*

Browning wasn't the only poet to notice this. In his glowing tribute, *The Throstle*, Alfred, Lord Tennyson (1809-92) rejoiced on hearing the song thrush singing in early spring:

> *Summer is coming!*
> *Summer is coming!*
> *I know it! I know it! I know it!*
> *Light again, leaf again,*
> *Life again, love again!*

## By another name

Up until 50 years ago, in many parts of England the traditional name for the song thrush was the *throstle*. (In fact, many bird lovers rebelled at the change and insisted on using the old name for a long time.) Various derivatives were used in different parts of the country: *Throg, Throggie* or *Throllie* in Yorkshire, *Thirstle* in the West Country, *Thrustle* in Shropshire.

The throstle often appeared in English poetry and literature. In *A Midsummer Night's Dream*, Shakespeare has Bottom commend: *The throstle with his note so true.*

'*At once a voice arose among*
*The bleak twigs overhead,*
*In a full-hearted evensong*
*Of joy illimited*'

from *The Darkling Thrush* by **Thomas Hardy** (1840-1928)

## ALL CHANGE

Reflecting on how he would miss the pleasure of hearing a thrush (*mavis*) singing in his poem *The Fallen Elm*, John Clare (1793-1864) wrote:

*The mavis sang and felt himself alone*
*While in thy leaves his nest was made,*
*And I did feel his happiness mine own*

A sense of 'things ain't what they used to be' was evident when the social reformer, William Morris (1834-96), penned his praise of a thrush:

*Oh thrush, your song is passing sweet*
*But never a song that you have sung,*
*Is half so sweet as thrushes sang*
*When my dear love and I were young.*

## PURE DISTRACTION

Writing movingly about a French battlefield in WWI in *A Thrush in the Trenches*, Humbert Wolfe (1886-1940) recorded how a thrush's song brought a welcome but temporary halt to the terrible conflict:

*Suddenly he sang across the trenches,*
*Vivid in the fleeting hush*
*As a star-shell through the smashed*
*black branches,*
*A more than English thrush.*

## The path of true love

Even the often cutting wit of Oscar Wilde (1854-1900) was susceptible to the song thrush's tune. In *From Spring Days to Winter*, he equates the path of many relationships with the song thrush's musical year:

*In the glad springtime when*
*leaves were green,*
*O merrily the throstle sings!*
*I sought among the tangled sheen,*
*Love whom mine eyes had never seen,*
*O the glad dove has golden wings!*

*Between the blossoms red and white,*
*O merrily the throstle sings!*
*My love first came into my sight,*
*O perfect vision of delight,*
*O the glad dove has*
*golden wings!*

*The yellow apples*
*glowed like fire,*
*O merrily the throstle sings!*
*O love too great for lip or lyre. . .*

*But now with snow the tree is grey,*
*Ah, sadly now the throstle sings!*
*My love is dead: . . .*

'*A thrush alit on a young-leaved spray*
*And, lightly clinging,*
*It rocked in its singing*
*As the rapturous notes rose loud and gay;*
*And with liquid shakes*
*And trills and breaks*
*Rippled through blossoming bough of May*'

from *The Music Lesson* by **Mathilde Blind** (1841-1896)

## Superstition and customs

● If country wisdom is to be believed, the prolonged singing of thrushes from bare trees or rooftops in January heralds a storm. (The mistle thrush used to be called the storm cock because of its habit of singing in high winds and rain.)

● In Scotland and East Anglia, another old name for the song thrush was *mavis*, probably from the Old French for a mewing seagull, *mauvis*. Many girls were called Mavis in the hope they would grow up with lovely singing voices like their feathery namesake.

*Its love song to the morn*
*I have heard the mavis singing*
*Mary of Argyle* by **Charles Jeffreys** (1807-1865)

● In winter, thrushes are partial to mistletoe berries, which is how the *mistle thrush* (right) got its name. Not only does the thrush deposit seeds it has swallowed in its droppings but it also strops its beak across nearby branches to dislodge seeds stuck to it in the very sticky berry juice.

*The thrush when he pollutes the bough*
*Sows for himself the seeds of woe*
**Anon.**

Unfortunately, this habit used to backfire on the thrush because mistletoe berries were used to make a sticky bird-lime which was spread on branches to trap them.

# The Collared Dove

*The collared dove came, saw and conquered the British Isles in less than 50 years, more quickly and comprehensively than Caesar's Roman troops or William's Norman army*

If you live in any town or village in Britain, there is likely to be a collared dove less than a mile away from you right now. If you cannot see it, you will probably hear it cooing soon. Such familiarity and abundance is all the more remarkable considering that abouty 50 years ago there were no collared doves to be found in Britain at all.

## INCORRIGIBLE PIONEER

From a starting population of two in Norfolk in 1955, there were more than 400,000 collared doves living throughout Britain by the turn of the century. During this swift spread over the country, collared doves prospered by exploiting people's property for food, roosts and nesting sites.

▶ *Prolific breeding and stalwart defence of the nest against predators, such as crows and magpies, go a long way to account for the collared dove's amazing record as a resourceful coloniser.*

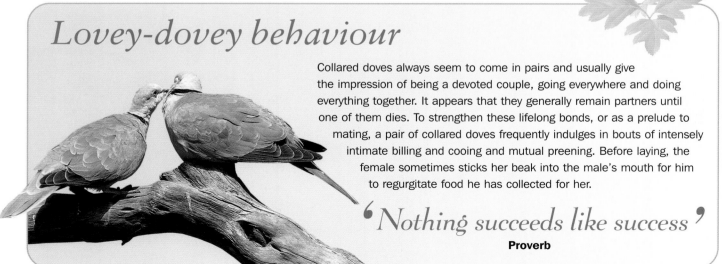

## Lovey-dovey behaviour

Collared doves always seem to come in pairs and usually give the impression of being a devoted couple, going everywhere and doing everything together. It appears that they generally remain partners until one of them dies. To strengthen these lifelong bonds, or as a prelude to mating, a pair of collared doves frequently indulges in bouts of intensely intimate billing and cooing and mutual preening. Before laying, the female sometimes sticks her beak into the male's mouth for him to regurgitate food he has collected for her.

**'** *Nothing succeeds like success* **'**
**Proverb**

# Going with the Grain

DURING THE LATE 1950s, birdwatchers waited with bated breath to see what effect the arrival of this newcomer would have on the native birdlife. It very soon became apparent that the collared dove was an innocuous invader; it had slotted neatly into a previously unexploited niche without ousting a native resident or regular winter or summer visitor.

The opportunity going begging could be summed up in one word: grain. Until the collared dove arrived there were no medium-sized, grain-eating, tree-nesting birds in Britain. Now it has very successfully filled that gap in the market.

## BUCKING THE TREND

Collared doves feed freely wherever plentiful amounts of grain are spilt on the ground. They also take grain as it is ripening in the fields. In fact they have a prodigious appetite for seeds and grain. One of the main reasons they do so well is that they wolf down the food faster than house sparrows and finches, which have to split the seeds first.

Collared doves normally feed on the ground, scavenging seeds that have fallen or been blown there.

They eat a largely vegetarian diet, taking grains, fruits and berries as well as seeds. Occasionally they pick up insects, such as beetles, too.

In the modern-day bird world, the collared dove has an unusual claim to fame: it is thriving in spite of the heavy use of pesticides and changes in agricultural practice. It has bucked a trend which has seen other birds

▲ *A collared dove visits a garden bird-bath to drink and bathe. Doves can drink by dipping their beaks into the water and sucking it up, then swallowing. Other birds have to tilt their heads back to let the water drain down their throats.*

that used to rely on spilt grain, such as the house sparrow, running into trouble and declining in numbers. For how long remains to be seen.

## Thanks very much

Collared doves owe at least part of their stupendous success to being opportunistic feeders. Many of the early recorded sightings were around chicken coops, where the doves were sharing the hens' corn. Today, pairs of collared doves regularly base themselves around garden bird-tables which are kept well stocked with grains, seeds and scraps.

As veteran camp followers, collared doves waste no time in exploiting any situation where grain and seeds are freely

available, whether it is on bird-tables or in farmyards, in zoo enclosures or around grain stores and flour mills. Most poultry farms and grain silos have a flock in residence nearby.

Three or four years after collared doves were first spotted in Hull on the Humber Estuary in 1959, large flocks of them were making regular feeding flights from their evening roosts in the suburbs to a flour mill and a lorry park that handled grain in the docks.

# Two by Two

THE BLEND OF TREES and open spaces in parks, churchyards and gardens evidently suits the collared dove. It now ranks among the most abundant and wide ranging of all garden birds – and is certainly one of the larger species to visit bird-tables regularly.

## SHOWING OFF

The main key to the collared dove's meteoric rise to stardom is its prolific breeding. Courting collared doves indulge in lots of cooing, bowing and chasing each other from telegraph pole to television aerial, from tree-top to telephone wire.

Unlike most birds, doves can fly virtually straight up in the air. When the male wants to impress a female, he noisily claps his wings together to gain height rapidly, then flamboyantly parachutes down, with his wings and tail fanned out, on a spiral flight path to land on the perch again. Then he tips forward, cocking his tail straight up in the air, as if he is bowing to her.

## NESTING PLATFORM

Collared doves are especially drawn to the year-round cover provided by evergreen conifers in churchyards and gardens for roosting and nesting. Urban collared doves also construct their nests on sheltered ledges on the outside of buildings and among the girders under bridges. In rural areas, they roost and nest in abandoned farm buildings.

Once a pair has selected its nest site, the male starts gathering twigs and brings them back to the female. She sits on the pile and arranges each one quite haphazardly into a flimsy platform around her. Collared doves have even been known to collect lengths of wire and pieces of wire mesh to incorporate into their nests.

▲ **UNDERSIDE**
*The feathers under the wings are white; the tail half black, half white.*

▲ **TAKING TURNS**
*The doves' behaviour provides a way of telling male from female – when incubating eggs, he always takes the afternoon shift while she sits on the nest overnight.*

> ' *Some vanquish by a single blow, others by efforts successfully repeated* '
> **Ancient Chinese Proverb**

## Getting off to a good start

Newly-hatched collared doves – or squabs as they are called – arrive in the world blind and sparsely covered with yellow down. At first they are fed on a very nutritious milky diet produced by both parents. During the breeding season, the walls of the crop (a storage pouch in the bird's gullet) thicken and the lining sloughs off to form a curd-like cheesy substance, known as crop milk, which is rich in proteins, fats, minerals and vitamins. The squabs grow incredibly quickly and can double their weight every 48 hours.

Crop milk production generally falls off after the first week, as the parents start weaning the squabs on to seeds. By the end of the second week the crop milk has dried up altogether. (Apart from mammals, only doves and pigeons, flamingos and penguins feed their young on a form of milk.)

◀ **THREE'S A CROWD**
*In less than three weeks, two squabs and one parent barely fit in the nest together – the tiny pink hatchlings have grown into energetic grey fledglings.*

▲ **PILE OF KINDLING**
*The collared doves' nest looks a bit like a heap of twigs which have been loosely and rather precariously arranged across some branches or on a ledge.*

## DOUBLE SHIFTS

The female lays one or two smooth white eggs; when there is a second egg, it is laid roughly a day and a half after the first. Both birds share the incubation; the eggs remain covered by one of the parents for 99 per cent of the time until they hatch 17 to 18 days later.

The hatchlings have unusually long, swollen beaks, which they thrust down their parents' throats to retrieve the crop milk that the adults regurgitate on demand. Fed on this rich diet at first, then partially digested grain, the squabs grow very quickly. They fledge in 17 or 18 days, but are fed by their parents for another three weeks.

## SECRETS OF SUCCESS

Theoretically, the ability to make a nourishing milk for their chicks frees the collared doves from having to rely on a seasonal food supply, such as caterpillars, for feeding their chicks. So they can breed at any time. In the British climate, a pair of collared doves generally produces four sets of twins a year, between March and October. In warmer regions they are known to breed all year round.

The minimum period between clutches is 32 days, which means that a pair may have two squabs growing up in one nest and two new eggs to incubate in another nearby. Such prolific breeding and a high survival rate – on average, half the chicks survive – are fundamental to their rapid spread and multiplication.

## Powdered down

Collared doves spend a lot of time preening. You often see them sitting in a summer shower, stretching out their wings and freshening up before rearranging their feathers with their beaks. Like other doves, a collared dove has special powder-down feathers – small white feathers which grow continuously and keep crumbling to produce a white dust which covers the whole bird and helps to keep the other feathers clean and waterproof.

# The Indian Invader

IN JUST 50 YEARS, collared doves have gone from being a meganotch on a keen birdwatcher's binoculars to a common garden resident, regarded by some as a disturber of the peace.

Collared doves originally came from India and Sri Lanka. During the 1600s they pushed westward, across Afghanistan, Asia Minor, Georgia, Armenia and Turkey, where their advance stalled until about 1912. Then, out of the blue, collared doves started to move steadily northwest again. What kindled this latest spark of wanderlust is not clear but it was probably some kind of spontaneous genetic change (mutation).

## PIONEERING ZEAL

By 1928 collared doves had reached Hungary where their spread gathered momentum. During the fastest period of expansion, from 1932 to 1952, collared doves were pushing north by about 60 miles each year, along a 150-mile wide corridor, advancing 1200 miles through war-torn Europe. Colonisation seems to have occurred in jumps of several hundred miles at a time, with subsequent backfilling and catching up.

By any standards, such progress was meteoric. Collared doves turned up in Czechoslovakia by 1935, on to Austria in 1938 and Germany and Italy by 1944, reaching Holland in 1947, then Denmark and the southwestern states of the USSR in 1948. Sweden and Switzerland fell in 1949, France in 1950 and Belgium in 1952. Before long they had hopped over the North Sea – or rather one had.

## GREAT EXCITEMENT

The first unofficial sighting of a lone collared dove in Britain was near Manton in Lincolnshire in August 1952. An unfamiliar dove was spied feeding happily among some chickens and identified as a male collared dove

*'A tiny spark of fire may set alight a whole prairie'*

**Old Chinese Saying**

## War and peace

At the start of the 17th century, the vast Mughal Empire in Afghanistan and India was ruled over by Emperor Akbar, the grandson of the founder of the Mughal dynasty, Prince Babur. While his grandfather had celebrated his successful invasion of India in 1526 by laying out the Garden of Fidelity in Kabul, the mighty Akbar indulged in the peaceful pastime of breeding doves as a diversion from fighting to defend or expand his empire. (In India, doves were sacred – Kamadeva, the Hindu God of Love, was always depicted riding on a dove.)

There is a certain sweet irony that, for all their war mongering, in 200 years the Mughals failed to conquer the whole Indian peninsula, while descendants of the doves they had bred succeeded in advancing peaceably over Europe and Britain in less than 100 years.

◀ *For a bird that originally hailed from India, the collared dove is remarkably impervious to long cold European winters. It does not fly away to warmer climes but sticks it out through snow and frost.*

'*To exceed is not necessarily to excel*'

**Proverb**

by a local postman, Reg May, who was a keen ornithologist. Hundreds of birdwatchers scrambled to catch a glimpse of the newcomer.

The first pair bred near Cromer in Norfolk in 1955. They've been on the march ever since. Their progress was closely monitored: they were seen in Surrey in 1956 and on Lewis off the west coast of Scotland in 1960. As early as 1964 there were an estimated 300 breeding pairs; that had risen to 100,000 by the early 1980s, when numbers were thought to be stable. Not so, as there are in the region of 200,000 pairs in Britain today.

### FREED SPIRIT

The scientific name of the collared dove, *Streptopelia decaocto*, literally means collar (*streptos*) dove (*peleia*). According to Greek myth, Decaocto was a poor, miserable servant girl. Hearing her prayers for mercy, the gods transformed her into a dove to relieve her misery. To this day, the dove's mournful call is said to echo the sadness of her former life.

## Unpopularity polls

● The collared dove's monotonous cooing and greedy appetite for grain mean that, in recent years, it has come to be regarded as a pest.

● Collared doves are also blamed for fouling buildings and footpaths, possibly spreading disease, damaging the masonry and causing a hazard to pedestrians. Nests can block guttering and downpipes. However, they may just be the scapegoats, when feral pigeons are the real culprits.

● In a straw poll taken among the members of staff at the British Trust for Ornithology, the collared dove was among the five birds least likely to be taken to a desert island.

● The collared dove's persistent cooing can be mistaken for a cuckoo's call and is blamed for bogus reports to *The Times* newspaper about hearing the first cuckoo of the year.

● It looks as though the collared dove is now set on colonising the USA. Although it only arrived in South Florida from the Bahamas in the early 1980s, it is rapidly expanding its range north and westward and is reported to be breeding in Georgia, Louisiana, Arkansas, Indiana and Colorado. Americans are already calling it the *beige starling* – a derogatory comment on its local abundance and noisy cooing.

# The House Sparrow

*The house sparrow may be a bit of a beggar and a gangster – it is noisy and bumptious too – but you have to admire its vivacity and confidence*

House sparrows are familiar and abundant worldwide. These adaptable little birds have forged a very successful career out of being camp followers, finding food and shelter around human settlements. Today, they are equally at home rifling through the rubbish bins of a city park, monopolising bird-tables in suburban gardens or jostling with the hens for their grain in a farmyard.

## RECIPES FOR SUCCESS

The house sparrow is a quick-witted, sharp-eyed opportunist, ready to exploit any situation for an easy crumb. Rather than being territorial, sparrows prefer to breed in small loose colonies and get together in noisy flocks to feed, bathe and roost.

▶ *The cock sparrow is a cool customer in more ways than one. He looks smart and he is sharp too, good at getting what he needs to survive in a hostile world.*

## Dusting down

All house sparrows revel in a spot of dust bathing during the summer to dislodge or discourage ticks and mites from clinging to their feathers. Here a female house sparrow is shuffling about in the dry earth, working dust into her dull brown feathers and throwing grit over her back with her wings. In the process, she is scraping a shallow crater in the ground.

To the exasperation of many gardeners, sparrows often choose the loose, neatly raked soil of a newly seeded lawn or flowerbed as their bathing ground, leaving the levelled surface pockmarked with hollows. Then, to add insult to injury, the impudent little birds often have the audacity to devour the seeds as well! One cheeky bunch of house sparrows regularly used to use a large bowl of gritty sugar in a worker's canteen as their dust bath!

# Cheeky Scavengers

SPARROWS FORAGE FOR most of their food by hopping jauntily about on the ground. Their stout beaks are well suited to a diet based on cereals, which they take from wherever they can find them – growing on an ear of wheat in a cornfield, scattered in a chicken run or in the more refined form of bread and cake crumbs on a bird-table. In the late summer and autumn, sparrows attack the seeds of wild plants, fruit and berries.

During spring and early summer, when house sparrows have chicks in the nest, the busy scavengers become eager hunters. They start catching aphids, caterpillars, sawfly grubs and other insects in order to feed their rapidly growing nestlings a diet that is richer in protein than grain and seeds alone can provide.

## ALL TOGETHER

For most of the year, house sparrows feed, roost and travel in flocks of 10, 20, maybe up to 50 birds, composed mainly of clan (family) members. The group stays in touch by making lots of penetrating – some say infuriating – *chi-chir-rip* and *chi-chip* calls. All their cheeping and rowdy squabbles often draw attention to the flock.

When a flock suddenly takes off together, there is an audible whirring of wings. Once in the air, sparrows fly briskly but they are thrifty pilots, doing only enough flapping to skim the hedge-tops or just clear other obstacles in their flight path. They rarely fly continuously for more than five to ten minutes at a time.

▲ *A few lucky sparrows are busy pecking seeds from a clump of dock. Generally these days, sparrows are in real trouble on farmland where modern intensive farming has all but eradicated weeds.*

'*Did not the sparrows watching round*
*Pick up the insects from your ground*
*Thus providence when understood*
*Her end and aim is doing good*
*Sends nothing here without its use*
*Which ignorance loads with its abuse* '

from *Summer Evening* by **John Clare** (1793-1864)

## Petal pinchers

In spring, yellow flowers such as primroses and crocuses are the most common. Their colour attracts early flying moths to pollinate them. House sparrows are also drawn to these yellow blooms, where they proceed to shred the petals into small pieces. This cock house sparrow is attacking the yellow flowers on a head of red-hot poker. Although all these flowers do contain nectar, the chances are that the sparrows are more interested in seeking out any insects hidden inside.

# Home from Homes

*female*

*male*

IN A SHELTERED nesting site under the eaves, house sparrows save time by making a higgledy-piggledy nest and stand a good chance of rearing all their chicks without being harassed by predators or humans.

Every spring, the cock house sparrow selects the place to build a nest. True to his name, he usually chooses a safe, weatherproof site under the eaves of a house or high up in a creeper on the walls. Failing that, a pair of house sparrows may adopt an old house martin's nest beneath the eaves before its owners get back from spending the winter in Africa; if push comes to shove, the aggressive sparrows will even evict the house martins in residence.

## COUNTRY NESTS

In the countryside, when buildings are in short supply, sparrows nest in equally impregnable positions, at the top of tall trees. There they fashion rough ball-shaped nests from straw and feathers. When thatched roofs and hay stacks were more common, house sparrows simply loosened up the straw to make a small cavity and added a few feathers to form a nest.

**▲ FAITHFUL MATES**
*The bond between the cock and the hen sparrow is long-term, often for life. The pair spends six months each year building a nest and rearing at least one but more likely three, and sometimes four broods together. The rest of the time they live in a small family flock.*

## COURTSHIP DANCES

Courtship displays begin early in March with some energetic sparrow dances. Having selected a nest site, the cock bird stays there, chirruping non-stop with wings shivering and tail raised, to attract his partner's attention – or, if he is single, to appeal to an unattached hen house sparrow in the neighbourhood.

When a hen sparrow starts to take an interest, the cock bird stiffens his tail and throws back his head so that his black bib is clearly visible. Then, holding his drooping wings out, he hops excitedly around the hen bird.

## Untidy nesters

Both cock and hen sparrow are involved in collecting dried grass and feathers to build their nest. They fly back to the nest site trailing long streamers of straw or with a feather banner in their beaks. When building in a nest-box or under the eaves, they cobble together a scruffy makeshift mound of straw and feathers on which to lay three to seven greenish-white eggs with grey blotches.

*'Yea, the sparrow hath found an house where she may lay her young'*

**Psalm 84: 3**

## Family life

female

Having established their partnership, a pair of sparrows starts building a nest. To reinforce their pair bond as they work, the cock bird presents bundles of straw to his mate, tapping her beak each time. Bill touching is also a prelude to mating.

Once she has laid her eggs, the hen sparrow does most of the incubating. Like other birds, she develops a large area of bare skin on her chest, called a brood patch, against which she warms her eggs. Off the nest, it is covered by feathers on her flanks. Although he does not have a brood patch, the cock bird takes his turn on the nest too, but only to cover the eggs while his mate takes a break to feed, drink and stretch her wings.

The chicks are naked when they hatch, 11 to 14 days after egg-laying. Fed on insects by both adults, the nestlings grow rapidly and are ready to leave the nest in roughly 17 days, when they join the family flock.

If she is impressed by his display and the site, her wings tremble and she lowers her body submissively.

The male's noisy wooing may also attract any unattached young cock sparrows in the area. They gather around to court the same hen. If one gets too close to her, she is likely to peck him. When the chirping reaches fever pitch, the hen at the centre of the attention can usually stand it no longer and flies off, pursued by her suitors. The song-and-dance wooing routine has to be resumed later.

▶ **PATERNAL PROVISIONS**
*The male sparrow does the lion's share of caring for his fledglings. While in the nest, the chicks are fed on insects but once they can fly, their father shows them where to find easier sources of food, such as crumbs from under a picnic table or on a bird-table.*

▲ **AT HOME WITH THE SPARROWS**
*Straggly strands of straw and loud chirruping are both signs that a pair of sparrows have stuffed their nest under the eaves and are busy raising their latest family. Sparrows are notorious for blocking gutters and downpipes with their nests.*

▼ **GROWING COLOURS**
*Juvenile house sparrows chase their parents about, cheeping loudly and begging for food with quivering wings. At first they all look like paler copies of their mother, until the young males get their first bib after an autumn moult.*

male

fledgling

# The Blackbird

*With his bold dark looks and deliciously rhythmic voice, the cock blackbird is probably the most easily recognised and best-known bird in British gardens*

From urban jungles to wildest moorland, from woodland and hedgerows to churchyards and gardens, it is virtually impossible to go anywhere in Britain without seeing or, more likely, hearing a blackbird.

### VIRTUOSO SOLOIST

Stationing himself on the highest tree, building or TV aerial around, the male blackbird pours out his musical song in rich contralto tones. It may not be the best voice in the bird world but, as the poet William Henley (1849-1903) put it so well:

*The blackbird plays but a boxwood flute*
*But I love him best of all*
*Because his song is all of the joy of life.*

Indeed he sings his melody so casually that it almost fizzles out at the end.

▶ *With a perfect golden beak and ring around his eye, not a shiny feather out of place, this handsome male blackbird is in prime condition to woo and win a mate.*

## White blackbirds

White blackbirds turn up quite frequently, especially in towns. A few are all-white but retain their yellow beaks and eye-rings so are not true albinos; most just have patches of bleached feathers on the head, wings or tail. The whiteness seems to be caused by a combination of breeding, diet and disease.

As Isidore of Seville (now patron saint of computing and the Internet) explained in his 7th-century bestiary about the nature of all God's animals, a white blackbird symbolised purity and was devoted to chastity. But, since whiteness runs in families, piebalds are evidently not always celibate.

An Irish man who has never seen a white blackbird, but is familiar with the national proverb *'There'll be white blackbirds before an unwilling woman ties the knot'*, may well give up wooing his reluctant girlfriend too soon!

# Changing the Menu

LIKE MANY BIRDS, the blackbird varies its diet according to what is plentiful and available at different times of the year. During the spring and summer, blackbirds spend a lot of time finding food on the ground. They prefer to eat earthworms, but feed on spiders, caterpillars, ants and snails as well.

## WELL-STOCKED CARPET

The garden lawn is the ideal hunting ground for a blackbird. It can hop across the short grass more easily than through the tall stems of a wild-flower meadow. Sometimes it stops, with its head tilted to stare at the ground, then suddenly prods the earth with its beak and deftly whips out an earthworm.

Always wary, a blackbird never ventures far from a thicket, hedge or shrubbery into which it can dive, grumbling noisily, if it is disturbed. Despite such twitchiness, blackbirds are notorious bullies when it comes to food, often terrorising other birds and stealing their prized catches.

## AUTUMNAL TASTES

As soon as berries begin to ripen and turn red on garden shrubs and in the hedgerows, the blackbirds are first in the queue to plunder the spoils. In autumn they eat a huge number of berries from honeysuckle, hawthorn, roses and bryony in the hedges and from bushes, such as cotoneaster, in the garden. Tassles of red berries on a rowan tree are great favourites.

During the winter, busy blackbirds can sound like feet shuffling through dried leaves as they impatiently toss leaf litter aside in search of snails, earthworms and insects hidden there.

▲ *Evidently on to a good thing among the daisies, this female blackbird may have paused to add one more worm to her wriggly beakful before flying back to her nest to feed her hungry chicks.*

## Feast of windfalls

During the autumn and winter months, blackbirds greedily tuck into windfall apples to supplement their hedgerow harvest. In summer they can make themselves unpopular with some gardeners – but not all, apparently – by pilfering soft fruits from raspberry canes, strawberry beds and cherry trees.

*' I value my garden more for being full of blackbirds than of cherries, and very frankly give them fruit for their songs '*

**Joseph Addison** (1672-1719)

# Family Matters

AFTER A LOT of skirmishing in the run-up to the breeding season, blackbirds buckle down to become diligent parents, working hard to rear at least two, often three and, exceptionally, four broods a year.

In autumn and winter, blackbirds relax their territorial grip and often flock together to feed and roost. The cock birds have an opportunity to size each other up and chase rivals noisily in and out of borders and bushes with aerobatic derring-do. Such scrambles usually culminate in boisterous mock jousts, where there is a lot of posing and screeching but few real fights. By spring, the males have divided up the garden, hedge or grove between them again.

## GOOD IMPRESSION

Come March and spring, the business of finding a partner starts in earnest. Each male picks the highest point in his territory from which to sing his jubilant melody, broadcasting for a mate and warning other blackbirds to steer clear of his no-go area.

In one-to-one courtship, the cock bird displays to a hen by dipping his golden bill, lifting his rump feathers and fanning out his tail. A flirtatious female throws back her head so that her beak and tail are pointing up to the sky and parades in front of him.

A paired-off cock and hen police their territory vehemently and vociferously during the breeding season. Few intruders of any kind are tolerated but other blackbirds get particularly short shrift. Predators are challenged too, including weasels, magpies and owls.

▶ **GUARD DUTY**
*During the breeding season, the male blackbird divides his time between protecting his territory, particularly from trespassing blackbirds, and tending to his mate and their chicks.*

▶ **GREAT EXPECTATIONS**
*With two parents stuffing earthworms down their necks all day long, blackbird chicks grow up fast. Just 14 days after hatching, they have their first set of feathers and are ready to launch themselves from the nest.*

*male*

▼ **DINGY FEMALE**
*Unlike her black mate, the female blackbird is a deep earthy brown on top. With her paler throat, speckled chestnut breast and brown beak, she is frequently mistaken for a song thrush.*

*female*

▲ **ALL HER EGGS IN ONE BASKET**
*Like that of the song thrush, the hen blackbird's nest is strong and bulky. She reinforces a frame of entwined roots and moss with mud, then adds a lining of dried grass to cushion her three to six blue-green, chestnut-brown freckled eggs.*

▼ **NOT YET A BLACK BIRD**
*Just-fledged young blackbirds look like browner, spottier versions of their mothers. The juvenile males always have black tails, while the tails of juvenile females are dark brown. After a late-summer moult, juvenile males spend their first winter looking sooty brown.*

*juvenile*

### FEMALE INITIATIVE

Nest built and eggs laid, the hen patiently incubates her clutch for 14 days. She only leaves briefly to find food or chastise trespassers. As soon as the chicks hatch, both parents go into super-caring mode. From dawn to dusk, they work tirelessly, taking away empty egg shells and excreta sacs as well as providing a regular food delivery service.

When the fledglings are ready to leave the nest, the parents cut their rations and fly about nearby, calling to them. Eventually, the boldest chick topples over the rim and finds it can fly, in a clumsy sort of way. In due course, the rest follow their sibling.

### WATCHING BRIEF

The fledglings are still helpless for 36 hours and emit feeble hunger cries to

attract their parents. This is why any apparently abandoned young bird should not be picked up and carried away; one of its parents is almost bound to be nearby taking care of it. In the blackbird's case, it is the male that looks after the youngsters for the next three weeks, as they get the hang of flying, feeding and roosting. Meanwhile his partner prepares for their next family.

# Gathering moss

The hen blackbird usually takes the lead in nest building. She selects a safe, secluded site, often in dense creeper against a wall or fence or in leafy trees or bushes. Then she collects nesting material and fashions a deep cup-shaped cradle. The more moss a hen blackbird can cram into her beak on each trip, the sooner her nest will be finished. After collecting a beakful of dried grass, some crafty female blackbirds have been seen flying to a puddle and rubbing the hay in mud before using it, ready-pasted, to bind and reinforce their nests. To help blackbirds find enough nesting material in your garden, you can leave small piles of moss and straw around and create a muddy patch in a flowerbed.

# Bye Bye Blackbird

FROM SPY PLANES and secret pirate codes to the title of a song recorded by the Beatles, the blackbird's name has been borrowed many times for its popular and powerful imagery.

Of all bird song, the blackbird's phrasing sounds most like human music. Famously, a blackbird really sang in a pop hit when The Beatles released their *White Album* in 1968:

*Blackbird singing in the dead of night*
*Take these broken wings and learn to fly*

Legend has it that Paul McCartney was woken by a blackbird singing and jotted down its tune. The song was recorded with Paul singing and playing guitar – and a real blackbird singing the backing. Many thought the lyrics referred to the Civil Rights Movement in America at the time.

It wasn't the first blackbird title to get into the hit parade. The haunting blues melody and lyrics of *Bye Bye Blackbird* were originally recorded in 1926 by Gene Austin. It was later popularised by such illustrious singing stars as Eddie Cantor, Frank Sinatra and Peggy Lee:

> *Pack up all my cares and woe,*
> *Here I go, singing low:*
> *Bye, bye blackbird.*

▲ *Musical notation of a snatch of blackbird's song*

## Blackbird spy plane

When it comes to flying, the American SR-71 Blackbird Spy Plane puts the feathered blackbird in the shade. It is the fastest, highest-flying plane in the history of aviation. It can travel at more than three times the speed of sound nearly 16 miles above the Earth's surface and has flown from London to Los Angeles in less than 4 hours.

' *The blackbird blows his yellow*
*flute so strong*
*And rolls away the notes*
*in careless glee* '

from *June* by **Francis Ledwidge** (1887-1917)

## BY MANY NAMES

According to St Isidore of Seville, the *merula* part of the blackbird's Latin name, *Turdus merula*, is derived from *mera volans*, which means *to fly at will*. He also said it used to be called *medula* because of its melodic song.

By the 17th century, the name of blackbird was already familiar. But Shakespeare favoured its old title of *ouzel* in *A Midsummer Night's Dream* when he had a defiant Bottom sing:

*The ouzel cock so black of hue*
*With orange-tawny bill*
Act III, Scene 1

*Woofell* was yet another alternative name for the blackbird in use in the 17th century when the English poet Michael Drayton (1563-1631) wrote:

*The woofell near at hand*
*hath a golden bill*

In Scotland, the blackbird was called a *merle*, possibly after *merlons*, the solid uprights of a battlement which, from a distance, look like blackbirds sitting in a row on a wall.

# Folklore and legend

● It is said that in 6th-century County Wicklow, St Kevin used to spend hours in silent prayer. One day a blackbird laid an egg in the Irish saint's outstretched hand and he stayed in that position until it hatched.

● In northern Italy, the last three days of January are often very cold and known as *'the days of the blackbird'*. Local legend has it that blackbirds were once white. Long ago, a blackbird sheltered from the cold in a chimney but its feathers turned black in the smoke, and blackbirds have been sooty ever since.

● The proverb *'To whistle like a blackbird'* means to do something easily.

● In his fable, *The Story of a White Blackbird*, the French romantic poet and writer, Alfred de Musset (1810-57) tells how a lonely white blackbird falls deeply in love with the white blackbird of his dreams. He discovers his beloved has duped him only when the tears he sheds expressing his love for her wash away her white make-up to reveal her dull brown feathers. Disgusted with her and himself, he vows to forsake the world for a remote place *'Where a blackbird is free to be white if he choose!'*

● If a blackbird is the first bird a young girl sees on 14 February, St Valentine's Day, she is said to be likely to marry a clergyman.

● St Gregory blamed the blackbird for leading people astray. He cited the case of St Benedict, who, after being visited by a blackbird, nearly broke his vow of chastity when he dreamed of a beautiful girl. Apparently he was able to resist the spell only by hurling himself naked into a bed of nettles.

# Four-and-twenty blackbirds baked in a pie

*Sing a song of sixpence,*
*A pocket full of rye;*
*Four-and-twenty blackbirds*
*Baked in a pie!*
*When the pie was opened*
*The birds began to sing;*
*Was that not a dainty dish*
*To set before the king?*

*The king was in his counting house*
*Counting out his money;*
*The queen was in the parlour,*
*Eating bread and honey.*
*The maid was in the garden,*
*Hanging out the clothes;*
*When down came a blackbird*
*And pecked off her nose*

Would you believe this innocent children's rhyme originated as a coded message to recruit pirates? It dates from the early 18th century when monarchs authorised privateers to cruise the high seas in search of treasure ships to plunder. Pirates were freelance maritime raiders.

When in port, the notorious pirate Captain Blackbeard had to be secretive about advertising for sailors to join his illegal and dangerous but lucrative way of life. So *Sing a song of sixpence, A pocket full of rye* announced a handsome payment of sixpence a day plus a leather pouch holding a litre of whisky – every sailor's dream.

The *four-and-twenty blackbirds* are Blackbeard's men and *baked in a pie* refers to how the pirates lured a passing vessel to its fate by pretending that their ship was crippled. Then they'd break cover and overpower the unsuspecting crew.

# The House Martin

*Every summer, house martins become our close neighbours, building their mud-cup nests under our roofs and scudding across the skies to sweep up airborne insects*

If you want to see house martins you have to look skywards. From late April to late October, that is where these little swallow-like birds are busy: stalking insects in the air over farmland, water and along the fringes of woodland, and skimming over rooftops in towns and villages all over the country.

### HIGH UP

When house martins are flying near buildings, scan the eaves to look for their muddy nest-cups stuck high up on the walls. In autumn, it is almost impossible to miss house martins, as they start thronging and chattering on telephone wires before leaving for their winter resorts in Africa.

▶ *The best way to distinguish a house martin from a swallow, sand martin or swift is to look out for its prominent white rump as it lands at its nest or streaks across the wild blue yonder.*

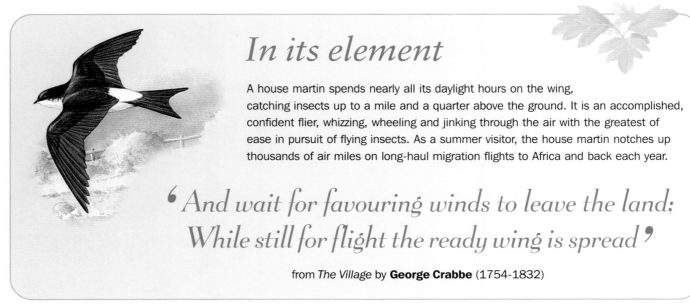

## In its element

A house martin spends nearly all its daylight hours on the wing, catching insects up to a mile and a quarter above the ground. It is an accomplished, confident flier, whizzing, wheeling and jinking through the air with the greatest of ease in pursuit of flying insects. As a summer visitor, the house martin notches up thousands of air miles on long-haul migration flights to Africa and back each year.

'*And wait for favouring winds to leave the land; While still for flight the ready wing is spread*'

from *The Village* by **George Crabbe** (1754-1832)

# Master Masons

HOUSE MARTINS USUALLY select north-facing walls on which to build their nests, so that the chicks inside won't cook on sunny days. Both partners collect mud from the banks of rivers, streams, ponds, puddles and farm gateways near the nest site, which they form into small usable pellets with their beaks.

## BUILDING SITE

Starting just below the eaves, a house martin builds its nest from the base up. Landing on a bare wall and fixing those first few mud pellets can be the trickiest part of the build. They prefer to work on a rough surface but can use brickwork or plaster, as long as there is a protruding nail or suchlike to pin the foundations on.

The house martins overlap the pellets, layer by layer, like bricks in a wall, and press them in place with their throats. They can't build too quickly because each course of pellets has to dry before the next is laid to stop the cup slumping.

Starting early on fine days, they build during the morning and spend the rest of the day feeding. About 2800 blobs and 14 days later, the

clay basin is complete. The finished nest has a small entry hole tight under the eaves and is lined with grass and feathers.

▲ *Gloriously squelchy sticky mud is just what a house martin needs when it is gathering muddy pellets to use for building its nest.*

‘ *There was a house, a house of clay, Wherein the inmate sat all day* ’

from *The House of Clay* by **Dinah Maria Craik** (1826-1887)

## Nesting colonies

Before there were houses, house martins used to build under rocky overhangs on cliffs and gorges; these days most nest under the eaves of houses or in window recesses. House martins are sociable birds and usually build their nests close together. On mainland Europe, nests may be plastered on top of one another in favoured sites – sometimes up to 40 or 50 pairs form a house-martin metropolis.

When it is finished, a house-martin's nest is an astounding feat of architecture and engineering. Two little birds have fashioned a snug, secure upside-down dome, about 15cm (6in) in diameter, out of mud. Even more astoundingly, they've managed to get it to stick to a vertical surface, on a wall, right up under the eaves.

# Close Families

ONCE THE NEST is finished, the female lays a clutch of four or five glossy white eggs. Both parents incubate the eggs for 14 to 16 days. When the chicks hatch, the adults toil all day long, flashing across the sky, gleaning a variety of flying insects – mostly small flies, beetles and aphids – and bringing them back to the nest. On warm days, flying insects are swept up on currents of warm air rising from the ground, and spiders hang-gliding on cobweb chutes may also join the aerial plankton.

### READY TO FLY

Depending on the weather, young house martins stay in the nest for 22 to 32 days until they are well developed and fully equipped to fly.

The parents encourage the fledglings to leave the nest by hovering at the entrance and calling to them to come out. For a while, the adults continue to feed their young, skilfully and swiftly passing insects over to them in mid-air and when they are perched on telephone wires.

### EXTENDED FAMILY

To raise three broods in one summer, a pair of house martins may rely on young from an earlier clutch helping to feed their younger siblings. At the end of the breeding season, the whole family may roost together – as many as 14 birds have been found in one nest. Alternatively, a new nest may be built as a dormitory annexe for the fledged young.

▲ **FAMILIAR VIEW**
*House martins are most frequently seen darting and dashing about, high up in the sky.*

‘ *Did not those birds some human shelter crave,*
*And stow beneath the cornice of his cave,*
*Their dry tight cups of clay? And from each door*
*Peeped on a morning wiseheads three or four.* ’

from *The Birds* by **Sir John Collings Squire** (1884-1958)

## Solar treatment

Flocks of house martins often gather on south-facing roofs in late summer to bask in the bright sunshine and soak up the warmth radiated by the tiles. They can famously tolerate temperatures as high as 27°C (80°F). House martins get chilled during the cold nights of early autumn and this solar therapy may be their equivalent of a soak in a warm bath to loosen up their flight muscles.

The house martins may also be trying to burn off a heavy burden of irritating body lice and mites picked up in the nest. On one occasion, a nest in Surrey was found to contain 452 living parasites including fleas, bird flies, martin bugs and fowl mites. Scorching the parasites out of their feathers helps to get the house martins' plumage into peak condition before they start migrating.

▶ SHUTTLE SERVICE
*Between them, a pair of house martins and their family helpers keep up a non-stop delivery of freshly-caught insects to their nestlings from dawn till dusk.*

▲ YOUTHFUL IMPATIENCE
*When nearly fledged, house martin chicks find their way to the tiny entrance at the top of the nest cup, poke their heads out and chirp loudly.*

Very late broods, with chicks still in the nest into October, often end in disaster. All goes well, considering the parents are working in cooler conditions and shorter days, until the adults can no longer ignore their migratory urge. Then one day, they suddenly leave for Africa, abandoning their nearly fledged chicks, which inevitably die.

### ALL DEPENDING ON...

The house martin's breeding success depends on a combination of factors. Finding a suitable nesting site is the first step. Some people now put up wire mesh under the eaves to stop house martins nesting there.

Older house martins often return several years running to existing nests, which already occupy the prime sites. You can tell which ones are being renovated: the new mud used to plug cracks and holes stands out as darker and shinier than the well-baked clay of the old part.

An ample supply of sticky mud to build or repair the nest is vital; in a dry spring, nesting may be delayed by a lack of mud. Then, once their chicks hatch, the house martins need plenty of warm dry days to bring out swarms of flying insects to catch and feed to them.

After breeding, and before migrating, house martins of all ages prefer to roost in their old nests or in trees. Only a few choose to join swallows and sand martins massing in reed beds each night. Eventually, they all depart for Africa in the autumn.

## Hard to tell

It is tricky to pick out the juvenile house martins from the adults when they are all flying about at high speed. From afar, a house martin looks black and white. But closer to, an adult turns out to have a more beautiful glossy blue-black crown and back than a younger bird, which looks browner and duller.

One key area for recognition is the house martin's plain white throat: it does not have the brown breast band of the sand martin or the red chin of the swallow.

*juvenile*

# The Lucky Martlet

THE GOOD FORTUNE bestowed by house martins nesting on a building was once highly prized. Long ago, when house martins failed to nest under the eaves of St Mary and All Saints Parish Church in Bingham, near Nottingham, parishioners were worried. To ensure their church was always blessed in future, they had a house martin at its nest carved into the stone above the church porch.

## HERALDIC MARTLETS

The house martin's little legs are just about long enough to hold its body clear of the ground so its feathers don't get caked with mud. The legs are covered in feathers, which may help to prevent heat loss as the house martin flies at high altitudes over mountains on its migration journeys. The short legs are fine for clinging to the nest but no good for walking: a house martin usually lands and takes off from the same spot, often without taking a single step.

In ancient heraldry, the house martin, or martlet as it was known, appeared as a legless bird on coats of arms. Frequently, martlets decorated the crest of the fourth son of an aristocratic family, symbolising one who had no rightful claim to any land – in other words 'he didn't have a leg to stand on'!

▲ *Chattering house martins look rather like notes on a musical manuscript when they congregate on telephone wires prior to migration in the autumn.*

' *This guest of summer, the temple-haunting martlet, doth approve, By his lov'd mansionry, that the heaven's breath smells wooingly here* '

from *Macbeth, Act I, Scene 6* by **William Shakespeare** (1564-1616)

# Folklore and legend

- There is quite a long and convoluted explanation for the house martin's scientific name, *Delichon urbica*. *Delichon* is an anagram of *chelidon* from *khelidon,* the Greek for swallow. This way of officially naming a bird may seem a bit flippant but is an accepted method of nomenclature. The Australian kookaburra is a large member of the kingfisher family: in its scientific name, *Dacelo novaeguineae, Dacelo* is an anagram of *Alcedo*, the name of the common kingfisher.

- *Urbica* comes from the Latin word for town, *urbs*, and alludes to the house martin's habit of nesting on buildings in towns and villages.

- In Britain the choice of a common boy's name, Martin, for the house martin was almost certainly a mark of its familiarity. The use of this name was probably originally inspired by the French name for the swift, which was Martinet, Martinette, Martnet or Martlet.

- In 1544, William Turner called it Rok Martinette, after its habit of nesting on cliffs, and Chirche Martinette. Shakespeare also knew it as the 'temple-haunting' martlet

- There are many punch lines to this old proverb, all of which imply that the house martin is one of God's favoured birds whose good fortune rubs off on anywhere it builds its nest:

  *The martin and the swallow –*
  *Are God Almighty's bow and arrow* or
  *Are God Almighty's bird to hollow*
  (meaning to keep holy) or
  *Are God Almighty's scholars* or
  *Are God Almighty's mate and marrow*
  (meaning good companions).

---

In French heraldry, the martlet used to be known as *la merlette*, which literally applied to a female blackbird but was often depicted looking like a swallow. Martlets appeared on the shield of the noble Norman family of Arondell, whose name came from *hirondelle*, the French for swallow, and after whom the ancient town of Arundel in West Sussex was named.

### POWER STRUGGLES

There are times when a pair of house martins has no sooner completed its nest than along comes a couple of house sparrows to hijack it. In many cases, possession is nine-tenths of the law: the house martins are ousted. Rumours used to abound that the house martins took their revenge by plastering the usurpers into the nest so that they could not escape.

### CHUCKLING STREAM

House martins chatter all the time: around the nest, in the air and when perched on telephone wires. To some this babbling sounds like '*the soft chuckling of a running burn*' but to others it is an irritating cacophony.

*' No jutty, frieze, buttress nor*
*coigne of vantage,*
*But this bird hath made his pendant*
*bed and procreant cradle '*

from *Macbeth, Act I, Scene 6* by **William Shakespeare** (1564-1616)

## Noisy neighbours

Underneath a lamppost is probably the last place to stand if house martins have chosen to build their nests beneath its canopy. Chirping birds are flying in and out all the time; a few rowdy quarrels flare up and begging young create a lot of noise and mess. Although it was once a lucky omen when house martins nested on a house, they are not always popular these days. But the law is on their side: it is an offence to disturb or destroy their nests during the breeding season.

# The Jay

*A jay takes fright very easily and, as one of the noisiest birds in the woods, it is usually heard, rather than seen, flying off to the shelter of the trees*

A dedicated woodland bird, the jay is totally at home among mature trees, especially oaks. In spite of its striking colours and markings, a jay usually remains fairly invisible because it spends most of its time under the cover of dense foliage, where it slips through the branches with the greatest of ease.

### WOODLAND ALARMIST

As self-appointed sentries, jays are excitable and vociferous birds. You are only likely to know that a jay is nearby when you get too close. Then, on taking flight, it utters a tirade of angry ear-splitting squawks, *kraak-kraak*. As confirmation that you have disturbed a jay, you can hardly miss the flash of white rump as it hightails it deeper into the wood.

▶ *The watchful jay is always on the look-out for danger in the woods. At the first sign of intruders it rattles off a volley of jangling calls to warn other wildlife.*

## Quiet interlude

The only time that rackety jays are dumbstruck is during the breeding season when they need to keep the location of their nests secret to deceive magpies, tawny owls, squirrels or even other jays that would steal their eggs or chicks. If you hear a jay's jangling screams in June or July, it is unlikely to be anywhere near its own nest; it is probably robbing another bird of its eggs or chicks. After the young jays have fledged, normal noisy service is resumed, with family troupes scouring the woods, following each other's harsh squalls.

*‘ From bush to bush slow sweeps the screaming jay, With one harsh note of pleasure all the day ’*

**John Clare** (1793-1864)

# Jay Marriages

IN SPRING, ROWDY assemblies of 20 to 30 excited jays gather in the tree-tops to find a mate. After some hectic bouts of follow-my-leader and a few choruses of soft crooning, a male jay confronts a female in a clearing. With his crest raised, feathers fluffed and wings slightly spread, he sways to display his markings. Such boisterous courtship gatherings – or marriages as they are called – end in jays pairing up and forming lifelong bonds.

## NEST IN SECRECY

Paired off by the end of April, a male and female jay build a well-concealed nest low down in thick undergrowth or dense ivy growing up a tree trunk. They weave a platform of sticks and twigs, bound together with a little mud, then line it with a thick layer of rootlets and hair.

The female jay usually lays four to six blue-green eggs with a few grey-brown specks at the rounded end. As soon as the clutch is complete, she starts incubating her eggs. She sits low on the nest and is hard to spot. While she is sitting, her mate feeds her.

The eggs hatch after 16 days but the female continues to brood her featherless chicks for the next few

days, as they soon get chilled if left exposed. At first, the male finds all the family's food until his mate can join him. The nestlings eat greedily and grow fast. After two weeks, all but their tail feathers are sprouting; in 19 to 20 days they are fledged and ready to roam the woods with their parents.

Despite its flamboyant plumage, the jay is often misidentified: it pays to think twice about which bird the

▲ *Amazingly, gawky young jays rarely fall out of their twiggy nest as they launch themselves at a parent, silently begging to be fed. The adults collect caterpillars, which they store in a throat pouch before taking the feast back to their chicks.*

flash of pink or black-and-white plumage you have just seen in the trees belongs to. Without a better look, a jay could easily be a nuthatch or great spotted woodpecker.

## Feather raising

Like many birds, jays enjoy splashing about in water to freshen up their feathers before preening. Any shallow pool or clean puddle is a good bath.

The most reliable indicators of the jay's mood are the cream-and-black streaked feathers on its crown. Although normally worn slicked back, when a jay is angry, alarmed or excited, these animated feathers are raised into a spiky crest. Depending on motivation, such crown-lifting is accompanied by a

variety of posturing and chattering calls to reinforce the message.

If you are ever lucky enough to catch a jay unawares, and can spy on it for a while without it realising you are there, you can witness how alert it is. It twists its head from side to side all the time, keenly scanning its surroundings for anything untoward. At the same time, the restless jay is likely to be lifting and lowering its fanned out tail or swinging it from side to side.

# Acorn Hoarders

JAYS USUALLY FEED on the woodland floor, eating beechnuts, hazelnuts, sweet chestnuts and pine seeds, as well as their great favourites, acorns. In autumn, mature oak trees produce thousands of acorns, many of which are picked up by jays to be stored away in their secret larders.

To eat an acorn, a jay holds it steady with its toes, then tears off the casing with its strong beak to reach the edible core. The jay is also fond of eating any berries, cherries, plums, pears and soft fruit it comes across in hedgerows, gardens and orchards.

## FAMILY FOOD

When it is feeding chicks in the nest, a jay adds animal protein to its diet and starts catching earthworms, snails, spiders and insects, especially caterpillars, beetles and earwigs. In the process they destroy many pests, including click beetles (adult wire worms) and winter moths.

During the breeding season, the jay is a keen mouser: it kills a mouse with two or three blows to its head before swallowing it whole. Jays are also notorious for stealing eggs and chicks from other birds' nests: a jay can clear a nestful of young thrushes or blackbirds in less than ten minutes. Poaching game-birds' eggs and chicks always makes them very unpopular with gamekeepers.

**▲ THE UNDERCARRIAGE**
*To a birdwatcher, the underside of the jay in flight is as distinctive as the top. The juxtaposition of pink and white plumage, black tail and broad, rounded wings are definitive.*

## Acorn collecting

In September and October, when the acorns ripen, jays methodically scour oak trees and the woodland floor for the latest crop. Instead of eating only what they require at the time, and leaving the rest for other birds and animals, the jay secretes the lion's share of the harvest.

• Incredibly, a jay can carry up to nine acorns at a time, thanks to its unusually large throat pouch. Generally it only takes three or four acorns per trip, plus one in the beak.

• It transports the acorns to different hiding places, often within half a mile, but sometimes as far as nearly two miles from where it picked up its booty.

• By creating its own larders in this way, a jay can store away enough food to last it for the whole year. Over the course of a winter, a jay relies on these stores to keep it going and is amazingly accurate at remembering where they are.

• The following summer, when the uneaten acorns begin to sprout, the new growth sometimes jogs the jay's memory and it quickly roots up the acorn underneath.

*'As sweet as any nut put by, Selected by a squirrel's eye'*

from *The Lily of Our Valley* by **W H Davies** (1871-1940)

# Anting antics

Most birds replace their old worn feathers with new ones at least once a year in a moult. But without daily attention, the feathers lose their insulating and waterproofing properties and flight becomes inefficient. In addition to regular bathing and preening routines, during the summer jays indulge in anting to keep their feathers in prime condition.

● The jay crouches down on an anthill and fans its tail out on the ground so a swarm of ants can crawl all over its feathers. It shows no sign of distress while the ants are running over it. Sometimes it picks up some ants in its beak and rubs them over its plumage, squirting a fluid out of them, and may even eat some of them.

● Most ants in Britain produce noxious chemicals, such as formic acid, to defend their colonies, attack their enemies and immobilise their prey. The jay may use such poisons as an insecticidal shampoo to purge itself of parasitic ticks and mites. Or the chemicals may serve as a feather conditioner.

◄ **SEED DISPERSER**
*By ferrying acorns to various secret locations around a wood, the jay plays an important role in distributing and seeding new oak trees. It will retrieve most of the acorns later, but the ones it forgets become the next generation of oak trees when they germinate.*

► **BURYING TREASURE**
*The jay's favourite hiding places for nuts and acorns are under leaves, among roots and moss or in tree holes. Jays have excellent memories and recall the location of most larders. Even when the ground is covered with snow, they know exactly where to dig.*

CHAPTER 3 · AUTUMN

# The Dunnock

*The dunnock has made a successful career out of staying in the background and being seen as an unexciting bird when in reality it is far from quiet or dull*

The modest dunnock seems to have turned unobtrusiveness and drabness into a way of life. A dunnock may appear to be very shy because it does nothing to draw attention to itself as it weaves its way through hedges or shuffles across the ground. In reality, it is just getting on with things in its own sweet way. Its quietness is a bit of a myth too: the soft song may be colourless but it is heard more than most, at any season.

## IN ANY HEDGE

Dunnocks often pass unnoticed but there are plenty out there, living in the shelter of hedgerows and bushy places everywhere: in woods, parks and gardens, as well as on farmland, scrub and wasteground.

▶ *It is a pleasant surprise to see a dunnock standing out in the open on a bramble stem where its beautiful warm brown and ashy colouring can be admired.*

## Cinderella of the bushes

The dunnock may be modest, retiring and often overlooked, but it is among the top 10 most common and popular garden birds in Britain. Many spend much of the year creeping about in the undergrowth on their own. After families break up in late summer, it is unusual to see more than two or three dunnocks in the same place over the winter.

*'The hedger\* lonesome brustles at his toil'*

from *Signs of Winter* by **John Clare** (1793-1864)

(\*Hedger is an old nickname for the dunnock)

# The Hedge Mouse

FOR MOST OF THE year the dunnock forages on the ground, staying out of sight under a hedge, in leaf litter or around the fringes of a lawn. It rarely ventures far from a border's edge, so it can beat a hasty retreat to cover if disturbed, rather like an inoffensive mouse. Its Dutch name of *heggemus*, meaning hedge mouse, suits it well.

A dunnock has the fine pointed beak of an insect-eater. During spring and summer, it industriously searches for flies, beetles and tiny caterpillars that have fallen to the ground from the overhanging branches of trees. Dunnocks also collect huge numbers of small earthworms, spiders and small snails. Food-hunting takes on a fresh urgency when there are many hungry chicks in the nest during the breeding season.

### DISAPPEARING DUNNOCKS

In the summer, when hedgerows and thickets supply all the insects and creepy-crawlies they need, dunnocks often vanish from gardens. But they usually reappear again in the autumn when they come in search of seeds and scraps. Sometimes they will land on bird-tables, especially those with a roof, but are more often seen feeding on the ground beneath. There they can neatly peck up crumbs of bread, cake, biscuits or nuts which have been knocked off the bird-table.

▲ *This is where you might expect to get your best view of a cautious dunnock, as it crouches and shuffles diffidently among the daisies on a garden lawn.*

> '*And the bird-loving dame can do no less Than throw it out a crumble on cold days*'
>
> from *Hedge-sparrow* by **John Clare** (1793-1864)

## Braving the winter

In Britain, the dunnock is one of the few insect-eating birds that stays around during the winter. During the colder months, it supplements its insect diet with seeds from low-growing weeds such as plantain, chickweed and sorrel, plus crumbs from the bird-table. Such adaptability is one key to the dunnock's success.

The dunnock also does a lot of preening and bathing in colder weather to keep its plumage in tip-top condition so it will provide better weatherproofing and insulation to keep out the wet and cold.

More female dunnocks die in cold winters than males as the cock birds are slightly larger and claim superior rank when it comes to grabbing food. Sometimes there is a surplus of male dunnocks going into the spring, which may be one reason for some unusual breeding trios. All in all though, dunnocks often emerge from harsh winters in better shape than many other small birds.

# The Hedge-hatcher

DUNNOCK-WATCHERS WERE amazed to discover that this seemingly dull little bird has an outrageously unorthodox sex life. In the dunnock's world, it seems as if 'for richer, for poorer' is ignored in favour of promiscuity. Unusually among birds, both the male and female dunnock are able to vary their partnership arrangements and breeding behaviour according to the quality of their habitat.

### COMPLICATED LIAISONS

When there is plenty of food, a male dunnock may reckon that the hen bird will be able to rear her brood with little help from him. He may couple with two or three females that year, each of which builds her nest and rears her family in his territory.

In leaner years, a female dunnock may recognise that she is going to need more help in raising her family than one male can provide. While she lets her nominal partner mate with her frequently, she may also enlist the help of a toy boy. Her mate tolerates the presence of this young pretender on his patch as long as he keeps a low profile and helps to rear his family. The female can be fickle and reward the junior male with a chance to mate with her behind her partner's back. This also encourages him to stay and help rear her chicks.

### MIXED BROODS

Tests on chicks in dunnocks' nests show that they often have different fathers. Despite or perhaps because

> ‘ *It makes a nest of moss and hair and lays*
> *When e'en the snow is lurking on the ground*
> *Its eggs in number five of greenish blue*
> *Bright beautiful and glossy shining shells* ’

from *Hedge-sparrow* by **John Clare** (1793-1864)

**▲ FREE LOVE**
*The dunnock's drab brown and grey plumage and shy-violet manner belie its promiscuous behaviour during the breeding season. While the male woos any willing would-be consort, the female is also out to seduce as many partners as she can.*

## Anti-cuckolding strategy

male

female

The dunnock's mating display is an elaborate, noisy dance: with his wings drooping, the cock bird excitedly chases his partner around in ever-decreasing circles, singing passionately all the time. Eventually she stoops down, with ruffled feathers and quivering wings, and lifts her tail to signal that she is ready to mate. If her first suitor is slow to accept her invitation, the fickle female may dash off to mate with another willing male nearby before rushing back to him.

But the first male has his own cunning ruse to avoid wasting his time rearing a rival's chicks. As the excited female raises her tail, the male pecks at her exposed backside, causing the female to eject a white droplet of sperm from a previous mating. Only when the channel is clear does her partner mate with her.

◄ **FLYING OFF**
*In the air, the dunnock manages to look unhurried even though it is usually fluttering, low and fast, straight for cover. Sadly dunnocks are often hit by cars as they make hedge-to-hedge dashes across busy roads.*

► **TRIO OF CARERS**
*Tucked safely away in a clump of brambles, five ravenous dunnock nestlings beg for food from one of their parents or their mother's lover cum chick-minder. Dunnocks are very wary when visiting or leaving their nests. They always checking carefully whether the coast is clear before ducking into or out of the hedge.*

of their unconventional partnership arrangements, dunnocks make very diligent parents and uncles.

Stuffed with a feast of insects, the hatchlings grow very quickly. In just 12 days, the sooty-coloured downy chicks are fledged and ready to leave the nest. As soon as the first brood is launched into the world, the adults start building a fresh nest in which to raise brood number two.

**CUCKOO'S FAVOURITE**
Cuckoos are infamous for shirking their parental responsibilities. Rather than build a nest of her own, a hen cuckoo lays her eggs in the nests of other small birds. Unfortunately for dunnocks, she often picks on them to foster her chick. Even though her mottled grey egg stands out like a sore thumb among the host's lovely blue eggs, the hapless dunnocks don't

seem at all concerned. They just get on and incubate it along with the rest. Once it hatches, they are unable to prevent their monstrous guest from kicking their eggs or chicks out of the nest. Nor do they attempt to retrieve their eggs or feed the ejected chicks. Instead, they lavish all their parental care on one cantankerous cuckoo chick and sacrifice their chances of raising a brood of their own.

# Out of the blue

Hen dunnocks usually build their nests low down in the thickest part of a hedge or bush or among a tangle of brambles. The nest is a neat cup of dried grass and moss woven on to a base of fine twigs and lined with hair or wool. The hen dunnock generally lays four to six exquisite plain turquoise eggs, each of which is quite pointed. Before her clutch is complete, she may hide her dazzling eggs under a cover of nest lining to stop them catching the eye of a female cuckoo or nest-robbers. She incubates them on her own for about 12 days.

# The Coal Tit

*The charming little coal tit shares the endearing qualities of agility and cheekiness with its larger cousins, the great tit and the blue tit*

Looking like a faded miniature great tit, with all the restless energy and acrobatic prowess of a blue tit, the coal tit is the least familiar and numerous of the three common garden tits.

### TREE TIME

Coal tits are first and foremost birds of woodland, particularly associated with conifer trees. They gravitate to parks, gardens, churchyards and old orchards with mature trees, especially when there are any pines, firs, cedars, larches or yews present.

In summer, a coal tit is hard to see because it spends much of its time hunting for insects in the tree-tops. It is more visible in the winter, when it visits bird-tables or forages in beech and alder woods with other tits.

▶ *The white patch on the back of the coal tit's neck is the key to distinguishing it from other black-capped tits.*

Continental
coal tit

Irish
coal tit

## Different colourways

There are two neighbouring races of coal tit that sometimes turn up on mainland Britain. The Continental coal tit (*Parus ater ater*) from western Europe has a bluer-grey back than the British coal tit (*Parus ater britannicus*) and is a rare winter visitor along the southeast coast of England. Many coal tits in western Scotland and Wales, especially in wintertime, resemble the Irish race (*Parus ater hibernicus*) which has a yellower tinge to the white plumage on its nape and cheeks.

*'Dear little wildwood bird! Mayhap There's wisdom under your black cap'*

from *The Snow Lies Still* by **W W Christman** (1937)

# Woodland Fare

VERSATILITY AND AGILITY in seeking out its food, plus an ability to store the surplus, stand the coal tit in good stead, especially over the winter. In the summer, while there are chicks in the nest, coal tits focus on catching spiders and insects, their eggs and larvae. They are partial to aphids, moths, caterpillars, weevils, flies and bugs that they hunt for in the upper branches of trees near the nest.

The coal tit takes advantage of its light weight and nimbleness to hover and snatch insects from leaves or to hang underneath a branch or twig to find food. It hunts over tree trunks more than other tits, hopping up and around the bark like a treecreeper.

Later on in the year, when insects are scarcer, quite un-tit-like, coal tits start feeding on the ground, picking up pine seeds, nuts and beech mast. They often form mixed flocks with other tits, scouring woodland, hedges and gardens for the seeds and nuts.

## HOARDING FOOD

Coal tits stash surfeit nuts and seeds in slits in the bark, among tassels of pine needles or patches of lichen, to eat later. Each beakful is stored separately rather than accumulated in a single large cache. Usually the reserves are kept for only a few days before being eaten. In the garden, great tits may steal the prudent coal tit's stored emergency rations.

▲ *In the winter, coal tits frequently join flocks of siskins and redpolls in feeding trips to alder and birch woods to pick the seeds from the mature female catkins.*

## Beating the bullies

During the winter, coal tits are frequent visitors to gardens, clambering over peanut-feeders and taking seeds and suet laid out on bird-tables. Because they usually get shoved aside by larger great tits and blue tits, coal tits have taken to slipping in when the coast is clear, grabbing a peanut or seed and flying off again quickly, either to eat or hide their prize elsewhere.

'*I have a generous table spread*
*With corn and nuts and fat and seed*'

from *The Snow Lies Light* by **W W Christman** (1937)

# The Hole Family

LIKE OTHER TITS, the coal tit prefers to nest in the shelter of a tree-hole, where its chicks can take their time growing up. Coal tits start breeding from March onwards, slightly earlier than the great tits and blue tits.

When courting, an amorous male approaches his prospective partner with his head held high so she can see his black chin clearly. They touch beaks before she moves on; he chases her and repeats the introductions for as long as it takes him to persuade her to become his mate.

### READY TO NEST

Once they are paired, both birds go in search of a suitable nest site. The coal tits' favourite nesting places are in abandoned woodpecker holes or natural tree-holes, quite low down on a dead or decaying stump. But if the entrance hole is big enough, they are all too easily outcompeted for

nesting space by blue and great tits. Consequently, coal tits are frequently forced to build in crevices between rocks or in stone walls, among the roots of a tree or in empty mouse or rabbit holes. They will also use nest-boxes with small entrance holes in the garden, particularly if these are placed near the ground, because blue

tits that would also use the boxes prefer to nest slightly higher up.

The female usually selects the final location for the nest. Working on her own, she spends the next 26 days assembling a cup of mosses and dead leaves bound together with spiders'

◀ **LIGHT AS A FEATHER**
*Climbing over or hanging under a fine twig of pine to probe between the needles for insects and spiders presents no problem for a featherweight coal tit.*

> ‘*Under the twigs the black cap hangs in vain*
> *With snow-white patch streaked over either eye*
> *This way and that he turns and peeps again*
> *As wont where silk-cased insects used to lie*’

from *The Blackcap* by **John Clare** (1793-1864)

*juvenile coal tit*

## On leaving the nest

From 16 to 19 days after hatching, the fledgling coal tits are ready to leave the nest. The juvenile's back is browner than the adult's, with yellower underparts, cheeks, nape and wingbars. Their small size, pale nape patch and the absence of a dark belly stripe helps to distinguish them from young great tits.

After leaving the nest, the youngsters huddle together in thick cover for several days, calling out to attract their parents' attention. (The fledglings from other tit families follow their parents about.) The young coal tits soon perfect the acrobatic skills that are the hallmark of all tits, and become independent within two weeks.

webs. She lines it with wool or fur from small mammals such as rabbits and dead mice and may add a few feathers. The male feeds his mate on a protein-rich diet of insects while she is nest-building and incubating the eggs. When she is disturbed on the nest, the female gives a long *hiss* to deter any intruders.

## BRINGING UP THE BROOD

The hatchlings are covered in fluffy grey down but totally helpless. For the first nine days after hatching, the female returns to the nest each night to keep the chicks warm. Otherwise, the adults always roost singly, often under overhanging branches, in old nests and tree-holes or in tangled ivy. The coal tit is the tiniest bird to roost on its own over the winter months.

The nestlings soon start pleading for food, opening their beaks wide to reveal a bright orange-pink lining to their mouths, framed in pale yellow flanges. For nearly three weeks, both parents spend all their time feeding their chicks. On average, they must find an insect every 2.5 seconds over a gruelling ten-hour day to keep up with the ceaseless demands of their rapidly-growing brood.

### ▲ TOP HOLE
*As far as the coal tit is concerned, this hole in a rotting branch on an old tree is prime real estate – a safe, weatherproof place to build a nest and rear a family.*

## Mossy cup

Like other tits, the coal tit rears a large brood. The female generally lays from eight to ten smooth white eggs with reddish-brown freckles – sometimes there are as many as 13 eggs in a clutch. She incubates the eggs on her own for 14 to 16 days. A pair of coal tits usually raises one brood each year, occasionally two.

# The Goldfinch

*If you see a blur of bright crimson and gold fluttering around a clump of ripe thistles, it is likely to be a party of dainty, colourful goldfinches on a feeding mission*

Just like wandering minstrels, goldfinches are always on the move, twittering in tinkly voices as they go. All summer, small flocks of these lovely birds flutter along the verges and hedgerows, down railway embankments, across pastures and waste grounds, and into gardens in search of teasels, thistle seeds and other fluffy weeds to eat.

## POPULAR MUSICIAN

The goldfinch's every action seems to be set to music. It sings as it flies, it twitters while it's feeding and it goes on singing its fluent, cheerful song, *widoowit-widoo-widoowit-widoowit*, all through the summer and well into autumn. When a goldfinch's voice rings out in August, long after most other songbirds have fallen silent, it is doubly welcome and delightful.

▶ *An eye-catching goldfinch is engaged in one of his favourite activities: deftly harvesting seeds from a head of teasel.*

## Young grey-pates

When fledgling goldfinches leave the nest they have yet to acquire the exotically colourful head-dress of their parents. Instead of the adults' jazzy red, white and black masks and fawn plumage, the youngsters' heads and bodies are covered in sober greyish-brown feathers with irregular darker brown streaks. (Because of their grey heads, juvenile goldfinches used to be known as *grey pates, grey kates* or simply *kates*.) The only hints of a more glamorous future are flashes of the gold bands on their black wings which identify them as goldfinches.

Such a subdued uniform buys the young birds two or three months of relative anonymity in the family flock. During this time they have a chance to learn the trade of thistle-plucking before moulting into adult colours in October. Here, a juvenile goldfinch is tucking into a thistlehead with youthful exuberance.

# Nesting Time

BY THE TIME THE goldfinches that spent the winter in Europe return to Britain at the start of April, residents and migrants are all ready to breed. Goldfinches nest in loose colonies: each pair defends a small exclusion zone around its nest but still forages in a flock. As seed-eaters, always on the look-out for new seed-heads to plunder, two birds have no hope of annexing a feeding territory large enough to sustain their family for the full duration of the breeding season.

## TIME FOR SEVERAL FAMILIES

Goldfinch chicks are rocked in a very deep, snug cradle, firmly anchored to the twigs at the end of a swaying branch near the top of a tree. The female goldfinch builds the nest, lays the eggs and does all the incubating. While she stays glued to the nest for two weeks, she relies on her solicitous mate to check on her regularly and bring her food.

Once the chicks hatch, feeding the nestlings is a team effort. The adult birds collect and swallow a mixture of seeds and insects which they cough up again at the nest. It appears that goldfinches time the arrival of their chicks to coincide with the hatching

of the small brown larvae of the larch casebearer moth (*Coleophora laricella*) from the end of May until late July. These caterpillars burrow into the soft young green needles of the larch trees and would cause lots of damage if the goldfinches weren't around to eat them.

A pair of goldfinches usually rears two broods each season. Over warm summers, when the thistles go on ripening and there is an abundance of food, they may slip in an extra

*▲ It is up-gapes-all when a parent goldfinch returns to feed its chicks a mixture of regurgitated seeds and insects. Growing fast, this brood already has the family hallmark of golden wing bands.*

brood so that their later chicks can take advantage of the glut of seeds. In some years, goldfinches may still be feeding nestlings as late as August, which is very rare among wild birds that breed in Britain.

## Immaculate nest

Some birds might think twice about building a nest on the spindly outer branches of a fruit tree or high up in a sycamore or chestnut tree – but apparently not the goldfinch.

The female skilfully weaves fine roots, grasses, moss and lichens into a thick-walled cup which is deep enough to hold her chicks safely while it is being tossed about in the wind. She anchors it tightly to supporting branches with cobwebs and lines it

with masses of plant down or strands of sheep's wool.

Into this comfy cradle one May morn, the hen bird starts laying five or six blue-white eggs with red-brown speckles. Then she sits on them for 11 to 13 days. When the chicks hatch, both parents busily fill their nestlings' gaping beaks with food. Fledglings are ready to leave the nest in 13 to 15 days. Then they join flocks to learn what food to eat and where to find it.

# The Thistle-tweakers

THE ANGLO-SAXONS used to call the goldfinch a *thisteltuige* – or Thistle-tweaker in modern parlance – which was a most appropriate name for a bird that spends so much of its time plucking downy-topped thistle seeds from ripe fluffy-white thistle-heads.

### UNIVERSAL THISTLE FINCH

Worldwide, the goldfinch goes by the name of Thistle-finch. In fact, the scientific Latin name for a goldfinch is *Carduelis carduelis*, which means 'thistle thistle'. The French call it *chardonneret* after *chardon*, a thistle; to the Italians, the thistle is *cardo* and the goldfinch, *cardellino*.

From mid-summer onwards, the seeds of ripe thistles are an important source of food for goldfinches. Flocks tour wasteland, pastures, hedgerows and wild gardens in search of fluffy thistleheads and other troublesome

▲ **AERIAL DANCE**
*Goldfinches flutter an airy ballet around ripe thistle-heads. Each alights briefly to pick out some seeds, scattering a few fluffy white parachutes on the wind in the process, before flitting on to another seed-head.*

## Thistle-plucking

The goldfinch's fine, pointed beak is the perfect tool for pulling tiny, closely-packed seeds from ripe thistles. This remarkably delicate, agile little bird can feed hanging upside down or perched on top of a thistle-head. Relatively short legs hold its body away from the spiky thistle-tops, while its strong feet and forked tail help to keep the bird balanced as it clings on to swaying seed-heads and bendy stems.

Unusually among songbirds, the goldfinch is adept at using its feet to pull a seed head within reach and to hold it steady while its beak extracts the seeds. A goldfinch often lands low down on a stem, then moves up so the seed-head bends over and comes within easy reach of a restraining foot.

Goldfinches seem to prefer seeds in a milky, nearly-ripe state. This means they change food plants all the time. In early summer, a goldfinch usually goes for the easy pickings of seeds which have floated away from ripe thistle-heads and landed on the ground. Seeds left on the plant come in handy later on in the year, when the ground is covered with snow or frost.

'*Out in the sun the goldfinch flits Along the thistle-tops, flits and twits*'

from *The Hollow Wood* by **Edward Thomas** (1878-1917)

weeds, such as groundsel, coltsfoot, ragweed, dandelion, knapweed and, later on, burdock. Goldfinches also feed on pine and alder seeds, as well as garden plants such as lavender.

## TINKLING TWITTERERS

Goldfinches usually travel around together. As they feed and flit from weed to weed, they call to each other repeatedly in their twittery voices. On the move, these chattery *tickelit* contact calls come over as '*wait-a-bit, wait-a-bit*', as though none of the birds wants to be left behind. Sometimes a sweet rippling chorus of tinkling notes, no louder than distant wind chimes, betrays an approaching party of goldfinches before the birds flutter into view.

In the air the goldfinch bounces along in a buoyant, springy fashion. As it is flying, the bold yellow wing markings, white rump and white-on-black pattern under its tail flicker in

the sunshine. When the goldfinch lands on a weed to feed, the red, white and black patches on its head come into sharp focus, clinching its identity. On its rare visits to the ground, the goldfinch hops about.

▲ **THISTLE HARVESTING**
*In their subdued juvenile plumage, these young goldfinches are quite hard to spot as they practise their newly acquired thistle-cropping skills on a large clump of fluffy thistle-heads.*

## Tweezer beak

Goldfinches are the only finches with beaks long and fine enough to reach teasel seeds embedded at the bottom of deep seed pockets in each compact head. In fact, it is mainly the males that feed on teasels as they have slightly longer beaks than the females.

When probing for teasel seeds, a goldfinch makes a curious buzzing *geez* sound. It is as though its head has to vibrate when the beak is poked into a pocket to shake a seed free before the bird can grip one between its tweezer-like beak and whip it out.

# Charm of Goldfinches

▲ *A flock of goldfinches is called a 'charm'. Although it looks very pretty flurrying along a hedge, the name was really inspired by the tinkling exchanges between the birds and comes from* charme, *the Old French word for song.*

THE THISTLE-FINCH HAS had many nicknames: the Scottish poet, Robert Burns (1759-96) recognised it as '*the gowdspink, music's gayest child*'; to another poet, John Clare (1793-1864) it was the Redcap; elsewhere it was called Goldie, Sweet William, King Harry or Fool's Coat (after a jester's multicoloured outfit).

## GOOD OMENS

Yellow birds were generally thought to be very lucky, denoting material and spiritual wealth. The first bird a girl sees on St Valentine's Day is meant to predict her future husband. If it is a goldfinch, he is likely to be a rich man. Because the goldfinch is such a sociable bird, it also promises social success and a long, happy, family life. In medieval times, the goldfinch was used as a charm to ward off the plague.

The word *goldfinch* was once used as slang for a golden guinea coin or for someone who always had a purse or pocket bulging full of gold and so was a prime target for thieves.

## MUSICAL TRIBUTE

The goldfinch's cheery little song has been an inspiration to composers, too. Antonio Vivaldi's (1678-1741) *Concerto No 3* for flute, strings and bass accompaniment is full of trilled notes. Because it sounds very much like the goldfinch's tinkling song this piece has always been known as *Il Cardellino* (*The Goldfinch*).

‘ *Sometimes goldfinches one by one will drop*
*From low hung branches;*
*little space they stop;*
*But sip and twitter, and their feathers sleek* ’

from *I Stood Tip-toe upon a Little Hill* by **John Keats** (1795-1821)

# Christian symbolism

● Because it eats prickly thistle seeds, the goldfinch was associated with the crown of thorns which Christ wore at His Crucifixion. The pretty little bird became a prophetic symbol of Christ's death on the cross. In the 15th and 16th centuries, Renaissance painters, including Raphael and Leonardo da Vinci, often featured a goldfinch in paintings of the Madonna and Holy Child to allude to the martyrdom of Christ at the end of His life.

In his *Madonna and Child and St John* (right), the Spanish Baroque painter Francisco Zurburán (1598-1664) depicts St John the Baptist as a child, holding up a goldfinch to amuse the infant Jesus.

● A goldfinch presented to the Christ child like this may have also been used to convey fertility and the dawning of a new age. An old Latin name for the vibrant goldfinch was *lucina*, the bringer of light. Consequently it was linked to Lucina, a pagan goddess of childbirth.

● Traditionally, any bird in a cage signified a soul trapped in its body. A goldfinch in a cage conveyed the liberation of that soul through the sacrifice of Christ on the cross.

● The goldfinch's red feathers were once thought to be a relic of when the bird tried to pull thorns from Christ's bloody head on the way to His Crucifixion.

## PLEASING PLAYTHING

According to the old Italian poet Dante (1265-1321) the goldfinch was a child's favourite pet. Tied to a long string, it was allowed to fly about but could never escape.

The goldfinch's ability to hold a thistle-head steady with its feet was turned into the captive bird's party trick. They were taught to pull a string that raised a tiny cart full of food or water up a slope.

## LIFE IN A CAGE

In William Hogarth's portrait of *The Graham Children* painted in 1742, which hangs in London's Tate Gallery, the pet goldfinch is scrabbling to get out of its cage. The children seem to think that it is joining in with the music from a serinette (a bird organ). In fact, it is frantically trying to escape from a cat which is creeping up on its cage.

By including the caged goldfinch, Hogarth has added a sombre note to this happy family scene. The bird should be safe in its cage, just as children are protected in childhood, but it isn't, indicating that such safe-keeping is fragile and transitory.

## Prisoners in chains and cages

The goldfinch's gaudy plumage and joyful singing have always fascinated people. Such extravagant beauty cost millions their freedom as highly sought after victims of a huge trade in caged birds. The Dutch artist, Carel Fabritius (1622-54) painted this forlorn goldfinch chained by its leg to an open perch in 1654, but the scandalous trade was still going strong in the late 19th century. In the autumn of 1860, records show that 132,000 goldfinches were trapped at Worthing in Sussex on their annual migration to Europe.

Despite the Protection of Birds Act in 1880, an illicit traffic in wild birds continued in Britain until the Wild Bird Protection Act of 1934 largely wiped it out (although there is still a small black market in goldfinches). By then wild goldfinches were becoming quite rare.

'*Freedom has a thousand charms to show, That slaves, howe'er contented, never know*'

from *Table Talk* by **William Cowper** (1731-1800)

# The Great Spotted Woodpecker

*Normally, a raucous* tchack, tchack *call echoing through the woods gives a great spotted woodpecker away before you catch sight of it*

Great spotted woodpeckers frequent mature broadleaf and coniferous woodland where there are a few old trees and rotting branches. Established trees in parkland and gardens also make an ideal hunting ground.

## STRIKING BIRD

On a woodland walk, listen out for a great spotted woodpecker's strident call or the rapid-fire tapping of its big beak on a hollow tree trunk as it hunts for food and drums to advertise its territory and attract a mate. If you are lucky, you may even catch sight of a black-and-white streak flying off between the trees.

▶ *When climbing a tree trunk, a spotted woodpecker leans well back, anchored by strong claws on its feet and braced against its stiff tail.*

*male*

## Head-basher

Woodpeckers can hammer away violently at trees without getting a splitting headache or suffering from concussion. How do they do it? For a start, the brain is protected by a reinforced thick bony skull that does not shatter when bashed against a tree 15 times per second. There is also a very effective spongy shock-absorbing layer between beak and skull to cushion the impact.

As further protection for the brain, the woodpecker has special muscles that pull the skull away from the beak at every strike. The woodpecker's neck muscles are extremely strong and well-coordinated, too, to hold its head perfectly straight on impact. Any twisting of the head could jar the brain disastrously.

# Drilling for Food

GREAT SPOTTED WOODPECKERS have an almost insatiable appetite for the insects and spiders they find lurking under the bark. When looking for food, a great spotted woodpecker lands on the trunk of a tree and hops upwards, working from side to side and pausing occasionally to listen for insect activity under the bark.

As the woodpecker climbs, it uses its strong beak as a crowbar to prise off the bark and expose the insects underneath. It also chisels into dead or dying trunks to reveal tunnels housing the grubs of wood-boring beetles. The woodpecker then uses its long tongue to reach into the holes and pull out the grubs.

## WOOD DRILLER

To peck out a hole in the trunk of a tree, the woodpecker goes hammer and tongs at the wood with its beak. Its head bashes into the trunk 15 or 16 times in one-second bursts, rather like a road-digging drill.

In autumn and winter, woodpeckers have to switch to eating nuts, fruit and seeds. They are especially partial to pine nuts and build up caches of pine cones to ensure against food shortages.

▶ *The woodpecker's long tongue darts out to pluck an ant from the bark or to probe a beetle hole for its resident grub.*

▼ *A crafty woodpecker wedges a nut into a cleft in the bark. This either acts as a larder for storing nuts and pine cones or an anvil on which to crack them open.*

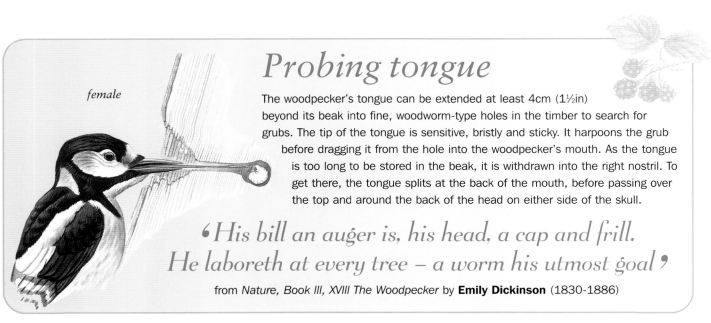

*female*

## Probing tongue

The woodpecker's tongue can be extended at least 4cm (1½in) beyond its beak into fine, woodworm-type holes in the timber to search for grubs. The tip of the tongue is sensitive, bristly and sticky. It harpoons the grub before dragging it from the hole into the woodpecker's mouth. As the tongue is too long to be stored in the beak, it is withdrawn into the right nostril. To get there, the tongue splits at the back of the mouth, before passing over the top and around the back of the head on either side of the skull.

‘*His bill an auger is, his head, a cap and frill. He laboreth at every tree – a worm his utmost goal*’

from *Nature, Book III, XVIII The Woodpecker* by **Emily Dickinson** (1830-1886)

# Nesting in Tree-holes

THE GREAT SPOTTED woodpecker is a thoroughly tree-based bird – as well as finding food under the bark, it also drills nesting holes in the timber in which to rear its young.

In March and April, a male great spotted woodpecker starts advertising for a mate by drumming out low-pitched, long-distance messages with its beak on a hollow branch. Each woodpecker has a unique signature tune. Once he has paired up with a female, the male continues beating out the rhythm to define the extent of their territory. Woodpeckers are the only birds in Britain to augment their natural voice with mechanically made sounds like this.

### CARVING OUT A NEST
Once bonded, it takes a pair of great spotted woodpeckers two to three weeks to hack out a roomy nesting chamber in a hollow tree trunk. Like other woodpeckers, a great spotted's beak serves as a powerful, self-sharpening chisel when it is fiercely and repeatedly hammered into bark and rotten timber. While the great spotted woodpecker is drilling it uses its very stiff tail feathers to brace itself against the trunk. It works at least 3m (10ft) above the ground, to create a small entrance hole, which is about 6cm (2½in) in diameter. The cavity within the tree trunk creates a roomy ready-made nesting chamber.

A lot of sawdust is thrown out while the woodpecker is drilling. To stop the fine wood chips clogging the bird's airways, its nostrils are narrow slits, covered with wiry feathers. Most of the sawdust generated by the drilling is discarded around the base of the tree, although a little is left in the bottom of the nesting chamber to absorb the chicks' droppings.

*female*

*male*

▲ **IN HOT PURSUIT**
*Woodpecker courtship is very energetic, involving a flirtatious aerial race through the tree-tops, followed by a corkscrewing chase around a tree trunk.*

▶ **COSY NESTING CHAMBER**
*From mid-May to the beginning of June, between five and seven creamy white oval eggs are laid in the sawdust-lined tree-hole. Both parents share the incubation for the next 16 to 17 days. When the chicks hatch they are naked, blind and very noisy.*

*male*

*male*

▲ **SPOTTED IN FLIGHT**
*The great spotted woodpecker flies strongly, in a typically bounding, roller-coaster style of flapping and gliding. Its white shoulder patches are obvious when it is in the air. From below, the red rump patch is also clearly visible.*

▶ **RED-HEADED FLEDGLINGS**
*The nestlings grow rapidly on a nourishing diet of grubs collected by their diligent parents – in this case the female. The youngsters are distinguished from the adults by the scarlet caps on their crowns.*

*nestling*

*female*

# Housekeeping

A male great spotted woodpecker leaves the nest after a feeding trip to its chicks. To keep the nesting hole clean and hygienic, he carries a beakful of sawdust-covered droppings away with him.

**GREAT SPOTTED OR LESSER SPOTTED WOODPECKER?**
*There is another, less common black-and-white woodpecker, the lesser spotted woodpecker (Dendrocopos minor), living in British woodland and parks.*

*Although the two species of woodpecker look superficially similar, the great spotted is bigger, with prominent white shoulder patches and a striking red patch under its tail which the lesser spotted lacks. The male great spotted also has a scarlet patch on the nape of its neck whereas the male lesser spotted has a scarlet crown. Another way of telling the two apart is to watch the back in flight – the great spotted has a plain black back while the lesser has white bars across its back (right).*

# The Woodpigeon

*The woodpigeon is portly in more ways than one: its breast is not only plump but also covered in a warm blush of port-wine stained feathers*

In spite of the 'wood' in its name, the woodpigeon's distribution is no longer limited to traditional wooded countryside. Although it is still commonly seen on farmland that is broken up by large hedges, copses and woodland, many have adapted to life in urban sprawl and nest in cities. In country areas, woodpigeons are still wary, flighty birds, but in parks and gardens they have become remarkably tame.

### WILY SWAGGERER

Waddling over the lawn on its short legs, a chubby woodpigeon may look rather bumbling and self-important, like a Captain Mainwaring of the bird world. But woodpigeons are far from stupid: they are very successful exploiters of the countryside.

▶ *A tubby woodpigeon certainly looks as though it has been living off the fat of the land, raiding crops in the fields.*

## A flock of clattering doves

*flock of flapping woodpigeons*

When disturbed, woodpigeons clatter out of trees and hedges with clapping wings, brushing all the branches noisily aside. The flapping wings generate a loud wheezy whistling sound, *wich wich wich*, that acts as an alarm call. The clattering wings are also used as part of the male's roller-coaster courtship display, when he repeatedly flies up steeply, clapping his wings, then glides down to show off his white wing bars.

'*And up with yet a louder noise Woodpigeons flusker*'

from *The Meadow Grass* by **John Clare** (1793-1864)

# Amorous Partnership

AFTER MUCH BILLING and cooing, a pair of woodpigeons builds a twiggy platform on a branch in a tall tree or high hedge, or on a rocky shelf or ledge on a building. The female then lays two quite small glossy white eggs which look a bit like squashed table-tennis balls. The male and female incubate them for 17 to 19 days. The eggs are rarely left uncovered: the female incubates them overnight, the male during the day.

### THE MILKY WAY

Young pigeons, or squabs as they are called, have just a few wisps of straw-coloured down and are very gawky. For the first four or five days, the nestlings are fed on a special protein-rich pigeon's milk – a white curd that sloughs off from the lining of both parents' crops – before being weaned on to a diet of regurgitated seeds.

Having outgrown the nest in three or four weeks, the squabs start to perch on nearby branches, waiting to be fed. They can fly at about 35 days old. The juveniles are duller brown than the adults, without white patches or greeny shimmer on their necks.

▲ *As if afraid to rock the boat, a pair of well-grown squabs sits quietly in the nest waiting to be fed. Even when a parent returns, they stay still until called to feed.*

▶ *To feed, the squabs stand on either side of their parent and thrust their beaks down the adult's throat. Then all three move rhythmically up and down to pump food from the crop.*

*bowing display*

## Smoochy courtship

Male and female woodpigeons are indistinguishable on looks alone so, before pairing, two pigeons go through an elaborate ritual to check that his or her partner is of the opposite sex. The male hops towards the squatting female with his head lowered, his tail raised and fanned. His throat is puffed out as he groans a soft *coo coo coo*. Then the pair-bond is reinforced by mutual caressing and courtship feeding.

*caressing*

❛ *Curr dhoo! Curr dhoo!*
*Love me and I'll love you* ❜

**Traditional Country Ditty**

# Pesky Pigeons

THE WOODPIGEON'S GREEDY appetite gets it into all kinds of trouble with farmers and gardeners, as it forages mainly on arable land, consuming a predominantly vegetarian diet. A woodpigeon is partial to all kinds of grain, green and ripe, and is one of the few birds that eats leaves: it nibbles away with relish at young cabbages, turnip tops and clover seedlings. Woodpigeons also eat large quantities of wild weed seeds, ivy, hawthorn and elderberries in the hedgerows and beechnuts and acorns from the woods. Sometimes they slip in the odd earthworm, snail or insect.

### BIT OF A GLUTTON

During the winter months, flocks of woodpigeons are seen feeding on the fields every day. But, by watching and following a flock closely, it turns out that the same flock is rarely seen on the same field two days running. With daylight in short supply in winter, a flock is on the move at the crack of dawn. Woodpigeons usually leave the wood flying directly down wind to minimise the amount of energy expended staying airborne. After a cold night's roosting, they probably feel peckish and are eager to find food as soon as possible.

During clear and bright weather, woodpigeons feed quite steadily. But when the air pressure begins to drop before a spell of wet and windy weather, they start scoffing with a greater sense of urgency, taking on board plenty of food to tide them over an uncertain period of poor feeding conditions when they may not find much to eat.

### MORE THAN A SIP

Woodpigeons drink a lot of water because they do not get very much moisture from the dried seeds and grains they eat. Unlike other birds, a pigeon is able to suck up water, using its beak as a straw, rather than scoop it up and throw back its head to let the liquid drain down its throat.

> '*Under the oak at early dawn*
> *Are five-and-twenty pigeons*
> *Vexing with squirrels on the lawn,*
> *And acorns their religions*'
>
> from *Highgate Dawn* by **John Drinkwater** (1882-1937 )

▲ **EMPEROR PIGEON**
*From a tree, a woodpigeon can keep an eye on the cornfields in which it feeds and see the woodland beyond where it might roost and nest.*

## Safe havens in gardens

Woodpigeons are now among the top 10 birds most commonly visiting garden bird-tables to take bread and scraps during the winter months. It looks as though this one has only just managed to squeeze on and is sharing the spoils with one of its smaller relatives, a collared dove. Normally, a woodpigeon looks far more comfortable plodding across the lawn picking up seeds and grains scattered there.

Not all the woodpigeon's visits to the garden are quite as innocuous: it is a notorious raider of vegetable plots, taking peas, beans and other seeds, and nibbling on cabbage and Brussels sprout leaves. A pigeon may be a pest, but at least gardeners are less likely to fire a shotgun at it than farmers, who shoot thousands every year to protect their crops and livelihoods from flocks of these voracious scavengers.

▲ **PLAGUE OF PIGEONS**
*A flock of woodpigeons makes itself extremely unpopular with farmers by trampling over a field of turnips and stripping tender leaves from rows of sprouting tops.*

**'** *They strut, they filch,*
*They to and fro*
*Make war to fill their bellies* **'**

from *Highgate Dawn* by **John Drinkwater** (1882-1937)

▲ **WHITE BARS**
*A clear white band on the wings is a woodpigeon's hallmark.*

▶ **HIGH FLAP**
*On take off and in display, a woodpigeon lifts its wings high over its back.*

# Whole foods

A woodpigeon swallows its food without breaking it up with its beak first. The grains, seeds, berries and shoots pass into a huge sack called a crop, which can hold a staggering 60 acorns or 233 hawthorn berries or 1000 grains of barley. The food is moistened in the crop before entering the stomach where it is churned by the muscles of the gizzard, ground up by small stones and grit and eventually broken down by digestive juices. During the breeding season, part of the crop's wall produces a nourishing curd, called pigeon's milk, to feed its young.

*the woodpigeon eats a variety of leaves, berries and seeds*

# Making Whoopie

IN BIRDING CIRCLES the woodpigeon is known as a Whoopie – a contraction of 'wood' and 'p' for pigeon – which captures some of the exuberance of its roller-coaster flappy flight.

In days gone by, country folk seem to have had a lot of fun composing jingles to mimic the woodpigeon's cooing. One such is:

*Take two-o coo, Taffy!*
*Take two-o coo, Taffy!*

There is an old tale of how a wily Welshman was about to rustle one of his neighbour's cows when he heard a woodpigeon cooing, apparently urging him to take two – so he did.

Others found the *coo-coo-coo*ing a rather melancholy sound. The poet, Jean Ingelow (1820-1897) felt '*The cushats cry for me*' (see opposite).

### PILE OF STICKS

There is another little rhyme about the rough twiggy platform that the woodpigeon constructs for its family:

*Coo-Coo*
*Me and my poor two*
*Two sticks across*
*With a little bit of moss*
*And it will do, do, do.*

An old legend tries to account for the woodpigeon's lack of nest-building skills. One day a magpie was trying to teach the young pigeon how to build a sturdy nest. But the youngster soon got bored and started to call out '*That'll doo-o! That'll doo-o!*' The angry magpie flew off, so the pigeon never learned how to build a stronger nest.

### MIXED FORTUNES

According to superstition '*He who is sprinkled with pigeon's blood will never die a natural death.*' But there again, bathing the feet of a feverish person in pigeon blood was said to help bring down their temperature.

'*And the deep mellow crush*
*of the woodpigeon's note*
*Made music that sweeten'd the calm*'

from *Field Flowers* by **Thomas Campbell** (1777-1844)

# Names for a country bird

● The woodpigeon's scientific name is *Columba palumbus*: *columba* is Latin for dove and *palumbus* for woodpigeon.

● The name pigeon probably dates from 14th- and 15th-century French words *peions* and *pyionys* which described a young pigeon. Both were probably derived from the Latin *pipionem*, a young cheeping bird.

● An early name for the woodpigeon, especially in Scotland, was the Cushat.

*Far ben the dark green plantin's shade,*
*The cushat croodles am'rously*

from *Bonnie Wood O'Craigielea*
by **Robert Tannahill** (1774-1810)

It came from *cuscote*, an even earlier name for the pigeon, which combines an echo of cooing and *scutan*, meaning shouters: literally the 'coo-shouter'.

● In southern England, thanks to a different pronunciation of *cuscote*, the woodpigeon was better known as a Quyshte or Quyste, and became the Queece, Queest, Quist, Quoice or Quoist, depending on local dialect.

● In many parts of the country, the woodpigeon was more familiar as a Culver, a name derived from the Old English *culufre*, meaning pigeon.

*Like as the culver on the baréd bough*
*Sits mourning for the absence*
*of her mate*

from *Sonnet LXXXIX*
by **Edmund Spenser** (c.1552-1599)

● A popular name for the woodpigeon in Scotland used to be the Cushie Doo.

*Sure maybe ye've heard the cushadoo*
*Callin' his mate in May.*

from *Birds* by **Moira O'Neill** (1864-1955)

◄ *Coming into land on a stubble field to guzzle some grain, a woodpigeon extends all the flaps on its wings and tail to slow itself down for a soft landing.*

## GLOOMY FORECASTS

If a pigeon was plucked indoors, all the feathers had to be burned as it was thought that using them to stuff a mattress or pillows would lead to an uncomfortable death. In Wales, the pigeon was always a portent of disaster, especially if it was seen flying near a coal mine.

' *At evening, casual flocks of pigeons make*
*Ambiguous undulations as they sink,*
*Downward to darkness, on extended wings* '

from *Sunday Morning* by **Wallace Stevens** (1879-1955)

## Massing pigeons

● By the autumn, there are hordes of woodpigeons all over the country: after breeding, the spring population may have trebled and thousands of migrants will have arrived from the Continent.

● In autumn after feeding out in the fields all day, grey 'clouds' of woodpigeons return to their woodland roosts. As the poet John Masefield (1878-1967) observed in his poem *Wood-Pigeons*:

*It is a beauty none but autumn has,*
*These drifts of blue-grey birds,*
*whom Nature binds*
*Into communities of single minds*
*From early leaf fall until Candlemas.*

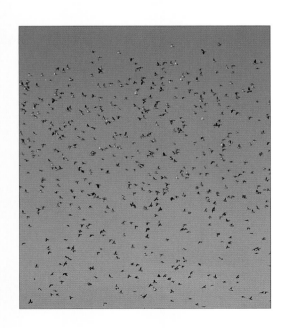

# The Goldcrest

*The goldcrest just pips the wren to an entry in the Guinness Book of Records as the smallest bird in Britain and Europe – indeed, it is one of the tiniest birds in the world*

Goldcrests are exasperatingly hard to see clearly. It is not just that they are tiny birds, they are fidgety too, usually dodging around in the topmost branches of lofty conifers. Pine plantations and forests are favourite habitats, but you also come across them flitting about yew and cedar trees in churchyards and gardens. In winter, goldcrests turn up in deciduous woodland, travelling with mixed bands of tits.

### WITHIN EARSHOT

Frequently it is the goldcrest's voice that gives it away. Goldcrests use a very high-pitched *see-see-see* call all the time – mere pinpricks of sound that keep them in touch with one another. The song may be quiet, but on a still day it can be heard from some distance away.

▶ *When a male goldcrest is excited he raises the golden feathers on his crown to reveal a fiery orange crest.*

## Carry on regardless

Living in the tree-tops, goldcrests do not encounter people very often. When you do see them, these tiny birds seem fearless, almost reckless. In reality, they are simply too busy foraging to waste time worrying about two-legged intruders. In theory, you can tell a male from a female by the colour of their crowns: the centre of his is orange while hers is pale yellow, but this is often hard to spot at a glance.

*' The goldcrest is not a shy bird but this seems due, not so much to tameness as to indifference: the indifference that small insects show to large things such as human beings '*

from *The Charm of Birds* by **Viscount Grey of Fallodon** (1862-1933)

# Feeding Time

MOST OF THE GOLDCREST'S time has to be spent finding food, especially when it is feeding a large brood of chicks during the nesting season or in the winter when insects are in short supply and hard to find.

Tall stands of evergreens in mature coniferous forests and woodland are its favourite haunts. The goldcrest has undoubtedly benefited from recent programmes of reafforestation which have involved the planting of vast expanses of conifer plantations.

Goldcrests are also attracted to larch copses, ancient yew trees in churchyards and established pines, cedars and even spiky monkey puzzle trees growing in mature gardens. The proliferation of *Leylandii* cypresses as garden screening has provided a new source of shelter for goldcrests to colonise, as well.

## WINTER ROAMING

As a goldcrest forages, it constantly flicks its wings and cranes its neck to inspect every stem, bud and leaf meticulously. The fine ridges on its toes give it a secure grip on slippery pine needles. It only ever pauses for a few seconds, before flying on to

examine the next twig. As they hunt, goldcrests utter high-pitched but soft *see-see-see* calls incessantly, as a way of locating other goldcrests among the leaves and needles.

Goldcrests mainly occupy pine woods during the summer. In winter, some stay in the overhanging shelter of the pine-needle clad branches. Others wander farther afield, often teaming up with tits, nuthatches and treecreepers to scour all types of

▲ *A goldcrest gives a stem of ivy the once-over for any small insects lurking there. Its restlessness and constant tail flicking are reminiscent of the chiffchaff, another small grey-green bird and a fellow member of the warbler family.*

woodland for food. Flock dynamics mean that the insects stirred up but missed by one bird are immediately snapped up by another following closely in its wake.

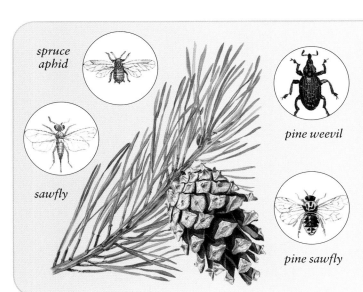

spruce aphid

sawfly

pine weevil

pine sawfly

## On the menu

Goldcrests are agile feeders, capable of reaching the parts of a tree that larger birds cannot reach. They hang upside down to pick aphids from the underside of pine needles and hover to catch flying insects in mid-air. The tiny bird can creep along to the tips of branches in search of spiders, mites and small insects – mostly flies, aphids, weevils and beetles – and their eggs and grubs. Occasionally it tussles with larger insect prey, such as moths and dragonflies.

When goldcrests do venture into gardens, they have a healthy appetite for greenfly on roses. Out of desperation in hard winters, they may be driven by hunger to visit bird-tables and will take fine breadcrumbs, fat and finely-grated cheese.

# Hanging Cradles

*male*

DURING MARCH, BOTH the male and female goldcrest begin putting their dainty nest together. Most are built in thick foliage out towards the end of a high branch of a pine tree. Gnarled yew trees in churchyards are another favourite place. Less frequently, they choose to build in dense ivy close to a tree trunk or in prickly gorse or brambly thickets.

Together the pair binds threads of spiders' silk to adjacent twigs to form the well-anchored handles from which they will hang the nest. On to these they weave a deep, thick-walled basket of moss and lichen, bound with silky cobwebs – painstakingly collected from among the pine needles – and lined with masses of feathers. Some pine needles may be woven into the rim to reinforce it.

The structure takes them almost two weeks to complete. It is amazing that two tiny goldcrests have the energy to build such an ingenious

nest and rear not one but two large broods each year.

## IMPORTANT POSITION

The nest is carefully aligned to offer least resistance to the prevailing wind. The high overhanging branches act as a canopy to shield the chicks from sun and rain and prying eyes. Despite being well-screened and suspended on flimsy twigs, seemingly inaccessible to all but the most determined and agile predators, the eggs and chicks are frequently plundered by hungry dormice and squirrels, jays and magpies.

## PHENOMENAL FAMILIES

Typically, the hen goldcrest lays a clutch of between seven and ten eggs, though it may be as few as five or as many as 13. She incubates them on her own for about

*female*

*adult male*

*juvenile*

> ‘ *Look, look, how he flits,*
> *The fire-crowned king of the wrens,*
> *From out of the pine!* ’

from *The Song of the Wrens* by **Alfred, Lord Tennyson** (1809-92)

## Spirited performances

When displaying to his mate or a rival, the cock goldcrest spreads his centre parting and raises his crest feathers on end to reveal the flame-coloured streak down the middle of his blond quiff. At the same time he bobs up and down, flicks his wings and calls insistently.

If he gets really agitated by a persistent rival or enemy, the male engages in a frantic aerial display, in which he loops, spirals or drops down in freefall from a high perch to

a lower one. Significantly, he is silent throughout this performance.

To impress a would-be mate, the male may hover above the branch on which she is perched. He holds his body almost vertical with his wings vibrating feverishly like a hummingbird. All the time, his head is looking down at the object of his desire. While hovering in this way, he does not so much sing as emit excited chirping sounds.

**◄ SPLITTING ITS SIDES**
*By the time a large brood of goldcrest chicks is nearly fledged, the nest is bulging at the seams and looks quite dishevelled. Eventually, the hammock sags so far that it splits, spilling out the fledglings unceremoniously on their maiden flights.*

**▲ SLINGING UP A HAMMOCK**
*Each end of the nest basket is securely anchored to adjacent pliant branches with spiders' webs, so that the cradle is suspended on silk threads between them like a hammock.*

16 days. When the eggs hatch, the chicks are scantily clad in sooty grey down and their mouths are lined with orange and edged in pink. In spite of the nest's ample insulation, the female stays with them for several days to make sure they do not get chilled.

The nestlings are fed by both parents on the typical goldcrest diet of insects, their eggs and grubs, mites and spiders. Keeping their numerous offspring well fed is a full-time job for both tiny birds. The young fledge, without gold crests, after 20 to 23 days in the nest.

## COPING WITH WINTER

In most seasons a pair of goldcrests manages to rear two large broods, and sometimes three. Such high productivity ensures that goldcrest populations recover quickly from losses incurred during icy winters.

Once they have fledged, the young goldcrests usually join up with other woodland birds, such as wrens and tits, to form large foraging parties for the winter. As autumn progresses, the resident goldcrests are joined by considerable numbers of migrants from northern Europe, where the winters are harsher than in Britain.

## *Peas in a pod*

Not surprisingly the tiniest bird in Britain lays the smallest British egg. The goldcrest's egg is no bigger than a slightly elongated yellowish pea, with reddish-brown spots. Each egg weighs about 13 per cent of the female's body weight, so a clutch of eight eggs will weigh more than she does. Individually, an egg may be a small start in life, but for the mother bird it is a massive investment.

*song thrush*

*goldcrest*

# The Tawny Owl

*Although poets insisted that the tawny owl called* tu whit, tu whoo, *its call is a real hoot – a haunting* hoo-oo *followed by a mellow* hoo-oo-oo-oo *echoing spookily in the dark*

Tawnies are the most common and familiar owl in Britain. But like most owls, they are easier to hear than see, because they hunt in the dark, at best illuminated by the silvery gleam of moonlight. During daylight hours, tawny owls rest quietly in trees in woods.

## GREAT HOO-HA

The hooting exchange between two tawny owls, be they mates or rivals, is the perfect accompaniment to a cold clear winter's night. On bright moonlit nights, their hoots echo and carry a long way through the woods. Hooting is catching: once one tawny owl gets going it sets off other owls within earshot. The sonorous calls spread out far and wide, rather like twilight barking.

▶ *Tawny owls and trees are inseparable: during the day an owl roosts on a tree's branches and at night it waits patiently up there for tiny mammals to scurry past.*

## Swivel-heads

With eyes that are bigger than its brain and have to be fixed facing to the front, a tawny owl is forced to turn its head to keep a watch on what is going on around it. The owl's extremely flexible neck can pivot through nearly a full circle, giving a good view forwards, backwards and sideways without having to move its body.

'*Now dark was on the prowl, Too-whit-a-whoo, from its hollow Called an owl*'

from *No Bed* by **Walter de la Mare** (1873-1956)

# Best of Mates

TAWNY OWL COURTSHIP is a tentative business of lowering the barriers of hostility between two well-armed killers to form lifelong pair bonds. Gingerly, a male tawny owl courts the female's cooperation by swaying from side to side, stretching up, raising his wings and ruffling his feathers, while grunting all the time. Nervously he shuffles along a branch, then backs off again until he gets the 'come-on' signal from her soft begging calls. After pairing, they lean against one another and preen each other.

## HAVING A FAMILY

Tawny owls breed from mid-March onwards. Hunting is easier then as the undergrowth on the woodland floor is still quite thin. The female lays from one to six round white eggs at two day intervals. She starts incubating after laying her first egg and the chicks hatch about 28 to 30 days after laying.

While the female owl sits on her eggs, her mate brings food to the nest. After the eggs hatch, she receives his catches and shreds them to feed to the chicks, to stop him from getting close to his young family. When the chicks are stronger and can swallow whole prey, she goes out hunting too.

▶ *Occasionally, tawny owls nest inside an old barn or building. Here the female is caring for at least one tiny chick, keeping it warm under her body and shredding carcasses for it to eat.*

▼ *Gaping scars in the trunk of a tree make ideal nesting holes for tawny owls. They add very little in the way of nesting material. As the females spend more time at the nest than the males, this tawny is probably a female tending her chicks.*

*fledgling tawny owl*

# Growing up

On hatching, tawny owlets are tiny helpless bundles of white down with blue eyes. They quickly grow into strange-looking balls of grey fluff and their eyes darken. The owlets often clamber about on the tree outside the nesting hole before fledging in about 35 days. They are strong climbers but even so young owls are often found on the woodland floor, apparently abandoned. If you find one, leave it alone: the parents will be nearby, dealing with the situation.

The first-born tawny owl gets a head start on its siblings and it usually grabs the lion's share of the food, producing a great disparity in size between the oldest and youngest chicks. If the supply of food from their parents dries up, the biggest chick is likely to eat the smallest one. For tawny owls, it is better that some chicks survive by sacrificing one of them than all die of starvation.

# The Night Hunters

A COMBINATION OF supersensitive sight and hearing, silent flying and lethal talons means tawny owls are superbly adapted for hunting and catching their prey in pitch darkness. By hunting over a fixed area night after night, year after year, a pair of tawny owls gets to know its territory well. Released into a new location, tawny owls are totally disoriented and literally fly into trees.

In its home territory, a tawny owl uses favoured vantage points and roosts from where it can map the best rodent runs, pinpoint where the songbirds roost, frogs hop and moles dig, as well as noting pockets of nuts and grains which its prey visits. Such local knowledge is invaluable for efficient hunting, especially in winter when prey numbers are depleted.

## TRESPASSERS BEWARE

Both owls keep an eye on movements through their part of the wood. The male controls his territory entirely by hooting. He can distinguish his mate's call from those of intruders and is quick to investigate a new hoot and make the stranger feel unwelcome. As a father, he is equally inhospitable to his offspring: once the youngsters have gained their independence he drives them off his territory.

## PATIENT HUNTERS

Tawny owls follow the watch-and-wait school of hunting. Rather menacingly, an owl sits scanning the woodland floor, just waiting until it hears a hungry little mouse snap a twig or put a paw on a crackly dry leaf. In a trice, the owl swoops down, snatches up the hapless mouse in its talons and carries it off to a perch nearby. There it crushes the skull in its beak before gulping its catch down whole, head first.

▲ **COMING IN FOR THE KILL**
*As a tawny owl swoops down on its prey, its broad, rounded wings help to steady its approach. It flies very quietly because a soft, velvety fringe around the edges of the flight feathers muffles the swishing of air over the wings.*

A tawny owl eats predominantly mice, short-tailed field voles and bank voles, young rats, shrews and the occasional mole. It also forages for earthworms and beetles on the

*prey transferred to beak for transport*

**▲ CATCHING LIGHT**
*Two pale saucer-shaped feather-lined depressions on the front of the head act as reflectors, deflecting every scrap of light into the supersensitive eyes.*

**▲ WHAT LARGE EYES!**
*With huge cylindrical eyes, the biggest that could fit into its skull, the tawny owl can practically see in the dark – its night vision may be up to 40 times better than humans.*

**◄ UNCANNY HEARING**
*The tawny owl's ear-holes are extraordinarily large; the right is larger and lower than the left, which helps the owl to fix the precise location of the faintest rustle. The ears are also specially tuned to the high-pitched notes of squeaking mice and shrews.*

# Owl pellets

After gobbling down whole rodents or birds each night, a tawny owl spends the day digesting its food. Later on, it sicks up the indigestible remains of the bones, fur and beetle wing cases all wrapped up in neat greyish-green 5cm (2in) pellets. On average a tawny owl produces two pellets every day. They collect under trees the owl has been roosting in and are a good clue it has been around.

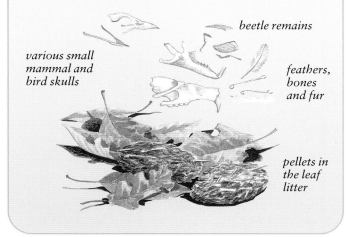

*various small mammal and bird skulls*

*beetle remains*

*feathers, bones and fur*

*pellets in the leaf litter*

> **'You glare as if you wish to bite**
> **All that you with your claws can smite.**
> **Your bill is strong and sharp and hooked'**

from *The Owl and the Nightingale* by **Anon.** (c1200)

**► KILLING FEET**
*The formidable talons grasp the prey and deliver the killer blow to the tawny owl's victims. Its feet and legs are so strong that a tawny owl can carry off a baby rabbit.*

## Skilled hunter

When a tawny owl closes in on its prey, all its powerful tracking senses are working overtime. At the last moment as it drops down on its victim, the owl extends its legs and thrusts its feet forward to grab the prize. The owl's large broad wings instantly switch from controlling and steering the descent to powerful flapping to pull itself up and away. After a successful strike, a tawny owl transfers the prey from its feet to its beak to carry it back to a perch or to its nest for the owlets.

ground and takes birds, frogs, toads and the odd fish whenever it can find them. It may even resort to a form of cannibalism, by capturing little owls if it comes across them perched out in the open on a fence or post.

An interesting double standard operates in favour of a bird of prey such as the tawny owl. By hunting under cover of darkness, it gets away with murder, while daylight nest-robbers such as grey squirrels and magpies are pilloried and despised for doing the same thing.

### THE MISSING SENSE

It is just as well that the tawny owl does not have a good sense of smell. If it did it would leave shrews and toads well alone, as both produce nasty substances to deter predators. The owl's nest can become rather putrid too, as surplus carcasses rot on the floor. These attract flies that buzz around the nest-hole and annoy the chicks, which snap at them with clicking bills.

# Tu-whit! Tu-whoo!

THE TAWNY OWL'S mellow hoot may not quite be *Tu-whit! Tu-whoo!* but it is a solemn anthem for a majestic lord of the night with a reputation for being a bearer of bad news.

Officially, the tawny owl is called *Strix aluco*. In Latin, this translates as 'the screech owl which hoots'. Many once knew the tawny owl as the Brown Owl or Wood Owl. Some called it the Brown Howlet, Hoolet or Yewlet. In French, the tawny owl is *l'hulotte*, which is derived from an obsolete verb meaning 'to howl'.

## BAD REPUTATION

Since ancient times, the magnificent tawny owl has been associated with death and decay. Not many poets had a good word to say about it. One very early poem, *The Owl and the Nightingale* dating from around 1200, records a fierce slanging match between those two singers of the night. The nightingale did not mince his words when he accused the owl of being a cruel, tuneless bully:

> *Your ugliness is many-fold*
> *Your body is short, your neck is small.*

## CORPSE BIRD

In 1619, Thomas Vautor described the tawny owl as an omen of death:

> *And sings a dirge for dying souls*
> *Te whit, te whoo, te whit, to whit*

In *Richard III*, William Shakespeare (1562-1616) has the king dismiss the third bearer of bad news:

> *Out on ye owls!*
> *Nothing but songs of death.*

Shakespeare also uses the tawny's hooting to signal winter, the cold dead season, in *Love's Labour's Lost*:

◀ *On a clear moonlit night, this pensive tawny owl is scanning the ground for small rodents scuttling underneath.*

## The watchful owl

There is little chance of taking an all-seeing tawny owl by surprise. The Irish poet, John Hewitt (1907-1987) brilliantly caught that sense of being spied on in his poem *The Owl*:

*that little feathered sheaf of life*
*that watched you watch*
*with steady eyes.*
*But when I came by easy stealth,*
*at last, within a yard or two,*
*the brown bird spread*
*enormous wings*
*and rose and quietly withdrew.*
*And we were left to carry home*
*a sense no mortal will devised,*

*that, for one instant out of time,*
*we had been seen and recognised.*

To some, such watchfulness seemed uncomfortable and sinister; others found it sage – a more charitable verdict that persists today in the image of a wise old owl keeping its counsel.

Tawny owls also keep a close eye on their eggs and chicks and defend them ferociously. Be warned: they have been known to launch dangerous attacks on people straying too close to their nests, however inadvertently. Tawnies often aim for the head and can inflict nasty injuries with their talons.

*Then nightly sings the staring owl,*
*To-who;*
*Tu-whit, to-who, a merry note.*

### FRIVOLOUS NONSENSE

At face value, in the whimsical poem *The Owl and the Pussycat*, written by Edward Lear (1812-1888), an owl was, for once, cast in the romantic lead. The ill-matched nocturnal hunters sailed away together:

*In a beautiful pea green boat,*
*They took some honey,*
*and plenty of money,*
*Wrapped up in a five pound note.*
*The Owl looked up to the stars above,*
*And sang to a small guitar,*
*'O lovely Pussy! O Pussy my love,*
*What a beautiful Pussy you are . . .'*

### TOWN OWLS

Although tawny owls are woodland birds, they thrive in towns and cities too, surviving mainly on pigeons and sparrows seized from their roosts. In *The Barrel-organ*, poet Alfred Noyes (1880-1958) claims the tawny owl as London's owl. (At least it is a tawny owl by call if not by eye colour.)

*. . . and after dark the long haloo,*
*And golden-eyed tu-whit tu-whoo of*
*owls that ogle London.*

'*And when the moonlight shineth through*
*Echoes the wild tu-whit tu-whoo*
*Of mournful owls, whose languid flight*
*Scarce stirs the silence of the night*'

from *The Lady of La Garaye* by **Caroline Norton** (1808-77)

## Folklore

● A well-known folk tale tells how a baker's daughter was punished after eating some of the bread her mother had baked especially for Christ when He was hungry on the way to His Crucifixion. After eating the dough, it blew up inside her, giving her greed away. For her selfishness, the girl was turned into an owl crying *Heugh, heugh, heugh*!

● The story goes that when the wren lost all her feathers, each bird gave her one of theirs, except the owl who refused because it didn't want to feel cold at night. So the other birds cursed the owl to be an outsider, existing in darkness for ever more.

● In Georgian times, *to owl* was to smuggle, an illicit activity usually carried out under cover of darkness. An owler referred to a person or ship smuggling sheep or wool from England into France.

● According to one 17th-century Scottish proverb:

*The gravest bird is an owl*
*An' the gravest man is a fule.*

CHAPTER 4 · WINTER

# The Robin

*By living in gardens and visiting bird-tables throughout the year, the chirpy robin has become one of Britain's most familiar and best-loved birds*

With its conspicuous red breast, a robin is instantly recognisable as it flits and hops around the garden, alights on a bird-table or sings from a tree. Its curtsying and tail flicking are also unmistakable. A strong singer, the robin has a rich melodic warble, *tic-tic-tic* warning call and shriller *tseeee* alarm cry – sounds which are often heard from dusk to dawn.

## BRAVE LITTLE BIRD

The robin is charmingly bold around people. The way it hangs around when anyone is digging the garden, eager to plunder the freshly tilled earth for food, is most endearing.

Such friendliness is largely limited to British robins. Over on mainland Europe, the robin is a much shyer bird, which usually lives in quiet woodland. There it follows in the tracks of wild animals, picking up any insects disturbed by their feet.

▲ *To a robin, the handle of a gardener's spade is the perfect low perch from which to pounce on earthworms and grubs in the newly turned soil.*

## Hunting for food

▲ *When not hopping about, a robin stands upright, ducking its head and twitching its wings and tail if alarmed.*

▲ *While looking for food, a robin tilts its head, not to listen for worms but to get a better view of the ground.*

Typically, a robin likes to scan the ground for its food from the safety of a sheltered low vantage point in a bush or hedge. As soon as it spots a likely victim, it darts down and grabs the insect, earthworm, woodlouse or spider before flying straight back to its perch.

When on the ground, the robin hops rapidly along, stopping regularly to keep an eye out for any prey or predator, such as a prowling cat. Suddenly, the little red-breasted bird will make a dash for some food it has spied, then fly up to the cover of a nearby bush or tree to eat it.

# Territorial Songster

IT MAY COME AS A surprise to find out that, most of the time, your friendly neighbourhood robin is singing its heart out in a nearby tree, not for joy or even to impress a potential mate, but to warn off rival robins.

## ROBIN REDBREASTS

For a robin, protecting its feeding and breeding rights on a small patch of garden or woodland can mean the difference between life and death. All year round, cock robins are prepared to defend their territories against any other intruding robins by singing, displaying and fighting if needs be. There is a brief truce only during the moulting season and in the coldest winter weather.

Both adult male and female robins have a distinctive patch of rusty-red feathers across their breasts and foreheads. To other robins this red breast acts as a warning. Particularly when puffed up, its meaning is clear: 'Keep away or else!'

## INDEPENDENT FEMALES

Female robins also set up their own territories during the winter, which they defend just as fiercely as the

males. In spring, male and female robins in neighbouring territories relax their exclusion zones, pair up and share an enlarged territory for the breeding season. Then it is the male's responsibility to defend their joint territory while his mate gets on with building a nest.

▲ *Usually a robin only has to crouch down, puff out its red breast feathers and throw back its head to see off another robin encroaching on its territory.*

## Fierce fighters

The robin is a very feisty little bird. If all its singing, posturing and feather-puffing fail to warn off a rival robin trespassing on its territory, the defending robin will go on the attack, swiping out with feet or wings to knock the interloper off its perch and drive it away, beyond its boundaries.

The clashing robins flutter face to face in a flurry of flapping wings, trading blows with their feet. Eventually they tumble to the ground where they roll over and over, vying to get on top. When one robin has pinned the other down, it pecks viciously around the eyes of its overpowered opponent, sometimes blinding or even killing it. Most scuffles last for less than a minute, before the loser (usually the intruder) flies off.

'*A single bush cannot harbour two robins*'
**Zenodotus** 250BCE

# A Year in the Garden

EVERY YEAR THE robin's life is a busy round of courtship, mating and chick-rearing, followed by a moult and a battle to survive the winter.

After getting together as early as December or January, a male and female robin may occupy the same territory but pay little attention to each other until the days start to lengthen and the weather warms up. In mid-March, the female picks out a secluded site, where she builds a nest, using leaves and twigs to form the cup-shaped base, which she lines with hair and moss.

## CONSCIENTIOUS PARENTS

Both birds are careful not to give the location of the nest away. At first the female visits it just once a day, usually early in the morning, to lay one egg each time until her clutch is complete. Then she starts sitting on them. Incubation lasts for 11 to 14

▲ **COURTSHIP FEEDING**
*While the female is nest building, the male robin woos her with food to reinforce their pair-bond and build up her strength for egg-laying.*

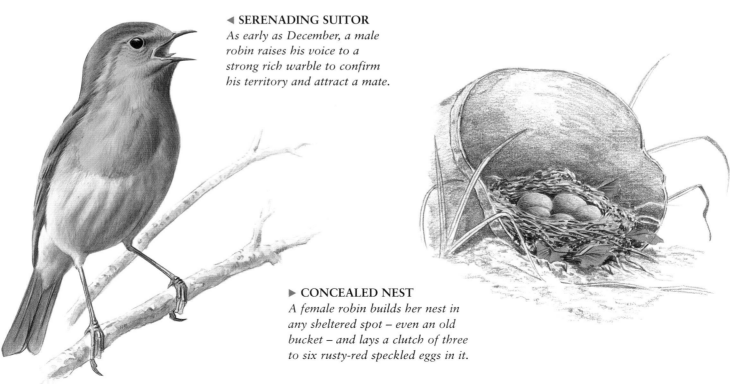

◄ **SERENADING SUITOR**
*As early as December, a male robin raises his voice to a strong rich warble to confirm his territory and attract a mate.*

▶ **CONCEALED NEST**
*A female robin builds her nest in any sheltered spot – even an old bucket – and lays a clutch of three to six rusty-red speckled eggs in it.*

**▲ HUNGRY MOUTHS**
*Blind and helpless on hatching, baby robins are soon clamouring greedily for food with gaping beaks, lined in orange with yellow rims. Their parents work tirelessly to keep them well fed. The young birds grow quickly – in 15 days, when they leave the nest, they weigh more than their parents.*

days. During this time, rather than visit the nest, the male calls her to him to feed her when the coast is clear.

After hatching, the chicks keep both parents busy feeding them. It's just as well that the robin has large eyes, so that it can be one of the first birds up and doing in the morning and one of the last to roost at night.

### AFTER THE FAMILY

When all their young are fledged, the parents split up and re-establish their own territories. Then the adult robins go into a sort of retreat for five or six weeks to shed their old feathers and grow new ones. During this moult, the cock robin falls silent – it is the only time of the year when he does not sing. Normal service is resumed in the autumn as the cock robins start singing again. Their cheery ditty is all the more noticeable then, because they are one of the few birds to sing in the winter.

**▲ FIRST PLUMAGE**
*A young robin becomes independent three weeks after fledging. Similar to adults in shape, it has plain brown dappled plumage, which serves as camouflage and saves it from being attacked by its parents. The red breast feathers only start appearing from the bottom up during the young robin's first summer moult.*

## Trials of winter

Robins struggle to survive during the short, cold days of winter. Finding enough food is a priority, so a well-stocked bird-table is a lifeline. Even then, the aggressive robin rarely drops its guard – in this case it is unwilling to share the feast with a visiting blue tit.

# The Legendary Robin

THE MUCH-LOVED robin redbreast has been bandied around in superstitions for thousands of year. It was also woven into proverbs and myths, and sung about in numerous ballads and nursery rhymes.

The robin certainly has a powerful hold on people's affections, especially at Christmas time. The tradition of posting good wishes to family and friends over the festive season dates back to about 1862, when Christmas greetings were printed on illustrated cards for the first time. From the start, robins of all sorts – comical, musical and cute – graced the front of the cards. Simple rhymes, based on the robin's friendliness, also urged people to support charities:

*'My wishes come by Robin's rhymes,*
*Since he has pleased so many times.*
*For London's poor are still in need,*
*Whom Robin's crumbs may help to feed.'*

Why robins were chosen to go on Christmas cards is unclear. At that time, postmen wore red waistcoats

*' A robin redbreast in a cage*
*Puts all heaven in a rage '*

from *Auguries of Innocence* by **William Blake** (1757-1827)

and were called redbreasts. Robins may have been used as a visual pun or tribute to the postal service. Or the robin's image may simply have fitted into a chain of superstitions, in which it had been seen as a sacred bird for generations. To this day, the impression lingers that the robin is a charitable, friendly little bird, which forms a warm alliance with humans. It is still thought to be unlucky to kill or injure a robin, to steal or destroy its eggs or keep it in a cage.

## GLASGOW CITY'S BIRD

Apparently the robin owes its place on Glasgow's city crest to a miracle worked by St Mungo, the patron saint of the city. In the 6th century, Mungo was being raised by St Serf in a Scottish monastery. One day, fellow students killed Serf's tame robin and blamed Mungo, to get him into trouble with his guardian.

Mungo was so distressed to see the limp body of the little bird that he picked it up and prayed over it until the robin came back to life. In 1271, this lucky robin was given a place on the Bishop of Glasgow's seal and then, 600 years later, it was incorporated into the city crest.

## How did the robin get its red breast?

Most of the many myths explaining how the robin comes to have a red breast suggest that the red feathers were awarded as a badge of honour, for help and favours performed for the gods and mankind. Take your pick as to which you like best

● The robin's breast was stained with the blood of Christ when it tried to pluck thorns from His head while He was on the cross.

● The robin was smeared with Christ's blood as it covered His face with leaves after the Crucifixion.

● Both Crucifixion myths may be reworkings of pre-Christian tales in which the robin was tainted with the blood of pagan sacrifice.

● The robin earned its red breast when it leapt in bravely to douse the burning feathers of the wren after this tiny bird had carried forbidden fire from hell.

● In ancient Welsh legend, the robin's breast was scorched red as the little bird carried water to quench the thirst of souls languishing in the fires of hell.

## NURSERY RHYMES

A few familiar nursery rhymes and folk songs celebrated the robin's role as a friend to both God and man. The lyrics of the well-known rhyme, *The Death and Burial of Cock Robin*, for example, reflected the widely held belief that to harm a robin in any way would bring bad luck.

*Who killed Cock Robin?*
*'I,' said the Sparrow,*
*'With my bow and arrow,*
*I killed Cock Robin.'*

*All the birds of the air*
*Fell to sighing and sobbing*
*When they heard of the death*
*of poor Cock Robin.*

To absolve their guilt, many creatures – the Beetle, the Dove, the Wren and the Owl among others – volunteered to assist at his funeral.

The rhyme may even hark back to a long-abandoned pagan custom of hunting robins at the summer solstice on the 21 June. To the Celts, this was a particularly significant time of the year, when the days started getting shorter and the summer gods gave way to winter ones.

## Babes in the Wood

In legend, the robin so '*loves mankind both live and dead*' that it can never leave a corpse unburied. This idea is echoed in the lyrics of an old English ballad, the *Babes in the Wood*. After being taken into the woods to be killed by two ruffians hired by their wicked uncle, the children are abandoned:

*Thus wandered these poor innocents,*
*Till death did end their grief;*
*In one another's arms they died,*
*As wanting due relief;*
*No burial this pretty pair*
*From any man receives,*
*Till robin redbreast piously*
*Did cover them with leaves.*

# Superstitions, proverbs and nicknames

- If a robin flew into a house, it was thought that someone inside would die soon. But in 1842 William Wordsworth (1770-1850) chose to defy any ill omens likely to arise from inviting a robin to come indoors to raise his spirits on his sickbed when he penned:

*'Stay little cheerful Robin! stay,*
*And at my casement sing,*
*Though it should prove a farewell lay,*
*And this our parting spring.'*

- It was believed that when a robin pecked at the window of a room where someone was lying ill, death would follow shortly.

- As long as a wish made on seeing the first robin of the new year was complete by the time the bird flew off, it was said that it would come true.

- If a robin sang in a bush, then the weather would be rough; but if the robin sang on an open branch, the weather would be warm.

- The Christmas robin may celebrate the fact that, unlike many other birds, robins go on singing heartily throughout the winter. As long as food supplies last, they sing in all weathers to defend their territories and to attract a partner for the next breeding season.

# The Long-tailed Tit

*A band of long-tailed tits has been likened to a flight of fairy arrows as the little birds breeze along with their extraordinarily long tails trailing after their tiny bodies*

The air buzzes with a chorus of high-pitched tittering *tsirrip-tsirrip* contact calls just before a flock of dainty long-tailed tits arrives. Suddenly a jittery squadron of minute birds with streamer-like tails appears, following each other erratically through the branches.

### HERE, THERE, EVERYWHERE
A tree or bush seems alive with their tiny, restless bodies and flickering tails as they caper over the thinnest twigs, seeking out insects to eat as they go. No sooner has the party arrived than it is drifting on again.

Favourite haunts are the fringes of broadleaved and mixed woodland with shrubby ground cover. They are also common on scrub and heathland and in hedges around farm fields.

▶ *Full-blown pussy willow gives a sense of how small and rotund a long-tailed tit's body is against its overlong tail.*

## Pottering through

A flock of 30 or more long-tailed tits is hardly ever still. It just keeps rolling on in short hops from tree to tree and bush to bush, along lanes and through gardens in a ceaseless search for food. In flight, they bob along with their tails waving like streamers behind them to serve as a rudder and a balance.

In the trees they are very acrobatic, tumbling around the thinnest twigs and flittering between branches. Members of the party are often quite scattered, with each little bird totally absorbed in its quest for minute insects, their eggs and grubs.

They keep in touch via incessant high-pitched hissing calls. At a given signal, the whole group is ready to abandon its search for food and flutter on to the next tree.

# All Together Now

THERE IS AN UNUSUAL 'all for one and one for all' spirit within a long-tailed tit flock. Family members are more than just travelling and feeding companions: they form part of a cohesive social group, with its own hierarchy, which is crucial to each bird's survival.

Where there is one long-tailed tit, there are sure to be others not far behind. The camaraderie of a flock provides each little bird with security and protection. When separated from its flock, a long-tailed tit becomes agitated. It starts calling loudly and searching distractedly for its missing companions. Meanwhile, the rest of the group becomes distressed too, and breaks off feeding and cries out frantically until they are reunited.

### STICKING TOGETHER

At breeding time, long-tailed tits take family loyalty and cooperation to exceptional lengths. If a pair fails to raise its first brood, it is often too late to start again, because a second clutch would miss the early-season glut of insects. Instead, the pair splits up and the female usually returns to her family flock. Then both birds

help to rear the young in other nests belonging to their brothers.

Such behaviour is not as self-sacrificing as it seems. Having failed to breed themselves, by assisting relatives to raise their large families, helper aunts and uncles are ensuring that their family genes are passed on to the next generation. Chicks reared by an extended family get more to

▲ *All year round, long-tailed tits feed on caterpillars, aphids, scale insects, ants, weevils and spiders found on leaves and among the lichen, moss and rough bark on trunks and branches.*

eat, are heavier on fledging and survive better. The helpful brothers and sisters also book their life-saving places in a flock for the winter.

## *Short-tailed pom-poms*

With their long tails and small bodies, it is easy to see why adult long-tailed tits used to be described as Feather Dusters, Lollipop Tits or Flying Teaspoons. But just-fledged juveniles have only rather short tails and fail to live up to any of these nicknames. In fact the youngsters look more like shaggy woolly pom-poms.

A juvenile long-tailed tit is also much darker and browner than an adult. Its nape and cheeks are a sooty brown, emphasising the pale, sometimes

raspberry-red eye-rings. The shoulders are tinged brown, instead of pale pink as in the adult birds.

In July, both adult and juvenile long-tailed tits start to shed their feathers. Unlike other British fledglings that lose only their body feathers, young long-tailed tits grow new, longer tail feathers as well. By October, the youngsters look just like the adults. Consequently, in a winter flock of long-tailed tits, it is impossible to tell which generation each bird belongs to.

*juvenile
long-tailed tit*

# Feathering the Nest

As soon as the days lengthen and warm up in spring, the overwintering flocks of long-tailed tits split up. Young females from one family group swap with those from neighbouring ones. The young males stay put and pair off with the latest intake of hen birds. The male's courtship display involves a fluttery flight. He climbs to a height of up to nine metres (30 feet), before fanning his tail and diving steeply back to the female.

## CHAMPION HOME-BUILDERS

Each pair of long-tailed tits stakes out a small territory within the range of its group. And both birds continue to roost with their extended family until their nest is ready. They pick out an inaccessible nesting site in a prickly bush – gorse, blackthorn, hawthorn or brambles are usually the favourites – and build no more than 3 metres (10 feet) above the ground. Occasionally they go for a penthouse site, high up in the fork of a tree or in ivy against the trunk.

Both the male and female spare no effort in creating a beautiful and intricate nest. Most of the building work is done in the morning. By the time they have finished, the partners will have flown hundreds of miles collecting building material which they painstakingly fashion into their globe-shaped nest. When finished, the structure is weatherproof to wind, sun and rain, although unfortunately not strong enough to repel predators.

## FINDING ROOM FOR THE TAIL

Long-tailed tits rear just one huge brood each year. In early April, a female lays eight to 12 (and rarely as

▲ **INDUSTRIOUS PAIR**
*Each long-tailed tit makes countless trips to woods, fields and farmyards, searching for hundreds of feathers with which to line its wonderful nest.*

many as 15) white eggs, which are sometimes speckled with red, and incubates them for 12 to 18 days. During the incubation, she is fed on the nest by her mate. While she is sitting in the nest her tail is brought up over her back so that its tip and her head plug the entrance hole. When she checks on the eggs or feeds the nestlings, her tail sticks out.

> ' *And coy bumbarrels\**
> *twenty in a drove*
> *Flit down the hedgerows* '

from *Emmonsails Heath in Winter* by **John Clare** (1793-1864)
(\* bumbarrel was a country name for the long-tailed tit at the time)

## A marvel of nest architecture

• The long-tailed tits start their nest by collecting moss, cobwebs and fibres of wool and hair which they weave to form a strong matted base. Then, working from inside, they build up the thin elastic walls, finishing off with a domed roof, leaving a small entrance hole near the top.

• The next step is for the two long-tailed tits to peel up to 3000 flakes of grey-green lichen from tree trunks and work them into the walls as a type of cladding all over the outside.

• Their final challenge is to collect lots of feathers to form a well-insulated lining to keep the chicks warm. About 1500 is average; the most ever counted out of one nest was 2680.

▲ **FAMILY HELPER**
*It is not unusual for three or more long-tailed tits to tend the occupants of a nest. The nursery assistant is usually an un-mated relative of the pair.*

**▲ IN ALL ITS GLORY**
*After 30 laborious days or more, a pair of long-tailed tits puts the finishing touches to its egg-shaped nest. It measures about 30cm (12in) around its girth, 35cm (14in) around from top to base and weighs roughly 30g (1oz).*

**▲ UNDER CONSTRUCTION**
*Working from inside, a long-tailed tit packs the lower walls of its nest in a gorse bush into a dense felt by paddling with its feet and pressing down with its breast, turning around and around all the time. Then it will go on to add a dome and a feather lining.*

## FAMILY CARE

The hatching of the chicks is timed to coincide with masses of caterpillars and other insects in early summer. Both parents care for their young, assisted by a variable number of helpers (up to eight have been seen), which are usually un-paired relatives.

After 14 to 18 days, the chicks are fledged. They continue to be fed by their parents and the aunts or uncles for at least another 14 days until they get the hang of fending for themselves. The family then remains together in a close-knit flock for the winter, tittering along by day and snuggling up closely together in a large feathery ball at night.

## Tight squeeze

The elasticity of the nest's walls is put to a severe test when there are 12 excitable chicks aboard and their parents join them to roost at night. In a scrum at feeding time, the hungriest chick is the most demanding and likely to get fed first. Here only three gaping long-tailed tit chicks have made it to the entrance. Although it must be very hot and stuffy inside, few youngsters are stifled in the nest. Eventually the nest walls burst under the strain, spilling the fledglings out for their first flight.

127

# The Starling

*So what if the starling wears a shimmery suit and behaves like a thug on the bird-table? Its go-getting approach to life makes it the most successful hustler in the bird business*

The bold, rumbustious starling evokes mixed reactions. To some people, starlings are just brash bullies that travel around in rowdy, fractious gangs. To others, their inexhaustible energy, bravado and smartness, cheekiness and petty squabbles are interesting and make them hugely entertaining to watch.

## REVERSE COMMUTERS

Flocks of starlings are commonly found foraging on farmland and in woodland, parks and gardens. The sight and sound of a huge babbling black cloud of starlings whirling back to their urban roosts at sunset on a winter's evening after a day's feeding in the local countryside has to be witnessed to be believed.

▶ *With his sheeny black feathers flashing blue, green and purple in the spring sunshine, a male starling burbles his merry tune from the top of a garden shed.*

## Costume changes

*winter plumage*

Over the course of a year, starlings appear in a confusing array of plumage: after an autumn moult, both males and females are heavily spangled with white or buff. During the winter, these pale spots get worn away so that by the spring starlings are a glossy metallic-black. This particularly applies to the males, as females have broader feathers with larger spots and may retain some speckling all the time.

'*The jolly costermonger\* of birdland – adorned with golden sequins*'

from *Birds of the Grey Wind* by **Edward A Armstrong** (1940)
(\* an old name for market stall holders who elected pearly kings and queens)

# Greedy Guzzlers

STARLINGS NORMALLY forage on the ground in small flocks. Each morning a group may fly 15 miles or more from where it roosted the previous night to plunder pastures or gardens.

## GARDENER'S FRIEND

Hungry starlings are valuable pest-controllers: they consume masses of root-nibbling wireworms and leather-jackets (cranefly larvae) living in the soil in gardens and fields. In half an hour, one starling swaggering stiff-legged over the lawn can eat as many as 20 leatherjackets. A starling can also snatch insects in mid-air rather like a swallow and hitch rides on the backs of sheep to pick off ticks.

## FOOD PIRATES

In winter, starlings eat more seeds and berries and make frequent visits to bird-tables and peanut-feeders. A typical raiding party of starlings suddenly lands in the garden with a noisy flurry, gobbles down any food on the bird-table, then dashes off again with a whirr of wings, cackling and gurgling all the time.

When hordes of starlings descend on a bird-table it looks as though

▲ *A windfall apple is a boon for a hungry starling when insects and worms are hidden under a blanket of snow.*

▶ *A parent starling keeps up the almost non-stop supply of earthworms, insects, spiders, centipedes, woodlice, snails and slugs to the chicks in its tree-hole nest.*

they are grabbing all the food. But it is a myth that starlings bully other birds; most of the food that they eat from feeding stations would not be taken by other birds in any case.

## Treasure hunting

Close-cropped grasslands are the starlings' favourite feeding places, especially during the breeding season. The well-trimmed grass in a garden is a perfect hunting ground, which is why you often see a band of starlings stomping over a lawn with their heads down, stabbing the surface with their beaks. When the earth is softish, they open their beaks underground and feel for earthworms and grubs moving in the soil. Unusually, a starling can also swivel its eyes forward to peer into a hole it has just made. Few other birds can do this.

Starlings generally feed in flocks of between 12 and 40 birds: many more and they risk attracting predators such as sparrowhawks; fewer and the flock fails to exploit the localised food sources in its feeding range properly. Each bird memorises the locations of good food sites and keeps an eye out for fresh ones.

# New Recruits

*female*

IN SPITE OF STARLINGS' boisterous ways, they make excellent parents to the next generation of movers and shakers. A male starling may select his nesting site as early as January but not pair up with his mate until early April. Having picked out a female he fancies from his flock, he woos her by sidling up to her on a branch and waving his wings about, crooning constantly.

## SAFE IN A HOLE

Starlings invariably build their nests in holes: these can be in trees or buildings, under the eaves of a house or on cliffs and quarry walls. Niches in church towers and spires are another favourite nesting place.

Starlings often return to the same nest site year after year. Always gregarious, several pairs may nest in loose colonies, with a number of nests in the same cavity. If starlings get into a roof space, they can create giant nests; over many generations these grow into some of the largest nests of any British bird.

Before the male starling starts courting his mate, he usually throws together a large, rough nest of straw, roots and dried grass. In March, you often see a starling ferrying straggly strands of straw back to his nest site in his beak. Later his mate collects feathers and hair to arrange as a soft lining in her partner's nest cup.

## FAMILY LIFE

From mid-April onwards, the female begins laying four to six beautiful pale blue eggs into the nest. When the clutch is complete, both adults share the incubation for 12 to 13 days until their chicks hatch. Then they start ferrying food to their nestlings every five minutes during daylight hours.

If all goes to plan the chicks are ready to leave the nest from 20 to 22 days after they hatched. Having successfully reared its first brood,

*male in summer*

> ' *Starlings used to sit there with bubbling throats*
> *Making a spiky beard as they chattered* '
>
> from *The Barn* by **Edward Thomas** (1878-1917)

▲ **MALE OR FEMALE?**
*It is blue for a boy and pink for a girl in the starling's world too. In summer, if the base of the lower bill is blue, the bird is a male; if pink, it is a female.*

## *Brown starlings*

At the beginning of June, lots of unfamiliar mousy-brown birds with pale throats suddenly start appearing on the lawn. The fact that these strangers chase around after starlings which have come to feed in the garden is a good clue that they are immature starlings. The youngsters rush up to the nearest adult with their beaks wide open, crouching and squawking at the top of their voices, demanding to be fed.

Over the rest of the summer, the young starlings' juvenile plumage becomes more and more patchy as the brown feathers are gradually lost, to be replaced with the black and pale spangled winter plumage of an adult starling. This youngster looks as though it is about halfway through its moult.

### ▶ CAVITY WALLS

*A family of fledgling starlings gazes out on the world from the threshold of the hole in a building where they have grown up. Soon they will be following their parents on food-finding missions.*

a pair of adult starlings is likely to go on and raise a second family each year. Usually there is an interval of about 50 days between the start of the two clutches.

### NIGHTLY GATHERINGS

As soon as their second brood has fledged and left the nest, starlings become communal again. Starlings are such sociable birds that it is very rare to see a single starling out on its own: normally there is a flock or family in tow. Several groups may forage together as a flock during the day and spend the night together with thousands of other starlings at a huge traditional roosting site.

*'Steal from the barn a straw till, soft and warm,*
*Clean and complete, their habitation grows'*

from *The Seasons: Spring* by **James Thomson** (1700-48)

### ▲ HOLES IN TREES

*The starling's preferred natural nesting site is a ready-made tree-hole: they often adopt a secondhand woodpecker hole.*

## Noisy brood

One of the chicks in this nest hatched so recently that the parents have not yet removed the empty eggshell and there is still an egg left to hatch. Clad in grey down, the tiny hatchlings open their beaks and start calling for food at once. The bright yellow gape and the paler yellow outline to their beaks make big targets for the adults delivering food in dark nest-holes. Every time one of their parents visits the nest to feed them, the nestlings screech until the food has been shared out between them.

# Cloud of Starlings

EVERY EVENING IN autumn and winter thousands of starlings take part in incredible aerobatic displays before bedtime. At dusk, flock after flock flies to a traditional roost site from the surrounding countryside. The sight of a single colossal black cloud of birds swirling overhead is one of the great wonders of the bird world.

The flight is phenomenally well-coordinated: each bird sticks close to the others nearest to it so that they can swoop, dive and whirl in perfect harmony without colliding. Then all of a sudden, the birds dive *en masse* into cover and settle down for the night. It is thought that the starlings use these mass gatherings to assess their numbers and operate some form of population control if necessary.

## NIGHT ON THE TOWN

By the late 19th century, it appears that starlings had discovered that the

▲ *As the sun sets in winter, starlings gather in their thousands, swirling and swooping swiftly over their favourite roosting site like a black cloud before settling down on a perch for the night.*

temperature in towns and cities at night can be as much as 5°C warmer than the surrounding countryside. In 1875, it is estimated that as many as 50,000 starlings congregated along Sauchiehall Street in Glasgow every night. Thousands more gathered at the railway stations in Birmingham,

> ‘ *And clouds of starlings ’ere they rest with day,*
> *Sink clamorous like mill-waters at wild play,*
> *By turns in every copse* ’

from *Sunset Wings* by **Daniel Gabriel Rossetti** (1828-82)

Newcastle and Bristol. In her poem *Starlings on the National Gallery*, Theodora Roscoe (1870-1962) tried to describe the cacophony of starlings huddled together on ledges and roofs around Trafalgar Square in London:

*Shrill whistlings pierce the traffic's ceaseless din,*
*A whistling as of wind through riggings taut.*

Similarly, the poet Robert Bridges (1844-1930) reflected on the huge hubbub of thousands of starlings arriving at a country roost in his poem *November*:

*They fly by the score*
*To the holly thicket, and there with myriads more*
*Dispute for the roosts; and from the unseen nation*
*A babel of tongues, like running water unceasing.*

At its peak, the heat and smell given off by thousands of roosting starlings became a health hazard. Fireworks and stuffed owls failed to deter them from using city buildings as their dormitories. Strips of plastic gel laid along the ledges did work by making footholds insecure.

## Names and legends

- In *The Boke of St Albans* (1486) Dame Juliana Berners was definitely understating the volume generated by roosting starlings when she declared the collective name for a flock of starlings to be a *murmuration*.

- The starling's scientific name is *Sturnus vulgaris* where *sturnus* was probably an amalgam of Latin and Greek words to convey twittering and *vulgaris* was common.

- The original English name for a starling was a Stare, from the Anglo-Saxon word *stœr* which itself probably came from the Latin *sturnus*. Until the mid-19th century, starling was simply the name for a young stare.

- The 19th-century nature poet John Clare (1793-1864) knew the starling as the starnel:

*There flocks of starnels too repair*
*When morning o'er the valley springs.*

- An Old English nickname for the starling is Dropfag. As the name was in use long before Sir Walter Raleigh brought tobacco back to England in the 16th century, it can't refer to cigarette ash; it may have meant spangled, like its plumage.

> *' They mimic in their glee,*
> *With impudent jocosity*
> *The terrible ululation of the owls '*

from *Starlings* by **Mary Webb** (1881-1927)

## Star performers

- Starlings are the Rory Bremners of the European bird world: they have an amazing gift for imitating other bird calls. While chattering, a starling may slip a totally incongruous snatch of a green woodpecker laughing or a duck quacking into its monologue, like an echo of a woodland or farmyard past.

- Starlings have a quick and retentive memory for mechanical sounds too. Just as former generations in the 1970s could mimic the intermittent electronic warbling of a trimphone to a tee, so today's starlings are whistling mobile phone call tunes everywhere.

- In *Henry IV, Part I, Act I, Scene 3*, William Shakespeare (1564-1616) implies that starlings can imitate human language when Hotspur threatens:

*Nay, I'll have a starling shall be taught to speak nothing but 'Mortimer' and give it him, to his anger still in motion.*

- Writing about his visit to Paris in 1765 in *A Sentimental Journey* the author Laurence Sterne (1713-68) recalled how, as he was expounding on the evils of the prison at the Bastille, he heard a childlike voice complaining '*I can't get out*' in his hotel one day. Along a corridor, he found a caged starling crying '*I can't get out –*

*I can't get out*'. Moved by the poor bird's plight, Sterne attempted to free it, only to find the door tightly secured with twisted wire. Eventually, he bought the starling in its cage from the hotel manager for a bottle of burgundy and took it home with him to England. The starling always remained a symbol of hopeless captivity to Sterne.

# The Pied Wagtail

*Pied wagtails are those smart little black-and-white birds that look a bit like Charlie Chaplin as they strut around, twitching their tails up and down all the time*

The elegant black-and-white pied wagtail is a familiar sight dashing and bobbing about as it charges across roofs and lawns, around car parks and over cricket pitches. It is often seen near water, by ditches, on the banks of a stream or paddling in the muddy margins of a pond. In fact, pied wagtails are found almost everywhere, except on mountains and in woodland.

## TRIPPING ALONG

The dainty pied wagtail is extremely nimble on its feet, briskly walking or chasing after flying insects. Without warning it may leap into the air or veer off in a new direction in pursuit of another juicy fly. All the time it is pumping its tail jauntily and emitting its squeaky *tschizzik-tschizzik* call.

▶ *The pied wagtail frequents damp places where there are plenty of insects flying about for it to catch.*

## Victimised by cuckoos

*fledgling*

A newly-fledged pied wagtail is greyer than either of its parents, with an olive-green tinge and a much shorter tail.

This young pied wagtail is lucky that it was not thrown out of its nest by a cuckoo chick. Despite the pied wagtails' best efforts to conceal their nests, they often attract the attentions of a female cuckoo, which then lays one of her eggs in their nest.

In his book, *The Charm of Birds*,

Viscount Grey described how one year a cuckoo targeted a pair of pied wagtails which regularly nested in the creeper on his cottage. After they had raised their gigantic foster chick, the pair built a new nest on the rear wall of the cottage. The cuckoo laid another egg in that nest and the luckless wagtails had to rear a second monster.

The following year the pair nested in the creeper once more, and again a cuckoo raided the nest. This time the pied wagtails abandoned it and never built there again.

# Signs of Breeding

BY LATE FEBRUARY or early March male pied wagtails are staking out their breeding territories. At this time they become pugnacious, attacking other males and even going for their own reflections in windows, hubcaps and wing mirrors.

As a prelude to erratic and excited courtship chases, each male sings a lovely warbling song. He approaches a likely female with his tail fanned, wings quivering and head bobbing. Then he tilts back his head to show off his black throat and breastplate.

## FAMILY EFFORT

The new pair selects a sheltered site – a cavity in a stone wall, wood stack or earth bank, on an ivy-covered tree trunk or a shelf in an outbuilding or farm machinery – to build their nest.

Working mainly in the mornings, a female pied wagtail builds a bulky nest of matted moss, grass and dead leaves and lines it with a thick layer of feathers, hair and wool. She lays a clutch of five or six greyish-white eggs with grey freckles. She does most of the incubation for 14 days but the male helps her to feed their brood. About 14 days after hatching, the fledglings graduate from the nest.

▲ *To this pied wagtail, a neat alcove in a piece of rusty old farm machinery was the most secure and secret place it could find to build its nest and rear its chicks.*

◄ *This juvenile pied wagtail is out on its own now, with only its reflection for company. It had just a few days of shadowing its father, as he caught food for the family, in which to learn where to find flies and how to catch them.*

## Winter uniform

*male in winter*

Many pied wagtails head south into Europe for the winter. Those that stay behind look greyer than they did during the summer. After an autumn moult, instead of the black throat and deep black bib of his breeding plumage, the male sports a white throat and thin black crescent-shaped cravat. His white cheeks become flecked with black and his back and flanks look slightly greyer. Only his rump stays black.

The spring transformation back to his crisp breeding colours is the result of a partial moult which is completed by the courting season. This spring moult takes place earlier abroad than it does in Britain, for returning birds are noticeably cleaner and trimmer than birds that have overwintered here. Each autumn, breeding is followed by a second, complete moult which restores the greyer winter plumage and replaces the worn-out wing feathers.

# Eager Fly-chaser

THE PIED WAGTAIL hunts insects on the ground or in the shallows of a stream or puddle. As it struts about on its long legs, its head jerks back and forth all the time, like a little clockwork toy, while its tail twitches up and down non-stop.

On spying an insect, a sprightly pied wagtail dashes after it, tripping erratically along on tippy-toes. Such headlong dashes are interspersed with sudden changes of direction and short fluttery zig-zagging sallies into the air – it can even hover briefly to snatch a fly in mid-air. It looks as if it is acting on pure impulse, torn between several tasty morsels, or being buffeted by the wind. But, in fact, few flying insects escape from its snapping beak.

### BRAVE MOVES

Pied wagtails snap up a lot of the flies which torment sheep, cattle and horses in fields and paddocks. The fearless little birds rush daringly between the legs of the hefty beasts. Sometimes they hitch a ride on the back of a sheep, dashing to and fro over the ewe's fleece, catching insects, while she wanders around.

When pied wagtails are feeding on dungflies gathered on cowpats, they defend temporary territories and drive away other wagtails to stop them scattering the flies. It seems that dungflies only occupy cowpats during the middle of the day. So in the morning and evening, pied wagtails gather in flocks to feed on swarming midges instead.

Pied wagtails are keen followers of the plough too, trotting along the ridges and disappearing into the furrows to pick up the grubs turned over by the blades.

### WINTER TERRITORIES

Pied wagtails are one of the few insect-eating birds to gamble on staying in Britain and finding enough food to keep them going through the cool winter months. In cold weather, the secret of the pied wagtail's survival lies in the supplies of insects to be found on the margins of water.

Individual birds establish a winter territory along a stretch of water, such as a river bank, and defend it against other wagtails. Each one feeds along a fixed route near the water's edge, searching for insects. From time to time, it returns to its starting point for another run at the tiny insects flying over the shallow water. To share the area with another pied wagtail would be counter-productive for both, and might tip the balance between survival or death.

> '*He stooped to get a worm*
> *And looked up to get a fly*'
>
> from *Little Trotty Wagtail* by **John Clare** (1793-1864)

## Finding flies in winter

The pied wagtails' hunt for insects takes them to some pretty unsavoury places, especially in winter when they cannot find enough insects in frozen ditches or icy ponds. Then a pied wagtail becomes a frequent visitor to sewage farms, where the filter beds and sludge tanks stay warm and make good breeding grounds for swarms of small winged insects.

Farmyards, pigsties and stables also used to be favourite haunts of pied wagtails in the winter, when the warmth of manure heaps attracted plenty of flies even in cold weather. Now that most water supplies on farms are piped, cowsheds have been cleaned up and insecticides are widely used, there are fewer flies around. These more hygienic conditions have been bad news for insect-eaters like the pied wagtail.

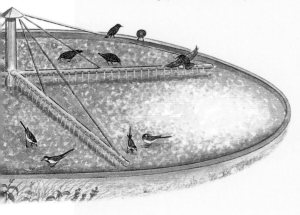

▶ **SPOTTING THE FEMALES**
*In spring and summer, it is easier to tell the difference between male and female pied wagtails than it is at other times of the year: his back is dark black and he has a full black breastplate, while she is grey on her back with a smaller bib.*

### ▲ DANCING ON HOT TILES

*On a bright day, a pied wagtail may switch its insect-trapping to a roof, where the warmth of the sun on the tiles attracts many flies. There it struts around with jaunty steps, occasionally darting or leaping up to catch a passing fly.*

*female in spring and summer*

*male in spring and summer*

# In the garden

A pied wagtail is frequently seen striding and scurrying over lawns, snapping up flying insects – it has been aptly described as the walking house martin (an aerial fly catcher). The smooth swards of well-tended grass make an ideal hazard-free hunting ground – apart from any marauding resident cats which may be about.

While in the garden, pied wagtails sometimes visit a bird-table and take chopped peanuts, mealworms, grated cheese or pinhead oatmeal.

# The Blackcap

*With his pretty, tuneful song and rapturous delivery, the cock blackcap is the ace singer among the warblers and a delightful member of the woodland choir*

Until recently, the blackcap had been thought of as a summer visitor to these shores. But ever since the mid 1950s, increasing numbers have been staying here for the winter too. In fact, the blackcap is often more visible over the winter, as it frequently visits garden bird-tables for much needed sustenance.

## UNDERCOVER STORY

During the summer, blackcaps prefer to live in open deciduous woodland with plenty of brambly undergrowth in which to feed, nest and roost. They also find shelter and plenty to eat among the tangled branches of old hawthorn and blackthorn hedges, in mature gardens and bushy parks.

▶ *As a male and female blackcap lean over to feed their chicks in the nest, they are easily distinguished by their crowns: his is black, hers is a warm brown.*

*cock blackcap in full voice*

## Woodland contralto

The cock blackcap has a beautiful voice which he uses most vigorously in April, when setting up his territory, although he will continue singing into July. His lively song begins slowly with a harsh twittering but ends on a loud outpouring of pure flute-like notes. The whole melody lasts only four or five seconds, but he repeats it frequently, with intervals of six to seven seconds between bursts.

*'In mid May the wood is filled with pure crystalline songs of grey Blackcaps'*

from *England's Birds* by **W Kenneth Richmond** (1936)

# The Larder

BLACKCAPS ARE basically insect-eaters, with a fine, pointed beak to prove it. In April, blackcaps start returning to their breeding grounds before many of the trees are in leaf. Even then, early-hatching insects, such as aphids on the sycamore buds, play a major part in their diet. To boost their energy levels, blackcaps may also take nectar from the flowers of goat willow in the hedgerows.

During the summer, the blackcap searches for insects, such as beetles, caterpillars and flies, and spiders among the leaves and branches on trees and bushes. It rarely uses up a lot of energy bothering to catch flies in mid-air. Chicks also get a regular delivery of small snails: the shells are a good supply of calcium for the rapidly growing nestlings.

## COLD RATIONS

In autumn, as supplies of insects decline, fruit starts to play a more important part in the blackcap's diet. Purple stains around its beak and vent are signs that a blackcap has been feasting on elderberries and blackberries, to lay down a fatty

energy reserve before embarking on its long, energy-sapping migration journey. During the breeding season, a blackcap weighs about 16g (½oz) but can double its weight after gorging on the sweet berries that ripen in late summer.

Blackcaps that spend the winter here rely on ivy, cotoneaster, holly and mistletoe berries. Many now also visit bird-tables over the winter, taking suet, cheese, scraps, bread,

▲ *Wild and cultivated berries are lifesavers for blackcaps spending the winter in this country – even if these berries are quite a mouthful for a hungry female blackcap.*

oats and peanuts. The fact that the blackcap is more vegetarian than most warblers, and is able to exploit bounteous bird-tables, has almost certainly helped a growing number survive the winter here.

---

## Family diets

Early clutches of blackcap chicks are reared on a glut of small green *Tortrix* and winter moth caterpillars hatching in May. Second broods are more likely to be fed on large, gawky craneflies and reputedly foul-tasting ladybirds.

'*I've oft this tiny minstrel met,*
*Where ivy flapping to the breeze,*
*Bear ring-marked berries black as jet*'

from *The Blackcap* by **John Clare** (1793-1864)

# Nettle-creepers

MALE BLACKCAPS arrive back in their traditional woodland breeding sites in a rush in late April or early May, several days before the females. After wandering about, sizing up possible territories, each male settles on one area. Then he breaks into song, first to proclaim exclusive nesting and feeding rights on his patch, then to advertise for a mate. Each spring, the cock blackcap's singing enhances the quality and volume of the chorus of bird song in woodlands no end.

## WOODLAND NESTERS

Before starting his courtship routine, a male blackcap constructs a number of makeshift 'cock nests' within his territory. He usually hides them low down in a jungle of thorny brambles or stinging nettles to provide extra protection for his brood. (His habit of building among nettles earned the blackcap its old nickname of Nettle-creeper.) Sometimes he also builds in evergreens, such as ivy and laurel, or in hawthorn, blackthorn or elder. Later on, when he has paired up, the cock bird escorts his hen on a tour of inspection of his 'nests'. She picks out her preferred location.

## ON TO THE NEST

After that, both birds work together to complete a neat but quite flimsy nest by weaving dried grass stems and fine twigs into a cup. To ensure a secure anchorage, they lace the grass into the surrounding vegetation. Finally they line the cup with fine rootlets and horsehair and decorate the rim with spiders' webs.

*male*

▲ **PATERNAL ROLE**
*A cock blackcap is involved in all aspects of family life, from helping to build the nest and incubating the eggs to brooding and feeding the chicks – and he still finds time to sing throughout the summer.*

> ' *And in the little thickets where a sleeper*
> *For ever might lie lost, the nettle-creeper*
> *And garden warbler sang unceasingly* '

from *Haymaking* by **Edward Thomas** (1878-1917)

## Energetic suitor

A courting male blackcap goes to extraordinary lengths to make sure that any females in the area notice him. He lifts his crown, puffs out his throat feathers, fans his wings and flicks his splayed tail as he warbles his jubilant melody with great gusto. Sometimes he faces the female, at others he turns side on to her. At times, the irrepressible little show-off sings with such exquisite rapture and excitement that he gets completely carried away and throws himself into some remarkable positions – he may end up hanging upside down from his favourite song perch.

Even after pairing up, a cock blackcap sings enthusiastically around his nest: while he is helping to build it, when he is approaching it to change incubating shifts with his partner and from a perch above the nest when the female is sitting on the eggs.

*female*

*male*

## ▲ ECONOMY FLIGHTS
*Blackcaps seem to save most of their air miles for long-distance migration flights. During the summer, flying is largely restricted to flitting about from one tree or patch of cover to another.*

By late May, the female blackcap has laid four to six eggs into the nest. The colouring of the eggs varies from a pale grey-buff background with dark grey spatters and dots to a pinkish shell with dark red markings. Both parents take turns to incubate the eggs, sitting for 12 to 13 days until the chicks hatch.

### PARENTAL RESPONSIBILITIES
The hatchlings are naked and need to be kept warm for the first week or so. The parents share out the chores equally: when one bird arrives back with food, the other leaves to find more, while the returning bird settles down to brood the nestlings. They grow at a phenomenal rate and are ready to leave the nest in 10 to 14 days after hatching.

For a couple of weeks, the fledglings stay together, perching within the shelter of a bush and keeping up a steady stream of double chirps so that their parents can find and feed them. At night the family roosts together, with the chicks lined up between parental bookends.

Blackcaps are evidently proficient parents because they record a high hatching and fledging success. In a good summer, a pair of blackcaps will raise a second brood, building a new nest to hold their next family.

### ▲ SO FAR, SO GOOD
*This female blackcap and her partner have been working flat out for the past month or so, slinging a nest between two bramble stems and rearing three chicks to within a few days of fledging.*

## Youngsters

A juvenile blackcap looks more like its mother than its father, but is even browner above and yellower on its underparts. Its crown is a muddier brown than the reddish brown of the adult female. Juvenile males acquire their black caps during their first winter. Some, like the one below, still show a little brown on their foreheads during their first breeding season. In her first year a young female has a yellower brown cap than an older hen.

*juvenile male*

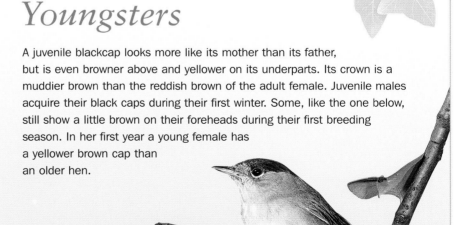

# Mock Nightingale

THE MALE BLACKCAP'S East Anglian nickname of the Mock Nightingale was praise of the highest order: the ultimate tribute that could be paid to the purity of his voice.

The comparative merits of the blackcap's sparkling spontaneous delivery and the nightingale's more technically brilliant song have long been hotly debated. The Reverend Gilbert White (1720-1793) was a fan of the blackcap. In May 1770, he noted in a letter that '*the Blackcap is a songster of the first rate. Its notes are deep and sweet.*'

Another keen ornithologist, the Reverend Francis Orpen Morris (1810-1893), noted that the blackcap can skillfully imitate other birds' songs as well, including '*the Robin, Nightingale, Blackbird, Thrush and Garden Warbler*'.

## NEW WINTER VENUE

Traditionally, blackcaps migrate to southern Europe and North Africa for the winter but, over the past 50 years, Britain has gradually become a more popular winter destination for some blackcaps that have spent the summer in parts of mainland Europe. The reasons for such a change in the blackcap's migratory behaviour have been the subject of much conjecture.

It is possible that in the 1950s a few blackcaps breeding in eastern Europe began reading the map upside down, as it were: instead of flying southeast one autumn, they headed northwest and ended up in Britain. Having survived a mild winter, they returned home the next spring and their descendants have been retracing their wing beats ever since.

But the first blackcaps to spend the winter here could equally well have come from Scandinavia. Instead of passing through Britain on their way south, some migrants may have spun out their stopover and stayed

> ' *The blackcap is a singing bird,*
> *A nightingale in melody* '

from *The Blackcap* by **John Clare** (1793-1864)

# Country names

- In its scientific name, *Sylvia atricapilla*, the blackcap is literally the 'black-haired woodland bird'. This is derived from *sylva*, the Latin for wood, *ater* meaning black, and *capillus*, which means 'hair on the head'. Many other warblers are *Sylvia* something too, but it was the tree-loving blackcap that earned them all this title from the Slovenian scientist Giovanni Scopoli in 1769.

- Other small birds, such as the coal tit, willow and marsh tits and reed bunting, also have black crowns. But it was only the black-capped warbler that was named after its black cap and always known as the blackcap warbler, which is now usually shortened to the blackcap.

- It is quite probable that the *swertling* mentioned by Aelfric (c.955–c.1010), the abbot of Eynsham, in his Latin to Anglo-Saxon vocabulary of 998 referred to the bird now known as the blackcap.

- Blackie Topper is the blackcap's most self-evident nickname.

- To account for the disappearance of some familiar summer birds during the winter before the idea of migration was accepted, the great Greek philosopher Aristotle believed that the garden warblers he saw during the summer transmuted into the blackcaps he saw around the Mediterranean in the winter.

- Favourite country names for the blackcap were the Hay Jack or Hay Bird because it built its nest from dried grass. In some places, the blackcap was also called Jack Straw.

- In Norfolk the blackcap was better known as the Mock Nightingale.

◄ *The cock blackcap's cheery singing is perfectly pitched for penetrating the dense undergrowth and carrying a long way through the woods.*

'*The black-caps croon and swing Deep in the night, and sing*'

from *The Farm* by **Edmund W Gosse** (1849-1928)

for the whole winter. In either case, a run of mild winters and cushy food sources – plenty of berries and well-stocked bird-tables – would have helped to establish the new trend.

### LESS TRAVELLING

The blackcaps wintering in the UK have an advantage over those that have to fly back each spring from southern Europe or Africa. For one thing, they have shorter and far less hazardous return journeys to their breeding grounds each spring. They will also get back earlier than more distant migrants and get the pick of the best territories.

An improved survival rate over the winter may also help to account for an increase in the total size of the breeding population. One estimate puts the immediate post-breeding population of blackcaps worldwide at a staggering 340 million.

## Winter movements

- Most of the blackcaps that breed or are reared in Britain and northern Europe each year are just summer visitors. They depart in the autumn, heading southwest to spend the winter around the western Mediterranean in Spain and North Africa.

- The farther north their starting point, the farther south the blackcaps travel: blackcaps from Scandinavia leapfrog those from Britain. Some years they fly over the Sahara Desert to reach Senegal in West Africa; other years they stop north of the Sahara.

- As the summer blackcaps leave, up to 3000 arrive to spend the winter

here, mainly in the South, East Anglia and the Midlands.

- Blackcaps that overwinter in Britain carry thicker plumage and more fat than the summer birds. They need good insulating layers of feather and fat to help keep them warm in cold weather.

# The Jackdaw

*When jackdaws establish a nesting colony in an area, you know about it – their raucous chattering and hectic comings and goings are impossible to miss*

Jackdaws are small crows that feed mainly on grassland in open farmland and parks. They roost and nest in holes in old trees, church towers and derelict buildings, coastal and quarry cliffs, and river gorges. In villages and towns, they use chimneys as nesting holes; narrow ledges and nooks on buildings or bridges serve as substitute cliffs.

## SECRETS OF SUCCESS

One key to the jackdaw's success and survival is its aptitude for exploiting man-made situations without being dependent on them. The very shrewd jackdaw has kept its options open: by eating a diversity of foodstuffs and nesting in a variety of locations it can take advantage of any and all opportunities as they arise.

► *An obvious grey shawl around its neck and very pale eyes distinguish the dapper jackdaw from other black crows.*

## Very rowdy crows

Both male and female jackdaws are extremely vociferous – there are days when it seems as though they never shut their beaks from dawn 'til dark. Their most overused calls are an explosive, hoarse *tchaak tchaak* and a high-pitched *kyaw*, which sounds a bit like the yelping of a small dog. A panic-stricken metallic screech – *karr-r-r karr-r-r* – warns of danger and raises the alarm.

*'The clamorous daws that all the day
Above the trees and towers play'*

from *Eve of St Mark* by **John Keats** (1795-1821)

# Field Faring

JACKDAWS SUBSIST mainly on animal matter: insects, including caterpillars, beetles and flies, as well as spiders, snails, slugs, earthworms and small frogs. They forage principally on the ground in pastures, ploughed fields and along the tideline. A jackdaw may also peck small prey from leaves or pick ticks off sheep or cattle by perching on their backs. If it finds a mouse or vole's nest hidden in the grass, it may eat the young rodents.

Like fellow crows, jackdaws are a menace to other birds in the breeding season, taking eggs and chicks from the nests of songbirds, seabirds, owls and kestrels. In the past, they were persecuted by gamekeepers for taking game-bird chicks.

## WINTER RATIONS

During the autumn a jackdaw has to supplement its diet with berries and fruit, grain and wild seeds. Jackdaws probably visit bird-tables more often than sightings suggest because they come to the garden early in the day to grab any scraps before there are many people about. The jackdaw will also scavenge for 'leftovers' on waste tips and at picnic sites.

▲ *A resourceful jackdaw has spotted some ticks on this red deer hind's ear and is busy plucking them off. It's good news all round: the jackdaw gets to eat some nourishing food and the deer ends up carrying fewer parasites.*

▶ *Jackdaws make a good living from filching corn and feed from troughs in free-range chicken runs and pig pens. This is a particularly useful and reliable source of food during the winter.*

# Feeding flocks

At any time of the year, jackdaws are seen foraging in ragged mixed flocks, primarily with rooks. Out of the breeding season, starlings often tag along with them; lapwings and gulls may also join the group in winter. The birds spread out over a field, often one being grazed by sheep or cattle, and search independently for food.

*' To sail inland, a dozen together, to the feeding grounds, and unearth the fat white slugs, (chork! chork!) '*

from *The Jackdaw* by **Edward Carpenter** (1844-1929)

# Holy Nesters

THE JACKDAW'S BREEDING season lasts from April to July. A male jackdaw usually pairs up with a lower status female from his flock. To impress her, the excited suitor struts up and down with exaggerated stiffness in front of a potential nesting hole. His wings are lifted and the feathers on the crown of his head are raised, giving him a high-browed appearance. As soon as a male and female jackdaw have paired up, the female gains the same status as her mate, a position she is quick to exploit – and others in the flock soon learn to recognise.

## NESTING PLATFORM

The jackdaw's nest is an untidy heap of twigs, piled up with dried grass and leaves. In some instances a huge amount of kindling is collected to fill the cavity and make it habitable. The central cup is lined with fine grass, hair and wool, which is either found snagged on barbed wire fences and thorny hedges or quite frequently plucked directly from the backs of sheep and cattle.

## GROWING UP

The female stays at the nest until all the eggs are hatched, keeping the helpless chicks warm. The hatchlings are skimpily clad in grey down, have brownish eyes and vast purplish-pink gapes outlined in yellow. Both parents work hard to find enough food to rear their young. Despite their best endeavours, in most years not all the chicks fledge. The last two to hatch are always smaller and disadvantaged when it comes to grabbing food.

As soon as their first feathers start to appear, the chicks begin preening and exercising, getting ready to leave the nest 30 to 35 days after hatching.

*young jackdaw*

> *' The church yard still its trees possest*
> *And jackdaws sought their ancient nest*
> *In whose old trunks they did acquire*
> *Homes safe as in the mossy spire '*

from *A Daydream in Summer* by **John Clare** (1793-1864)

▲ **WELCOMING PARTY**
*As the eldest chick grows stronger, it starts clambering up the side of the tree-hole in which it was raised. Then it waits at the entrance to greet a returning parent and get first bite at any food it is carrying.*

## Holes for all

In spring, jackdaws return to their traditional nesting sites, congregating around sea-cliffs and quarries, church towers, ruined buildings and chimneys, or old woodpecker holes and natural tree-holes, even rabbit burrows. There need to be a lot of nesting sites in one place as jackdaws are very gregarious and nest in large colonies. A jackdaw colony is a strong social unit, with a defined hierarchy, in which members rally round to help those in trouble – even helping injured brethren to feed – and unite to attack intruders. They are most hostile to fluttery black enemies, in the form of other nest-robbing crows.

**▲ CATTLE HUSTLING**
*Two jackdaws have alighted on the white saddle strip of a Belted Galloway and are vigorously pulling out tufts of its hair, which they will use to form a cosy lining for their nests.*

Juvenile jackdaws look more brown-black than their parents and have bluer-grey eyes for their first year.

## DARKENING THE SKY

By the end of June, most fledglings have joined the family flock, flying out each day to feed in the fields. At dusk, the sky near their winter roost is darkened by '*a cloud of drifting blackened paper*' when the returning jackdaws wheel, swerve, tumble and dive about. It always looks as if they are being buffeted in a chaotic flurry by the wind. In fact, they are just toying with the breeze, testing their flying skills. And all the time these evening conclaves are accompanied by a chorus of *tchaak tchaak* calls.

*'There is a bird, who by his coat, And by the hoarseness of his note, Might be supposed to be a crow'*

from *The Jackdaw* by **William Cowper** (1731-1800)

## One nestful

Clutches vary in size from between four to six greenish eggs with ash-grey or brown spots and blotches. The male is particularly vigilant when his mate is laying her eggs lest he be cuckolded by a maverick jackdaw. The female starts incubating her clutch when the second egg is laid. The male feeds her for as long as she is sitting on the eggs. A pair of jackdaws almost always raises only one brood a year.

# The Grey Heron

*The grey heron adopts the same frozen stance and look of rapt concentration whether it is hunting in a peaceful backwater or on a lake in the centre of London*

The stately grey heron is a big wading bird which frequents freshwater and saltwater sites all over Britain. In the countryside, herons are timid but in towns and cities they are amazingly unperturbed by all the hustle and bustle.

**WHERE TO LOOK**

More often than not, the ghostly grey heron is seen standing perfectly still, feeding in the water or on the banks of rivers, reedy lakes or rushy ponds, muddy estuaries, marshes and dykes. When disturbed, the heron rises ponderously from the ground with deep strokes of its large wings. During the breeding season, grey herons breed in established colonies of huge twiggy nests in the topmost branches of tall trees.

▶ *Add a fixed stare to a dagger-like beak, an S-curved neck and black pigtail and you have a grey heron.*

## Signs of youth

*juvenile*

The juvenile and immature grey heron is more uniformly grey than an adult, with less white on its head or neck. The front of its neck and underparts are more heavily streaked with black as well, and it shows no signs of its parents' wispy plumes at the base of the neck or a black crest trailing down its nape. A young heron's upper bill is dark rather than yellow like the lower one; adults have all-yellow beaks.

*'And sweeter the music of birds that soar, When the cry of the heron is heard on the wold'*

from a translation of an Ancient Irish verse by **Douglas Hyde** (1860-1949 )

# Heron Trees

ALTHOUGH THE GREY heron hunts on its own, it breeds in colonies called heronries, mostly at the top of tall trees but also in reed beds, on cliff ledges or on the ground. Most grey heron colonies contain between ten and 30 nests, but a few in England still exceed 100.

### ANCESTRAL PILE

Grey herons gather at a heronry in December or January. Experienced males occupy and refurbish the old nests. They see off rivals by raising their crests, stretching their necks, and lashing out with their beaks. Any newcomers and younger birds have to build on the fringes where they are more vulnerable to attack from crows and birds of prey.

In his courtship display, a male grey heron executes crazy zig-zagging dives and calls persistently to attract a mate. After pairing, the two herons preen each other and exchange twigs as a prelude to nest-building. The male collects sticks, or pinches them from another nest, for the female to arrange, before adding a fresh lining of dried grass or bracken. Then they mate on the nest or branches nearby.

▲ *Gangly grey herons attending to their twiggy nests in a heronry at the top of a tree may look precarious, but they are amazingly agile when moving about in the branches.*

▶ *Any time between February and May or June, a grey heron lays her four pale greenish-blue, pointed eggs in the nest: a huge basket of sticks and twigs wedged in the high branches.*

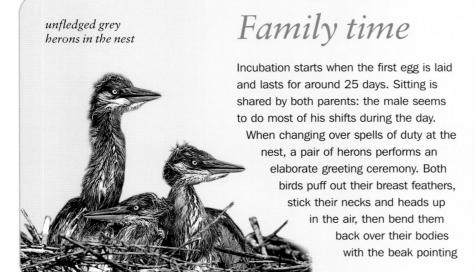

*unfledged grey herons in the nest*

## Family time

Incubation starts when the first egg is laid and lasts for around 25 days. Sitting is shared by both parents: the male seems to do most of his shifts during the day. When changing over spells of duty at the nest, a pair of herons performs an elaborate greeting ceremony. Both birds puff out their breast feathers, stick their necks and heads up in the air, then bend them back over their bodies with the beak pointing skyward. A bout of bill sparring follows before one bird leaves and the other settles down on the eggs.

The newly-hatched chicks are covered in long blackish-brown down with white tips, which is bristly on the top of the head. The youngsters grow rapidly and are clambering about in the branches by the time they are 25 days old. Fledging follows by day 50 but it takes another four years for them to reach adulthood and start breeding.

# Slick Catcher

GREY HERONS USUALLY hunt for food in ponds and along ditches, streams, shallow rivers, marshes and mudflats, where the water is clear and its prey more visible. They probably breed early in the year because water-weed cover is thinner then, which makes it easier to spot and catch enough fish to feed their growing families.

## FAVOURITE FARE

Wary and suspicious, the grey heron feeds mainly early in the morning and in the evening in quiet spots. When fishing, it uses a combination of stealth and speed to catch its prey. It eats a variety of fish, generally no more than 20cm (8in) long, including eel, trout, flounder and carp. Herons also catch frogs, lizards and snakes, ducklings and moorhen chicks, plus some shellfish and large insects, such as grasshoppers and dragonflies. It may take a few small mammals too, especially voles and an astonishing number of moles, which often tunnel through the soft damp earth near its hunting grounds.

The heron swallows most of its prey whole, after some deft sleight-of-beak to ensure that the catch goes down head-first. That way around, barbs cannot catch in the heron's gullet and choke it.

## COME BACKS

During the day, a grey heron takes a break from fishing to digest its early catches. It often rests on one leg in shallow water or on the bank.

## ▲ TRANSFORMATION
*As a grey heron takes off, it unfurls its broad wings, revealing the black flight feathers, gradually bends its neck back into its shoulders but leaves its legs sticking straight out under its short tail.*

## ▼ NO ESCAPE
*A wriggly eel is a bit of a beakful, even for an adult grey heron as it flies away to kill and eat the slippery fish on the bank.*

> '*Can fetch with their long necks out of the rush and reed, Snigs\*, fry, and yellow frogs, whereon they often feed*'

from *Polyobion* by **Michael Drayton** (1563-1631)
(*snig is an old country name for an eel)

*flying off with an eel*

## Capturing its prey

When hunting, a grey heron usually stands stock still for hours at a time. A pair of keen eyes are crucial: the heron gazes into the water until it spots a fish or frog swimming past, then tracks its prey and makes a lightning-fast lunge to catch it. An extra-long sixth vertebra at the base of the neck, which hinges forward at the top and backward at the base, acts as a pivot for the whiplash attack. The wriggling prey is mostly clamped in the beak, not speared, although young herons may misjudge their lunge and pierce their victims. A skilled adult heron only ever gives its thrust as much as it needs – even in shallow water it rarely hits the bottom – and hardly ever misses.

## ▲ PROVERBIAL MILLPOND

*Calm clear water makes an ideal hunting ground for a heron. The only thing that is likely to disturb this transfixed grey heron from its fishing is its own reflection on the glassy surface.*

Grey herons regurgitate pellets of the undigestible parts of their prey. When they have been eating small mammals and frogs, bones and fur come back up in pellet form. Even if a grey heron's digestive juices can dissolve the fish bones, leaving nothing to bring up, it will swallow grass or feathers as purgatives and disgorge them later.

### NOISY WELCOME

Parent herons fly up to 20 miles from the heronry to find food for their family. They carry their catches back to the nest in roomy pouches in their neck. On their return, their rumbustious offspring greet them with a ceaseless cacophony of beak-clacking accompanied by hysterical grunts, squeals, quacking, barking and some weird *kaka-kaka-kakak* calls, which sound rather like the roosting call of a blackbird.

In the first few weeks, while the chicks are tiny, the adults pour a regurgitated fish soup down their throats. Later when their offspring are stronger, the parents simply dump the fish they have caught in the nest and leave the youngsters to squabble over it and feed themselves.

# Powder puff

The grey heron has a long and complicated preening routine. While fishing, slime and scales from slippery wet prey are bound to rub off on the grey heron's feathers. The heron has an instant solution tucked away in its plumage: patches of specially crumbly feathers on its breast and its flanks. Such powder-down provides a dust which the heron uses to preen itself. It scratches away the mess with a comb-like ridged third claw on each foot and distributes powder with its beak.

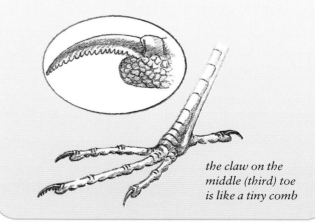

*the claw on the middle (third) toe is like a tiny comb*

# The Grey Sentinel

THE SOLITARY, STATIONARY grey heron had a reputation for being doleful and ghostly. Life can be hard for grey herons. All sorts of hazards may kill them: becoming entangled in barbed wire, flapping into overhead cables, choking on large fish, being attacked by foxes or getting shot.

Bad weather can take a heavy toll too. Grey heron nests buck and sway about in the roughest spring gales, sometimes so violently that the eggs or youngsters topple out or the nests themselves may get dislodged from the tree-tops. Strong winds may also prevent the adults returning to the heronry, leaving the eggs and chicks exposed to the elements.

Harsh winters claim the greatest number of lives. When streams and ponds freeze over, grey herons cannot fish through the ice and may starve to death. In prolonged icy spells, grey herons often head to the coast, where the saltier water in saltmarshes and estuaries is less likely to freeze than fresh water farther inland.

## HEALTHY SIGN

The presence of grey herons on a river or lake is generally a good sign. It shows that the fresh water is clean enough to support plenty of fish life for the grey herons to eat. As the top predator, a grey heron is vulnerable to toxic chemicals and pollution, which accumulate through the food chain and end up concentrated in the fish that it eats.

## PAST TIMES

Water bailiffs used to persecute grey herons for their fish-eating habits in lakes and rivers. Today, trout farmers still find that individual herons can become persistent pests. Herons are also notorious for taking goldfish and valuable koi carp from garden ponds. Laying a net over the water is the only way to stop them.

*' The moping heron, motionless and stiff,*
*That on a stone, as silently and stilly,*
*Stood, an apparent sentinel '*

from *The Haunted House* by **Thomas Hood** (1799-1845 )

# Old names and folklore

- The grey heron's scientific name is *Ardea cinerea*: *ardea* is the Latin name for a heron used by Virgil and *cinerea* means ash-grey.

- The name 'heron' is probably derived from *hragra*, a mutation of its strident *kraik* cry. There are records dating from around 1300, which refer to the heron as the *heyrun* or *hayroun*.

- The heron once masqueraded under many variants on the heron theme: Hern, Harn, Herl or Hegrie. Until the 17th century, herons were better known as Heronshaws, Henshaws or Handsaws.

- The grey heron used to be called Frankie in imitation of its *fraank* call.

- In the country, the male grey heron was once affectionately known as Jack Hern and his mate as Moll.

- Poachers in Wales used essence of heron leg to lure fish into their traps.

- The fat from a plump heron was used to cure arthritis and rheumatism because, despite standing in water all day, herons never suffered from either.

- In Northern Ireland, people thought incubating herons thrust their long legs through the base of their nest.

- It was said that grey heron's eggs were a watery green because the heron spent so much time gazing into pools and streams.

- Long ago, the heron was often mistakenly called a crane, although a heron flies with a bent neck and a crane with a straight one.

◀ *All hunched up, with its wings wrapped like a cloak around its legs to keep warm, a young grey heron shivers through an icy winter's day: a haughty hunter frustrated and imperiled by the freezing weather.*

According to one very early German scholar, Rabanus Maurus Magentius (c.780–856), herons were revered for flying so high, '*where they behold forever the countenance of God*'. To Ancient Egyptians the heron signified the southerly wind, as it migrated north each spring, following the River Nile to the Mediterranean Sea.

According to superstition, a heron waxed and waned with the moon: it was plump during a full moon but became gaunt at the change of the moon. In fact, herons can catch more fish and frogs by bright moonlight than on dark moonless nights.

### KEEP COUNTING

Grey herons nest communally, before the trees are in leaf, so are fairly easy to count. They are the subject of the longest running census of any British bird, conducted for over 70 years by the British Trust for Ornithology.

> ' *The heron mounted doth appear*
> *On his own Peg'sus a lancier,*
> *And seems on earth, when he doth hut,*
> *A proper halberdier\* on foot* '

from *The Falcon* by **Richard Lovelace** (1618-c.1657)
(\*a foot solder carrying a halberd, a combined battleaxe and spear)

## Heron hawking

- In falconry, the grey heron was a royal bird: only kings could hunt them, flying a cast of falcons – a pair of female peregrines – against it.

- The heron would rise steeply in a tight spiral to a great height to thwart the falcons' attempts to climb above it for a stoop – their lethal megafast dive.

- When attacked in the air by a bird of prey, a heron vomits up the contents of its crop, to lighten its load and facilitate a swifter retreat.

- Herons were regarded as a delicacy to serve at a grand feast. In the 15th century, over 400 were served after the enthronement of an Archbishop of York.

CHAPTER 5 · HELPING BIRDS

# Nature's Bounty

*Turn your garden into a feast for the birds as well as the eyes
with plants whose bright autumn fruit provides food in winter*

With many habitats lost due to intensive farming and urban development, birds have been forced look to gardens to find places to live and feed. Gardens in the UK cover about 670,000 acres, more than all of Britain's nature reserves combined. One mature garden can host as many as 60 different species. The blackbird is one of many birds that now favour towns over countryside.

To attract birds to your garden, you need to give them places to nest, such as trees, woodpiles or ivy-covered walls, and plenty to eat in the form of insects, seed-heads, berries and fruit. And offering them a bath goes down well too.

Gardening for birds is not just about what you plant, it's also about letting nature have its own way occasionally. Although insects and snails can often be pests, they do attract and support many birds. By not using chemical pesticides, you leave the birds more to eat.

◀ **AN APPLE A DAY**
*The redwing is one of many birds to feed on windfall apples in winter. Robins, song thrushes, blackbirds and starlings do too.*

▲ **BERRY HUNGRY**
*Shrubs such as cotoneaster provide food aplenty from autumn to winter for fieldfares and other berry-eaters.*

> ' *The thrill of England's*
> *winter days*
> *Of England's frost-sharp air* '

from *A Christ-Child Day in Australia* by **Ethel Turner** (1872-1958)

## Trees and shrubs

Mature trees provide a year-round banquet. The alder produces seeds that goldfinches and siskins eat; the oak, acorns for jays; and the ash, keys for bullfinches. Willow, birch, beech and hazel all produce seeds or fruit for birds to eat. In the dead of winter, windfall apples and pears are a godsend to birds, while, in autumn, birds flock to crab apple and rowan trees and berry-laden shrubs to feast.

Hedges make cosy shelters as well. Some prickly ones such as hawthorn and holly provide protection with food thrown in too. Yew, beech and wild privet hedges offer both food to eat and places to hide, roost and nest for many feathered visitors.

**▲ THISTLE A MERRY TUNE**
*Although it does eat seeds in the winter, this blue tit is just perching on a teasel, as only the goldfinch can reach its seeds.*

## VARIETY IS THE SPICE OF LIFE

Even a small garden can provide a variety of bird-friendly habitats, as long as the planting includes short and long grass, herbaceous plants, climbers, shrubs and mature trees. On the lawn, starlings, song thrushes and blackbirds hunt for earthworms, while robins scour freshly dug-over flowerbeds or aphid-covered rose bushes for food.

Among the trees, blue and great tits bustle about searching for insects as blackbirds kick through the dead leaves beneath on the lookout for other creepy-crawlies. Rockeries and stone walls also harbour plenty of insects for the birds to eat.

To give the birds something to eat all winter long, leave seed-heads on your plants until March. Flowers which produce seeds such as heather,

Michaelmas daisies, lavender and sunflowers supply a feast. Many seed-heads also harbour hibernating insects and spiders.

Thick leafy climbers and shrubs provide nesting and roosting places for birds. Ivy is especially good at offering cosy all-year-round cover with room service – the dark berries

ripen late-on in winter, providing precious food in the coldest months. Wrens, blackbirds, dunnocks and robins all shelter and feed on ivy climbing up walls and fences.

### Wild winter fare

These plants and trees will give the birds food from autumn to spring; just be sure to leave seed-heads on and any windfalls lying beneath the trees for the birds to find.

- **Apple tree** – apples
- **Beech** – seeds (mast)
- **Berberis** – berries
- **Cardoon** – seeds
- **Cotoneaster** – berries
- **Crab apple** – tiny red apples
- **Daphne** – berries
- **Grape vine** – grapes
- **Hawthorn** – red berries
- **Holly** – red berries
- **Ivy** – black berries
- **Mahonia** – black berries
- **Mountain ash** – red berries
- **Nigella** – seeds
- **Oak** – acorns
- **Pear tree** – pears
- **Pyracantha** – red berries
- **Roses** – many varieties sport large rose hips
- **Strawberry Tree** – red fruits
- **Sunflower** – seeds
- **Thistle** – seeds
- **Viburnum** – red berries

### Water for winter

Birds need fresh water more than ever during the winter. They must keep their feathers clean if they are to stay warm, because dirty, sticky feathers do not provide good insulation. A pond or other water feature provides them with something to drink, a place to wash, and a larder stocked with tiny insects. If there is no space for a pond, an upturned bin lid will do. To stop the water from freezing, float a ball on your pond or bird-bath – as the wind moves it, the ice will break. Do not use glycerine or de-icers since they stick to the birds' beaks and stop them from preening.

# Winter Feeders

*The right feeder and the right food in the right place will help the birds survive the winter and give you plenty to see*

▲ **WOODPECKER FEAST**
*Woodpeckers love suet. Push it into crevices in tree bark or holes drilled in a hanging log for them – you may attract nuthatches too.*

Two out of three households put out food for wild birds in their gardens and are rewarded with regular visits from starlings, house sparrows, chaffinches, greenfinches and tits, as well as dunnocks, song thrushes, blackbirds and robins.

You can make your guests feel at home by putting out food in their favourite spots. Acrobatic tits like to feed among the branches while pied wagtails, robins and thrushes generally stick to the ground. Woodpeckers prefer logs or tree trunks they can cling to, while dunnocks stay close to shrubberies. Bold starlings and house sparrows will feed almost anywhere they find food.

## HITTING THE SPOT

Put your feeder where it is easy to get at for refilling and cleaning and where you can see all the action. Make sure that the birds can feed in comfort and safety, out of the prevailing wind and away from predators. The best site is in the open but near a bush or tree so that they can hide if need be.

Where you have space, put out more than one feeding station. If you

> *' The birds sit chittering in the thorn*
> *A' day they fare but sparely;*
> *And lang's the night frae e'en to morn*
> *I'm sure it's winter fairly '*

from *Up in the Morning Early* by **Robert Burns** (1759-1796)

## Something for everyone

Feeding birds is like catering for a large party of fussy eaters – some prefer insects or suet, others only eat nuts and seeds. If you put out a variety of food, there'll be something for everyone. Commercial bird-seed mixes and sunflower seeds suit a wide range of species. Dunnocks, thrushes and robins like soft-bill mixtures (pinhead oatmeal and other soft seeds mixed with fat).

Some foods, including heavily-salted food, mouldy or rotting food or desiccated coconut, can harm birds. Peanuts may be contaminated with a fungal poison called aflatoxin, so buy them from reputable sources such as the RSPB.

**▲ BLUE TIT TREAT**
*Although blue tits are insect-eaters, they will nibble at apples in winter. This little tit is tackling an apple that's bigger than he is.*

**▶ DO-IT-YOURSELF FEEDER**
*Make your own hanging feeder by pouring melted suet mixed with seed into a small cup or coconut shell, then suspend it from a tree.*

have more than one feeder, make sure that they are hanging well away from each other and from any nest-boxes. This gives timid birds a chance to feed in peace while more aggressive birds are monopolising the other feeder or bird-table.

## CLEAN-UP CREW

Birds are messy eaters, so if you don't clean up after them you may get unwelcome guests: rats and mice! Put out food in the morning so the birds have a chance to eat it all by dark. From time to time, rake up the debris. Clean your table by pouring a kettleful of boiling water over it from time to time and disinfect it with a one-in-ten solution of disinfectant to water each year. Places where birds gather can get contaminated with *Salmonella* from their droppings – so move your feeding stations occasionally.

The RSPB recommends feeding birds all year round, so they emerge from the winter in good condition for breeding and stay fit. And in summer, you have the fun of seeing parents bring their offspring to your bird-feeder – just don't give them whole nuts, which may choke the nestlings.

## The right feeder

Some birds prefer to eat from a bird-table, others like pecking at fallen crumbs on the ground, while a few are agile enough to use hanging feeders. Finches perch as they peck at seeds from a hopper.

A bird-table lets you watch birds interacting: for example, the little robin fighting off larger birds to get his share. It should have a rim to keep the food from falling off, a roof to keep it dry, and a guard on the pole to discourage cats, squirrels and mice.

# Feeding the Birds in Winter

*Chaffinch*

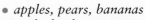

*Your bird-feeder will attract all sorts of birds if you put out the right foods. Some will be drawn by bird-seed or peanuts, others have more specialised tastes such as live mealworms*

## Foods birds love to eat

*Some birds are seed-eaters, others insect-eaters and some eat both. Put out bird-seed for seed-eating birds such as the finches. Insect-eaters, such as the robin and the woodpecker, need meatier fare such as suet. Thrushes thrive on a diet of rotting fruit, while the humble sparrow enjoys breadcrumbs.*

- *bird-seed mixture*
- *sunflower, hemp and other seeds*
- *unsalted peanuts and other nuts*
- *bird seed cake (seeds with suet)*

- *suet, bacon and bacon rind and other cooked meat or animal fat*
- *live mealworms and wax worms*
- *grated cheese*

- *apples, pears, bananas*
- *soaked sultanas, currants, raisins*
- *oats, cooked rice, bread, pastry*
- *halved fresh coconut*

**BLACKBIRD**
Bread, grated cheese, millet, windfall apples, seeds, berries

**BLACKCAP**
Berries, breadcrumbs, fat, rolled oats

**BULLFINCH**
Peanuts, seeds

**CHAFFINCH**
Fresh coconut, peanuts, seeds

**COLLARED DOVE**
Peanuts, grain, maize, millet

**DUNNOCK**
Niger seeds, grated cheese, pinhead oatmeal, uncooked pastry, rice (cooked and unsalted)

**FIELDFARE**
Berries from trees and shrubs, including holly, rowan, hawthorn and cotoneaster; windfall fruit under apple and pear trees

**GOLDCREST**
Suet, grated cheese

**GOLDFINCH**
Hulled sunflower seeds, niger seeds, peanuts, thistle-heads

**GREAT SPOTTED WOODPECKER**
Black sunflower seeds, suet pushed into holes or crevices in a tree, whole, shelled nuts, peanuts, fruit

**GREENFINCH**
Black sunflower seeds, peanuts, rice (cooked and unsalted)

**GREEN WOODPECKER**
Fat, live mealworms

**HOUSE SPARROW**
Black sunflower seeds, grain, millet, peanuts, rice (cooked and unsalted)

◄ **FOR THE NEXT GENERATION**
*Christmas or New Year is a good time to repair and put up nest-boxes. Fix them facing north, to save them getting too hot on sunny days. If you put out nesting material such as hair and wool, you will give the busy parents a head start. It is important to clean out the box well at the end of each nesting season.*

*If you have no space to put up a nest-box, plant climbers, trees and shrubs in your garden to give the birds natural cover for nesting and roosting. Conifers provide particularly good year-round shelter. Even a flowerpot wedged into an ivy-covered fence can make a cosy home for a family of robins.*

*Redwing*

**JAY**
Corn, fresh coconut, fruit, peanuts

**LINNET**
Grain, seeds

**NUTHATCH**
Black sunflower seeds, peanuts, suet pushed into holes or crevices in a tree

**PIED WAGTAIL**
Fat, suet, grated cheese, live mealworms or wax worms

**REDWING**
Berry-bearing trees and shrubs including holly, hawthorn and cotoneaster, windfall fruit under apple and pear trees

**ROBIN**
Dripping, suet, fat, grated cheese, rice (cooked and unsalted), peanuts, hulled sunflower seeds, live mealworms

**SISKIN**
Black sunflower seeds, peanuts

*Waxwing*

**STARLING**
Bananas, bruised and rotten apples or pears, fat, fat balls, grain, scraps, seeds

**THRUSHES:** SONG AND MISTLE
Bacon rind, bruised bananas, cooked and uncooked pastry, fat, fat balls, grated cheese, suet, windfall apples and pears

**TITS:** GREAT, BLUE, COAL AND LONG-TAILED
Bacon rind, suet, fat, black sunflower seeds, fresh coconut, mixed seeds, peanuts, other nuts, bruised fruit (apples, pears or bananas)

**WAXWING**
Berry-bearing trees including holly, rowan, hawthorn and cotoneaster

**WREN**
Bacon, suet, fat, grated cheese

*Fieldfare*

# The Blackbird

## Distribution

*Blackbirds are very common and widely distributed all over the British Isles and much of Europe. The British breeding population is largely resident, although during a spell of icy winter weather some Scottish birds may drift west and south as far as Ireland and France.*

*In September, British residents are joined by flocks of migrants from southern Scandinavia and northern Europe. Some of these visiting blackbirds stay for the winter and head north and east again in spring. Others fly on south, through France and Spain as far as North Africa.*

*Homesick settlers successfully introduced blackbirds into Australia and New Zealand.*

☐ areas where the bird stays all year
☐ areas where the bird is a summer visitor
☐ areas where the bird is a winter visitor

### HABITAT
Common everywhere – from woodland, hedges, gardens and parks to moorland

### NATURE WATCH
● At first glance blackbirds and starlings on a bird-table together may look alike. But blackbirds are plumper with a longer tail than the more upright starlings.
● In the breeding season, both the male blackbird and starling have yellow bills, but while the cock blackbird's plumage is glossy black, the starling's shimmers with purple and green.

## NAMES
**SCIENTIFIC NAME:** *Turdus merula*
**NICKNAMES:** Woofell, Amsel, Zulu

## IDENTIFICATION
**APPEARANCE:** adult male is all-black with yellow beak and eye-rings; female is earthy brown above with chestnut breast, paler throat and brown beak; both have dark brown legs; fledglings are browner and more freckled than the hen; in their first winter, young males are sooty brown with dull beak and eye-ring
**SIZE:** 24-25cm (10in) long
**WINGSPAN:** 34-38cm (13²/₃-15¹/₃in)
**WEIGHT:** 80-100g (2²/₃-3¹/₃oz)
**FLIGHT:** direct and low
**VOICE:** musical, fluty song delivered very nonchalantly; hysterical *chook-chook-chook* when disturbed; scolding *chik-chik-chik*; in flight *tsi*; *tic-tic-tic* at dusk when about to settle down for the night

## FOOD
In spring and summer, eats mainly earthworms and insects; during the autumn and winter it feeds on windfall fruit and berries galore, plus any earthworms, insects or snails it can find; a greedy visitor to bird-tables and steals food from other birds

## BEHAVIOUR
Bold and bossy to other birds but often nervous when disturbed by humans; a very noisy bird, issuing strident alarm calls; both males and females are fiercely and vocally territorial
**ENEMIES:** cats, cold or dry weather

## BREEDING
**PAIRING UP:** breeding season lasts from late March to July; a pair rears 2-3 broods each year, sometimes 4
**NESTING:** female builds a bulky cup of moss and roots, reinforced with mud, lined with grass, in a bush, tree or thick creeper
**EGGS:** 3-6 greenish-blue eggs with variable dusting of chestnut specks
**INCUBATION:** female sits for 14 days
**YOUNG:** newly-hatched chicks are covered in buff-grey down; mouths lined in yellow with yellowish-white flanges; fed mostly worms by both parents; fledged in 13-15 days; dependent on parental guidance for another 3 weeks
**MOULT:** adults/juveniles in late summer
**LIFE EXPECTANCY:** many die young; few make it to 5 years

## POPULATION IN BRITAIN
About 5 million breed each year; swollen by European migrants in winter

# The Blackcap

*In summer the blackcap is widespread over Britain. It is common in southern England, Wales and lowland Scotland, but rare in the Highlands and localised in Ireland where there are few trees. It is also found across Europe, including southern Scandinavia, east to Iran.*

*The blackcap is both a summer and winter visitor to this country. In autumn, most British and northern-European nesters fly southwest to spend the winter in Spain; a few turn south into North Africa and some cross the Sahara. Blackcaps nesting in eastern Europe fly southeast to the Aegean. The small winter population in Britain is a mixture of a few residents and some European visitors.*

☐ areas where the bird stays all year
☐ areas where the bird is a summer visitor
☐ areas where the bird is a winter visitor

## NAMES

**SCIENTIFIC NAME:** *Sylvia atricapilla*
**NICKNAMES:** Nettle-creeper, Hay Jack

## IDENTIFICATION

**APPEARANCE:** a large warbler; the male has the black cap, hers is rusty-brown; he is plain ash-grey underneath and olive-brown above; she is a browner-grey below and browner above; a juvenile looks like the female – a first-year male may still have a few brown feathers in his black cap
**SIZE:** 13.5-15cm (5½-6in) long
**WINGSPAN:** 20-23cm (8-9in)
**WEIGHT:** 16g (½oz), rising to 30g (1oz) when fat is laid down before migration
**FLIGHT:** flitters jerkily over short distances; more fluttery during displays
**VOICE:** loud clicking *tacc-tacc* calls when distressed or alarmed; cock bird sings a rich flute-like melody from April to July

## FOOD

In spring and summer, picks caterpillars, beetles, flies and spiders from leaves; in autumn and winter, eats fruit and berries and takes food from bird-tables

## BEHAVIOUR

Mainly solitary, except in the breeding season and when migrating; wary and timid, keeping to leafy cover; male sings more than most around the nest
**ENEMIES:** crows and squirrels; trappers in southern Europe during migration

## BREEDING

**PAIRING UP:** starts in late April-early May with males singing to establish territories and win a mate; rears two broods a year
**NESTING:** both birds weave a neat but flimsy cup of grasses and fine twigs lined with thin roots and hair; built low down in undergrowth, hedges and bushes
**EGGS:** lays 4-6 eggs which are very variable in colour and pattern
**INCUBATION:** partners share the sitting for 12-13 days
**YOUNG:** on hatching, the chicks are naked; their parents take turns to keep them warm and find insects and tiny snails to stuff into their pink-lined mouths; the nestlings grow fast and fledge in 10-14 days
**MOULT:** adults moult chiefly in breeding areas, between July and September, before flying south
**LIFE EXPECTANCY:** up to 10 years

## POPULATION IN BRITAIN

Up to 600,000 blackcaps breed each summer; some 3000 overwinter here

## HABITAT

Favours deciduous woodland with thick undergrowth and tall trees; visits parks and gardens during the winter

## NATURE WATCH

● The garden warbler shares many of the blackcap's haunts each summer. They look different – the garden warbler is a plain brown bird – but sound alike, eat the same insects and build similar nests.
● At a glance, a blackcap could be mistaken for a marsh or willow tit, but the tits' black caps are more helmet-like.

# The Blue Tit

## Distribution

*The blue tit is the commonest tit in the British Isles. It is now resident throughout the mainland and neighbouring islands, although it colonised the Outer Hebrides, off the west coast of Scotland, less than 40 years ago.*

*Blue tits are widely distributed on mainland Europe, except in northern Scandinavia and at high altitudes, and along the North African coastal strip. In summer, they extend their range farther north into Russia.*

*Very rarely, massive flocks of blue tits invade eastern England from northern Europe during the autumn months. They come in search of food and stay until the spring, when they return to where they came from.*

☐ areas where the bird stays all year
☐ areas where the bird is a summer visitor

### NAMES
**SCIENTIFIC NAME:** *Parus caeruleus*
**NICKNAMES:** Bluecap, Tomtit, Nun

### IDENTIFICATION
**APPEARANCE:** adult male and female have white face and blue crown, pale yellow front, greenish back and blue wings and tail feathers; short, conical beak; males brighter blue than female; juveniles are yellower and drabber
**SIZE:** length 11-12cm (4¼-4¾in)
**WINGSPAN:** 19-21cm (7½-8¼in)
**WEIGHT:** on average about 10-12g (⅓oz)
**FLIGHT:** bursts of rapid wing beats
**VOICE:** cheerful trilling song – *tsee-tseee-tsu-chu-chu*; quick scolding *tsee-tsee-tsee-tsit* call; female hisses *ps-s-sie* when disturbed on the nest

### FOOD
Mainly insects and spiders – caterpillars are crucial for rearing the chicks; also eats pollen and nectar in spring, wild fruits, seeds and nuts on bird-tables

### BEHAVIOUR
Lively, acrobatic little birds; youngsters live in flocks during the winter; adults are more solitary, except during the breeding season

**ENEMIES:** windows, cats, squirrels, weasels, woodpeckers and starvation

### BREEDING
**PAIRING UP:** male and female get together in late March or early April; 1 large brood is produced in May or June to coincide with caterpillars hatching on apple and oak trees
**NESTING:** female builds a nest-cup from moss and dried grass, lined with hair and feathers, in a hole in a tree or stone wall or in a nesting-box
**EGGS:** 7-15 white eggs with red-brown specks (more than female's own weight)
**INCUBATION:** female sits on the eggs for 12-16 days, while the male brings food
**YOUNG:** both parents feed the chicks, which are fledged after 16-22 days
**MOULT:** juveniles moult to adult colours in their first autumn; adults renew their feathers after the breeding season
**LIFE EXPECTANCY:** 2-3 years, as long as the fledglings survive the early weeks out of the nest and their first winter

### POPULATION IN BRITAIN
About 4 million breeding pairs in the spring; of the 20 million blue tits after the breeding season at least 12 million will die over the following 12 months

### HABITAT
Mixed woodland but has adapted well to thick bushy cover in gardens, parks, orchards, hedges and churchyards

### NATURE WATCH
● To encourage blue tits to nest in your garden, put up a nesting-box. Make sure the box has a small entrance hole to exclude other birds and predators.
● Being bold and inquisitive can land blue tits in trouble. To stop them flying into windows and breaking their necks, you can stick a silhouette of a hawk on the inside of the glass.

# The Chaffinch

## Distribution

*Chaffinches are evenly distributed throughout the British Isles. Their range extends all over Europe, around the Mediterranean to North Africa, west as far as the Canary Islands and Azores in the Atlantic Ocean and east across Asia to Afghanistan.*

*Resident breeders generally stay put during the winter. In late September or early October, they are joined by flocks of migrant chaffinches from northern Europe. Some stay until the spring, more than doubling the resident population; others carry on to winter quarters around the Mediterranean, notably in Spain and North Africa. Sometimes, these travellers are joined by young birds from southern England.*

☐ areas where the bird stays all year
☐ areas where the bird is a summer visitor
☐ areas where the bird is a winter visitor

**HABITAT**
Seen frequently and almost everywhere – in woodland, hedges, gardens and parks

**NATURE WATCH**
● Look for the chaffinch's white wing bars, or you might mistake a hen chaffinch for a female house sparrow.
● In winter, a cock chaffinch may be confused with a male brambling, except that a chaffinch's shoulders are white, not orange; in flight, his rump is moss-green, not a dazzling white; and his beak is pink not yellow.

## NAMES
**SCIENTIFIC NAME:** *Fringilla coelebs*
**NICKNAMES:** Bachelor Finch, Pink Twink

## IDENTIFICATION
**APPEARANCE:** white shoulder patches and band on wings and green rump; otherwise cock and hen look very different: in breeding season male has bright slate-blue crown and chestnut breast (he is paler and duller in winter); hen is plain pale olive-brown; juveniles are browner versions of the hen
**SIZE:** 14.5-16cm (5½-6½in) long
**WINGSPAN:** 24.5-28.5cm (9¾-11½in)
**WEIGHT:** 20-25g (⅔-⅞oz)
**FLIGHT:** strong and undulating
**VOICE:** rattling song which accelerates and descends with final kick *chip-chip-chip-chwee-chwee-tissi-chooeo*; low *chip-chip* in flight; *pink-pink* contact call

## FOOD
In spring and summer, eats insects and feeds them to the chicks; during the winter eats seeds and visits bird-tables

## BEHAVIOUR
Confident to the point of tameness around humans; territorial during the breeding season; congregates in flocks during the autumn and winter, often travelling around with other finches, buntings, sparrows, tits or larks
**ENEMIES:** nest-robbers, cats, weather

## BREEDING
**PAIRING UP:** breeding season lasts from April to July; usually produces only 1 brood each year
**NESTING:** female constructs a neat cup of moss, grass and bark, lined with hair and feathers, camouflaged with lichen
**EGGS:** 4-6 greenish-blue eggs lightly sprinkled with purplish-brown blotches
**INCUBATION:** female sits for 12-13 days
**YOUNG:** newly-hatched chicks covered in light grey down; mouths lined in carmine and orange and outlined in white; fed by both parents; fledged in 13-14 days
**MOULT:** in late summer, new feathers leave the males looking dull for the winter; the tips gradually wear away to reveal bright feathers in the spring
**LIFE EXPECTANCY:** mortality is highest among fledglings; on average, lives for 2-3 years

## POPULATION IN BRITAIN
Over 7 million breeding pairs each spring; estimated that numbers are increased by over 10 million migrants from the Continent during the winter

# The Coal Tit

## NAMES
**SCIENTIFIC NAME:** *Parus ater*
**NICKNAMES:** Coalmouse, Coaly Head

## IDENTIFICATION
**APPEARANCE:** smallest of the true tits; male and female look alike with black cap, throat and bib and white patches on the cheeks and nape; upper parts olive-grey; wings marked with two white bars; underparts pale buff darkening to brown on the flanks; juveniles have a yellower tinge
**SIZE:** 10-11.5cm (4-4½in) long; smallest of the true tits
**WINGSPAN:** 17-21cm (7-8½in)
**WEIGHT:** 8-10g (¼-½oz)
**FLIGHT:** fast, dipping and flitting
**VOICE:** high-pitched *tsee-tsee* contact calls; persistent fast, sweet and high-pitched *weecho-weecho* song

## FOOD
Eats insects, their eggs and larvae, and spiders it finds hiding among pine needles and leaves, and in crevices in bark all year round; it also eats spruce seeds when they are available; in winter it visits bird-tables for peanuts, seeds and suet to supplement its natural diet of insects, which are hard to find

## BEHAVIOUR
Typically tit-like – agile and acrobatic; gregarious when not breeding; stays with mate even when foraging with other tits, siskins or redpolls during the winter
**ENEMIES:** cats, birds of prey, bad weather

## BREEDING
**PAIRING UP:** from March to July; usually rears 1 brood each year, maybe 2
**NESTING:** female builds a snug nest of moss and dead leaves woven together with spiders' silk and lined with fur, wool and feathers in a tree-hole, mouse tunnel, chink in a wall or a nesting-box
**EGGS:** lays 8-10, maybe as many as 13, white eggs with reddish speckles
**INCUBATION:** female sits for 14-16 days; male may feed her on the nest
**YOUNG:** hatchlings are covered in grey down with an orange-pink gape outlined in pale yellow; both parents feed them for 16-19 days until ready to leave the nest, then for a further 2 weeks
**MOULT:** takes place after breeding
**LIFE EXPECTANCY:** from 2-3 years for the adults

## POPULATION IN BRITAIN
Up to 1 million pairs breed each year; numbers are steady

## Distribution
Coal tits are found in woodland throughout the British Isles. They are especially common in Scotland and Wales and generally absent from the less-wooded Fens and Scottish islands.

Local populations usually stay in the same area all year round. In harsh winters, there may be a slight drift to the southwest. British coal tits may also be joined by Continental coal tits for the winter, particularly in years when the beech-mast crop has failed in northern Europe and food is short.

The coal tit breeds throughout Europe, across the Mediterranean to North Africa and east into Turkey, over central Asia to Japan, and north into parts of Scandinavia and Russia.

☐ areas where the bird stays all year
☐ areas where the bird is a summer visitor
☐ areas where the bird is a winter visitor

## HABITAT
Common in woodland, particularly among conifers, in the summer; may move to birch and alder woods, gardens and parks in the winter to find food

## NATURE WATCH
● The coal tit does well in young pine plantations where there are plenty of insects for them to eat. If tree-holes are scarce, they will nest on the ground.
● Coal tits took several years to recover from the gales in the south of England in 1987 which skittled many conifers.

# The Collared Dove

## Distribution

*Since first breeding in East Anglia in 1955, collared doves have spread rapidly across the British Isles. They are now a common garden bird.*

*The collared dove breeding range extends from India to Turkey, across islands in the Mediterranean, through Europe to northern Norway and as far as isolated Iceland. They are still colonising Russia to the east and Spain, Portugal and Morocco in the west.*

*The collared dove was inadvertently released in the Bahamas in the 1970s and quickly reached Florida on the southeast coast of the USA. Eurasian collared doves, as they are called on that side of the Atlantic, are spreading rapidly across the United States.*

areas where the bird stays all year

## NAMES
**SCIENTIFIC NAME:** *Streptopelia decaocto*
**NICKNAMES:** Turkish Dove, Indian Ringdove

## IDENTIFICATION
**APPEARANCE:** males and females have uniformly pale grey-brown plumage with a pinkish tinge over the breast; large red eyes and dark grey beak stand out on pale head; wings and tail are darker brown; the main flight feathers are slate grey; juveniles are a duller brown, with scaly backs and wings, caused by pale fringes to their feathers, but no black collar mark
**SIZE:** 31-34cm (13-14in) long
**WINGSPAN:** 48-55cm (19-22in)
**WEIGHT:** 150-220g (5-7⅓oz)
**FLIGHT:** direct and fast with rapidly flicking wings
**VOICE:** monotonous three tone cooing *koo-koooOO-kuk*; emits a harsh *kwerr* on landing and in display flights and a *ghee-ghee* alarm call

## FOOD
Eats mainly grains and seeds from stores and fields; also feeds on fruit and berries and regularly visits bird-tables or seeds scattered on the ground in winter

## BEHAVIOUR
Often seen in pairs, perched in trees, on television aerials and telephone wires; in winter forms large foraging flocks and communal roosts of up to 1600 birds
**ENEMIES:** sparrowhawks, cats, diseases and bad weather

## BREEDING
**PAIRING UP:** often forms a lifelong bond with partner; in Britain, generally rears 4 broods from March to October; in warmer climates can nest all year round
**NESTING:** builds a flimsy platform of twigs high up in the branches of conifers and on sheltered ledges around and in buildings
**EGGS:** 1-2 white eggs in each clutch
**INCUBATION:** both birds share the incubation for 17-18 days
**YOUNG:** chicks (squabs) hatch with a skimpy covering of yellow down and huge beaks; at first both parents produce rich crop milk to feed them, then wean them on to seeds; fledged in 17-18 days but fed by the adults for 3 more weeks
**MOULT:** in the autumn
**LIFE EXPECTANCY:** up to 8 years, once the squabs have reached maturity

## POPULATION IN BRITAIN
Around 230,000 breeding pairs

## HABITAT
Generally, roosts and nests in evergreen trees in parks and gardens and on buildings in towns and villages but often commutes to farms, grain stores and factories to find food each day

## NATURE WATCH
● The black-and-white bar around the back of the collared dove's neck makes it easy to identify.
● Persistent three syllable *coo*-ing from a collared dove distinguishes it from the five-part *coo*-ing of the woodpigeon – and gets on the nerves of people all over the country.

# The Dunnock

## Distribution

*The dunnock is a common and familiar bird in towns and countryside, gardens, parks and hedgerows, throughout the British Isles. It also breeds in most of Europe and Scandinavia, except in the western parts of Spain and Portugal.*

*Unlike many insect-eaters, dunnocks are resident in Britain, Scotland and Ireland, although there may be a slight southerly drift in harsh winters. Dunnocks breeding in Scandinavia and eastern Europe move south for the winter. Occasionally, large flocks of dunnocks land up on the east coast in autumn.*

*After a few losses in the 1960s, the dunnock's distribution and numbers have stayed much the same for the past 30 years in the British Isles.*

## NAMES

**SCIENTIFIC NAME:** *Prunella modularis*
**NICKNAMES:** Shufflewing, Hedge-creeper, Hedge-sparrow, Hedgy, Hempie

## IDENTIFICATION

**APPEARANCE:** male and female look alike: both have warm chestnut brown backs streaked with black and slate-grey throat and underparts; head is also grey with brown crown and cheek patches; juveniles are browner with more spots and streaks
**SIZE:** 14-15cm (5$^{1}/_{2}$-6in) long
**WINGSPAN:** 19-21cm (7$^{1}/_{2}$-8$^{1}/_{2}$in)
**WEIGHT:** 19-24g ($^{5}/_{8}$-$^{7}/_{8}$oz)
**FLIGHT:** generally unhurried in short swift passage from one hedge to another
**VOICE:** sings a short, fast high-pitched but rather colourless warbling song all year round; issues a piercing *pseep* as a contact or alarm call and a *sissississ* flight call

## FOOD

Feeds mainly on the ground, taking insects, earthworms, spiders and small snails in the summer; during the autumn and winter also eats weed seeds and breadcrumbs and scraps that have fallen to the ground from bird-tables

## BEHAVIOUR

Except in the breeding season, the dunnock is a solitary bird; it creeps about flicking wings and tail, keeping low to the ground and never going far from cover
**ENEMIES:** cold weather, cats and cars

## BREEDING

**PAIRING UP:** from March to August; raises 2 or 3 broods each year
**NESTING:** nest building starts at the end of March; male accompanies female while she is collecting nesting materials to build a neat cup of twigs, grass and moss, lined with hair, low down in a thick, often thorny hedge or bush
**EGGS:** lays 4-6 perfectly plain bright turquoise-blue, rather pointed eggs
**INCUBATION:** mainly by the female for 12 days
**YOUNG:** hatchlings are covered in black down and have bright orange linings with two black spots inside their mouths; fed by both parents, sometimes helped out by a second male, they grow very rapidly and fledge in 12 days
**MOULT:** completed by late August
**LIFE EXPECTANCY:** up to 5 years

## POPULATION IN BRITAIN

Nearly 3 million breeding pairs

☐ areas where the bird stays all year
☐ areas where the bird is a summer visitor
☐ areas where the bird is a winter visitor

## HABITAT

Relies on hedges and thickets to provide shelter, nesting sites and food

## NATURE WATCH

● The dunnock is often mistaken for other small brown birds – house sparrows, juvenile robins and wrens. Remember the dunnock has a grey breast and is a shy loner – house sparrows hop about in flocks, young robins are brown speckled and wrens are smaller and more frenetic.
● The cock dunnock even sounds a bit like a deflated cock wren.

# The Goldcrest

## Distribution

*The goldcrest is widely distributed in the British Isles. The only places it is not found are in the fens of East Anglia and the Scottish Highlands.*

*In the autumn, the resident British population drifts south; some head off for Europe; the rest are joined by thousands of immigrants seeking refuge from icy winter weather in northern Europe. They arrive overnight along the east coast, exhausted from their exertions. It almost defies belief that, twice a year, in October and March, so many of these tiny birds manage to fly across the North Sea.*

*Goldcrests are also found over much of Europe, although not in most of Spain and Portugal.*

☐ areas where the bird stays all year
☐ areas where the bird is a summer visitor
☐ areas where the bird is a winter visitor

### NAMES
**SCIENTIFIC NAME:** *Regulus regulus*
**NICKNAMES:** Marigold Finch, Tot-o'er-Sea

### IDENTIFICATION
**APPEARANCE:** males and females have needle-sharp beaks, olive green backs, grey wings with two white stripes and buff underparts; the male has a golden crown outlined in black, which he raises to a fiery orange crest when excited or angered; the female's is pale yellow; juveniles look like their parents but have no colourful crest until after their first autumn moult
**SIZE:** 8.5-9cm (3½in) long
**WINGSPAN:** 13.5-15.5cm (5½-6¼in)
**WEIGHT:** 5-7g (⅙-⅓oz)
**FLIGHT:** fluttering and constantly flitting
**VOICE:** sharp, pin-point call *see-see-see* heard from treetops; *smallest of small songs – tweedly-tweedly-twiddledidee*

### FOOD
Searches trees for insects, mites and spiders; sometimes takes cheese and fat put out in gardens during the winter

### BEHAVIOUR
Britain's smallest bird flits restlessly through the branches of trees; male displays bright crest during courtship and when dealing with rivals and enemies
**ENEMIES:** prolonged cold winters

### BREEDING
**PAIRING UP:** from March to June; rears 2, maybe 3 broods a year
**NESTING:** both birds help to build a deep, thick-walled basket using moss, lichens and wool bound together with spiders' silk and lined with lots of feathers which they sling beneath pine twigs with more spiders' webs
**EGGS:** 7-10 off-white eggs with brownish-red spots at wide end
**INCUBATION:** female does most of the incubation for 16 days
**YOUNG:** chicks are covered in sooty-grey down, with orange gape outlined in pink; fed by both parents; leave nest after 20-23 days; juveniles gang up with great and blue tits to form mixed flocks which rove through the woods looking for food during the winter
**MOULT:** moult in the autumn
**LIFE EXPECTANCY:** up to 3 years; migration and winter kill many young

### POPULATION IN BRITAIN
About 800,000 breeding each year; numbers are literally decimated by harsh wintry weather

### HABITAT
Found in conifer plantations and woods, but also in beech and oak woodland, among yews in churchyards and mature cedars and cypresses in gardens

### NATURE WATCH
● During prolonged severe winters, in 1916-1917, 1946-1947 and 1962-1963, the population plummeted as goldcrests are too tiny to conserve much body heat during icy nights.
● Rearing two large broods each year usually helps numbers to recover quickly.

# The Goldfinch

## Distribution

*During the summer, goldfinches are common over much of England and Wales but scarcer in Ireland. Ironically for a bird that is so fond of thistles, goldfinches are absent from much of Scotland, as if the terrain and climate do not suit them.*

*Between mid-September and the end of October, about three-quarters of adult (especially females) and juvenile goldfinches leave Britain for warmer wintering grounds in western France, Spain, Portugal and North Africa. They migrate in flocks by day; many still fall victim to nets and guns on the way.*

*Goldfinches were introduced into New Zealand and Australia where they have become pests on strawberry farms.*

☐ areas where the bird stays all year
☐ areas where the bird is a summer visitor
☐ areas where the bird is a winter visitor

## NAMES
**SCIENTIFIC NAME:** *Carduelis carduelis*
**NICKNAMES:** Goldie, King Harry, Fool's Coat

## IDENTIFICATION
**APPEARANCE:** brilliantly colourful; adult males and females look similar, with red, white and black head markings but, close up, the red on the male's head extends farther behind the eyes; juveniles are dull greyish-brown without bright head markings; all have bold yellow bars on their black wings
**SIZE:** 12cm (4³/₄in) long
**WINGSPAN:** 21-25.5cm (8¹/₂-10in)
**WEIGHT:** 14-17g (¹/₂-¹/₃ oz)
**FLIGHT:** bouncy and buoyant
**VOICE:** contact call is a clear *tickelit* given when perched and in flight; humming *geez* when feeding; sharp *titt-wittit* when alarmed on nest; song is a set of tinkling twitters used by both sexes all year round

## FOOD
Favours thistle seeds and fluffy seeds of other weeds; has the only beak able to extract seeds from a ripe head of teasel; catches insects for chicks; eats seeds on bird-tables

## BEHAVIOUR
Travels around in flocks for most of the year; twitters constantly
**ENEMIES:** many are hit by cars as they fly along hedgerows and verges

## BREEDING
**PAIRING UP:** courtship begins in April; first clutch laid in early May; rears at least 2, maybe 3 broods a year
**NESTING:** female weaves a neat nest from grass, moss and roots, lined with plant down, at the end of a branch
**EGGS:** usually 5-6 blue-white eggs with red-brown freckles
**INCUBATION:** female sits on the eggs for 12-13 days, waited on by her mate
**YOUNG:** chicks are covered in dark grey down and have a purplish-red lining to their mouths with cream flanges; fed on regurgitated seeds and insects by both parents; fledged in 14-15 days, then join the family flock
**MOULT:** adults in summer after breeding; juveniles undergo a partial moult in October to get their adult colours
**LIFE EXPECTANCY:** few live beyond 3 years; over half die in their first year

## POPULATION IN BRITAIN
About 300,000 breed every year

## HABITAT
Leads a nomadic life, moving wherever weeds flourish in wild gardens, on wasteland, rough pastures and verges

## NATURE WATCH
● To tempt goldfinches into your garden, let it run wild in places or plant some teasels specially for them and leave lavender heads uncut for the winter.
● Goldfinches take husk-free sunflower kernels, millet and tiny niger seeds from hanging feeders or special low wire trays as well as from the ground.

# The Great Spotted Woodpecker

## Distribution

*The great spotted woodpecker is the most common woodpecker inhabiting mature woodland over England, Wales and Scotland (though not in the very far north). It is not found in Ireland.*

*It is present over a huge range, from Europe to Japan. Within this spread, there are minor local regional variations in markings, size and shape of bill.*

### Lesser spotted woodpecker

*The lesser spotted woodpecker is not found in northern England, Scotland or Ireland. Otherwise, the ranges of lesser and greater spotted woodpeckers overlap in Europe, with the lesser spotted pushing farther north in Scandinavia and Russia.*

☐ areas where the bird stays all year

## NAMES
**SCIENTIFIC NAME:** *Dendrocopos major*
**NICKNAMES:** Great spotted woodpecker, Pied woodpecker

## IDENTIFICATION
**APPEARANCE:** both male and female adults are black and white with a scarlet patch on the rump under the tail and conspicuous white shoulder patches; the male has a red patch on the back of his neck as well; juveniles are black and white with a red cap when first fledged
**SIZE:** 22-23cm (9in) long
**WINGSPAN:** 30-35cm (12-14in)
**WEIGHT:** on average 80g (3oz)
**FLIGHT:** typically undulating in the open
**VOICE:** strident laughing *tchack tchack*; in spring, males drum loudly on tree trunks to broadcast their territorial range

## FOOD
Thrives on tree-dwelling insects and their grubs; eats a more varied diet of seeds, nuts and fruits in winter when it visits bird-feeders – it is particularly keen on pine nuts

## BEHAVIOUR
Infamous for raiding other tree-hole nests, such as those of tits, for their eggs and chicks; unpopular with bee-keepers when they ransack hives
**ENEMIES:** ousted from their nesting-holes by owl squatters

## BREEDING
**PAIRING UP:** male and female get together in March and April to rear 1 brood each year
**NESTING:** both birds excavate a nesting chamber 25-30cm (10-12in) deep in the trunk of a tree, at least 3m (10ft) above the ground with an entrance hole about 6cm (2½in) in diameter
**EGGS:** in May lays 4-7 creamy white oval eggs in a sawdust-lined chamber at the bottom of the nesting-hole
**INCUBATION:** both parents take it in turns to sit on the eggs for 16-17 days
**YOUNG:** the chicks hatch featherless and blind; fed by both parents, they leave the nest 18-21 days later
**MOULT:** loses and replaces feathers after the breeding season; chicks begin to shed their pale grey down as they leave the nest
**LIFE EXPECTANCY:** 3 years on average

## POPULATION IN BRITAIN
Roughly 28,000 pairs breed each year; there are none on Ireland

## HABITAT
Prefers mature deciduous woodland and parks with dead or dying trees

## NATURE WATCH
● The outlook for the great spotted woodpecker in Britain appears to be bright. During the past 30 years, a series of mild winters and more peanut-feeders in gardens have helped to sustain larger populations.
● To encourage more woodpeckers to live in an area, woodland owners and managers are urged to leave some dead or dying trees standing for them to find food on and hack out nesting chambers.

# The Great Tit

## Distribution

*Great tits are ubiquitous – common and widespread all over Britain and Ireland. Most are resident in an area unless there is a population explosion after a mild winter. Then the overspill has to move on and find new places to live.*

*Apart from the green and yellow great tit* (Parus major major) *which is familiar to people as far apart as Britain, China and North Africa, there are three other groups: in India and Malaysia, the great tit* (P. major cinereus) *has a blue-grey back and whitish underparts; in the Far East great tits* (P. m. minor) *are greenish above and whitish underneath; a Turkestan great tit* (P. m. bokharensis) *living in central Asia is pale grey on top, white below.*

### NAMES
**SCIENTIFIC NAME:** *Parus major*
**NICKNAMES:** Tomtit, Ox-eye, Saw-sharpener

### IDENTIFICATION
**APPEARANCE:** male and female have a black head with white cheeks, yellow underparts with a black stripe down the centre, green upperparts with blue-grey wing and tail feathers; males are larger than females, with glossier, brighter plumage and a wider, longer belly stripe; juveniles are duller, greyer and yellower
**SIZE:** 14cm (5½in) long
**WINGSPAN:** 22.5-25.5cm (9-10in)
**WEIGHT:** 16-21g (½-¾oz)
**FLIGHT:** flight strong and undulating
**VOICE:** conversational birds with a large vocabulary of contact (*tsee-tsee*) alarm (*churr*) and begging (*zeedle*) calls; the male's spring song is *tea-cher, tea-cher*

### FOOD
Mainly eats caterpillars, beetles, other insects and spiders in the summer; switches to eating mainly seeds and nuts in autumn – it is especially fond of beech mast; it is a regular visitor to bird-tables and peanut-feeders in gardens over the winter

### BEHAVIOUR
A bold, bumptious, sociable little bird with a reputation for being a bully; highly vocal; often spends the winter foraging in woodland in mixed flocks
**ENEMIES:** sparrowhawks, weasels, owls, cats and cars

### BREEDING
**PAIRING UP:** February to June; highly territorial in the breeding season; usually rears only 1 large brood a year
**NESTING:** builds in a tree-hole, nesting-box or crevices in stone walls; female collects moss and grasses and lines the cup with wool and hair
**EGGS:** 5-12 white eggs with sprinkling of reddish speckles
**INCUBATION:** female sits for 16 days
**YOUNG:** chicks tiny, naked and blind on hatching with orange gape outlined in pale yellow; fed by both parents; leave nest after 19-21 days; juveniles gang up with other tits in mixed flocks which rove through the woods looking for food
**MOULT:** in the autumn
**LIFE EXPECTANCY:** few survive their first winter; some live for 10 years

### POPULATION IN BRITAIN
Estimated 3 million breed each year

☐ areas where the bird stays all year
☐ areas where the bird is a summer visitor

### HABITAT
A woodland bird, now just as commonly found in hedgerows, parks and gardens everywhere, all year round

### NATURE WATCH
● In the 1980s, great tits laid eggs with thin shells because acid rain caused by atmospheric pollution made the calcium needed to form eggshells less accessible.
● Just as great tits time their breeding to coincide with the hatching of scores of caterpillars in the woods, so sparrowhawks aim to have nestlings when young great tits are fledging.

# The Greenfinch

## Distribution

*The greenfinch is a common resident throughout lowland Britain and Ireland. As a sociable bird, it travels around and forages in flocks but rarely strays far from its home range.*

*In autumn, there may a slight southerly drift to escape the colder northern weather. Hardy residents are joined by huge numbers of greenfinches from the Continent, which cross The Channel to spend the winter here.*

*Greenfinches are found from northern Europe to the Mediterranean as far as northwest Africa and right across Asia to China and Japan. They have also been introduced to Australia and New Zealand, and to some South American countries.*

☐ areas where the bird stays all year
☐ areas where the bird is a summer visitor
☐ areas where the bird is a winter visitor

## NAMES
**SCIENTIFIC NAME:** *Carduelis chloris*
**NICKNAMES:** Greeny, Green Linnet

## IDENTIFICATION
**APPEARANCE:** a large, burly finch with heavy wedge-shaped beak and short forked tail; in spring and summer, males have olive-green backs and heads with ash-grey patches and brighter citrus-green underparts; after an autumn moult, looks browner for the winter; females are a duller browny green; juveniles look like streaky females; all have yellow flashes on wings and along the sides of the tail
**SIZE:** 15cm (6in) long
**WINGSPAN:** 24.5-27.5cm (10-11in)
**WEIGHT:** 25-32g (¾-1oz)
**FLIGHT:** strong but undulating
**VOICE:** pairs use a twittery *chichichi-chichit* contact call; males sing a drawling *breeeze*

## FOOD
A dedicated seed- and grain-eater; may be reduced to eating shoots and buds in the spring; feeds chicks on insects and spiders; visits bird-tables for seeds and peanut-feeders and will also take seeds scattered on the ground

## BEHAVIOUR
A sociable bird which nests in loose colonies and moves about in large flocks over the winter
**ENEMIES:** cats, sparrowhawks, magpies, bad weather and tidy farms

## BREEDING
**PAIRING UP:** April to July; rears 2 broods each year
**NESTING:** male and female put together an untidy nest of grass, moss and wool, lined with hair and a few feathers in hedges, dense bushes, conifers and thorny thickets
**EGGS:** 4-6 whitish eggs with a sprinkling of purplish speckles
**INCUBATION:** female sits for 12-14 days
**YOUNG:** hatchlings covered in white down, with a pink lining to the mouth and yellow flanges; fed insects and ground-up fresh seeds by both parents; fledged in 14-15 days
**MOULT:** between June and August
**LIFE EXPECTANCY:** up to 13 years, but vulnerable when young

## POPULATION IN BRITAIN
Around 700,000 pairs breed each summer; as many as 3 million may winter here

## HABITAT
Once frequented woodland fringes with access to farmland; now lives in hedgerows, churchyards and gardens all over the country throughout the year

## NATURE WATCH
● In autumn, hedge-flailing strips many precious fruits and seeds from wild trees and shrubs, depriving greenfinches of their natural diet and forcing them to rely increasingly on bird-table provisions.
● Unlike other birds, greenfinch numbers increased in the 1990s.

# The Grey Heron

## Distribution

*Although the grey heron is widespread and common around fresh and salt water throughout the British Isles, more are seen in southern England.*

*Grey herons generally stay in Britain all year round. In dry summers and harsh winters there may be a drift to the coast and a few may cross The Channel, seeking milder haunts. Grey herons nesting in northern Europe migrate in the autumn: many come to overwinter in Britain but some travel on to winter south of the Sahara.*

*The grey heron ranges across much of Europe, Africa and Asia, from Norway to South Africa. There are about 124,000 living in Europe, 3500 in Turkey and 22,000 in Russia.*

☐ areas where the bird stays all year
☐ areas where the bird is a summer visitor
☐ areas where the bird is a winter visitor

## NAMES

**SCIENTIFIC NAME:** *Ardea cinerea*
**NICKNAMES:** Hern, Frankie

## IDENTIFICATION

**APPEARANCE:** male and female look alike; upperparts are grey, underparts whitish; the long neck is white with black streaks; the white head has a wispy black crest; the dagger-like beak is yellow but turns orangey-pink during the breeding season; the legs are spindly; the juvenile is darker and greyer, with a darker beak, and has no crest
**SIZE:** 90-98cm (35-38in) tall – the tallest British bird
**WINGSPAN:** 1.75-1.95m (5¼-6½ft)
**WEIGHT:** 1.3-2kg (3-4½lb)
**FLIGHT:** unhurried beats of arched wings; can fly high and dive with surprising agility, twisting and turning to avoid attacks from birds of prey
**VOICE:** harsh, honking *fraank fraank* call in flight; noisy bill-clacking at the nest

## FOOD

Catches fish and frogs, moorhen chicks and ducklings from shallow water – fresh, brackish or salt; also takes snakes, lizards, voles, moles, grasshoppers and beetles living in or near the water's edge

## BEHAVIOUR

Nests communally in tall trees but otherwise is solitary; incredibly still and patient while fishing but remains wary and is quick to spot danger
**ENEMIES:** bad weather; electricity cables and barbed wire fences; foxes and crows

## BREEDING

**PAIRING UP:** breeds early, with elaborate courtship displays from January onward; usually rears only 1 brood a year
**NESTING:** a large twiggy basket, the nest is reused year after year; refurbishing an old nest is a pair-bonding exercise
**EGGS:** 4-5 pale greenish-blue eggs
**INCUBATION:** parents share the sitting from the first egg; perform a greeting display at every change-over; each egg hatches 25-27 days after laying
**YOUNG:** chicks have brownish-grey down; fed regurgitated fish by both parents, they can fly at around 50 days old; take 4 years to mature and start breeding
**MOULT:** in the autumn
**LIFE EXPECTANCY:** up to 25 years

## POPULATION IN BRITAIN

Up to 14,000 pairs breed each year; numbers are increasing but still suffer setbacks in icy spells or due to pollution

## HABITAT

Seen standing in or beside shallow rivers, streams, lakes and ponds, canals and ditches, on marshes and estuaries

## NATURE WATCH

● Small birds, such as tree sparrows, may build their nests among the loose stack of twigs and sticks in an old heron's nest.
● Over long distances, the grey heron flies high and may be mistaken for a large bird of prey because of the leisurely flapping of its dark wings.

# The House Martin

## NAMES

**SCIENTIFIC NAME:** *Delichon urbica*
**NICKNAMES:** House Swallow, Eaves Swallow, Window Martin

## IDENTIFICATION

**APPEARANCE:** male and female look alike; prominent white rump and pure white underparts differentiate it from a swallow and sand martin; upper parts are black but shimmer blue-black in sunshine; short legs and feet are feathered in white; juveniles are duller and slightly browner
**SIZE:** 12.5cm (5in) long
**WINGSPAN:** 26-29cm (10¹/₂-11¹/₂in)
**WEIGHT:** 15-23g (¹/₂-³/₄oz)
**FLIGHT:** soars and swoops strongly but is rather fluttery in direct flight
**VOICE:** very vocal around the nest and in the air, with a twittery song, chirping contact calls and *treep* alarm call

## FOOD

Catches insects and spiders flying or floating in the air at heights up to 2000 metres (6500 feet).

## BEHAVIOUR

Always gregarious, nesting in colonies, feeding and migrating in flocks;

a summer visitor here but no one is sure exactly where they are in the winter
**ENEMIES:** domestic cats, wet and dry summers, storms while migrating

## BREEDING

**PAIRING UP:** breeds from mid May to October, rearing up to 4 broods a year
**NESTING:** both partners use mud pellets collected from the edges of pools and river banks to build a clay basin with a narrow entrance at the top, lined with grass and feathers; under the eaves of buildings, beneath bridges and on cliffs
**EGGS:** 4-5 white eggs
**INCUBATION:** parents share the sitting for 14-16 days
**YOUNG:** chicks are skimpily clad in pale grey down and have a yellow lining to their mouths; both parents feed them insects; young from early broods may help feed siblings in later broods; nestlings are fledged in 22-32 days
**MOULT:** may start on migration or shortly after arriving in the tropics for the winter
**LIFE EXPECTANCY:** 5-14 years

## POPULATION IN BRITAIN

Anything from 250,000-500,000 pairs breed here each year but the numbers are declining

## Distribution

*House martins are widely distributed across the British Isles in the summer. Their nests are visible and familiar in towns and villages everywhere, except in the northwest of Scotland.*

*Later to return than the swallows and sand martins, house martins start arriving in April and leaving again in late August and September. The last stragglers do not go until late October. They winter in Africa, probably south of the Sahara Desert, although their exact whereabouts are not known.*

*The house martin breeds throughout Europe and is well known as far south as North Africa. It also ranges east, across Russia as far as Japan and southwards into the Himalayas.*

☐ areas where the bird is a summer visitor
☐ areas where the bird is a winter visitor

## HABITAT

Very familiar because it nests on human dwellings and feeds in the open air, flying over meadows, waterways and downwind of reservoirs

## NATURE WATCH

● You can buy prefabricated house-martin nests from larger bird-food and accessories suppliers to fix under the eaves of your house.
● In a dry spell, the house martins in your neighbourhood would appreciate you playing mud pies in your garden to provide some building material for them.

# The House Sparrow

## Distribution

*House sparrows are cosmopolitan birds, living alongside human dwellings all over the world. The estimated global population of house sparrows is around 500 million birds. In Britain, they are abundant but unevenly distributed, being thin on the ground over vast tracts of uninhabited farmland and heath in rural Wales, Scotland and Ireland.*

*By and large, house sparrows never travel far from their home range, staying together in small local flocks of clan members. On autumn and winter evenings, flocks may converge on a large communal roost in a tree.*

*House sparrows soon settled in when imported into South Africa, New Zealand, Australia and North America.*

□ areas where the bird stays all year

## NAMES
**SCIENTIFIC NAME:** *Passer domesticus*
**NICKNAMES:** Spadger, Sprog

## IDENTIFICATION
**APPEARANCE:** adult males and females look different: in winter the male is a grey shadow of his summer self with a brown beak; by spring, feathers have worn to reveal his grey crown, chestnut nape, white cheeks and black bib with mottled brown-black wings; females drabber, plain buff with highlight behind eye; juveniles similar to females
**SIZE:** 14-15cm (5½-6in) long
**WINGSPAN:** 21-25.5cm (8½-10in)
**WEIGHT:** 24-32g (1-1⅓oz)
**FLIGHT:** busy and low
**VOICE:** chatty birds with loud, harsh, repetitious chirping notes: *chi-chir-rip* and *chi-chip;* emits a scolding *cher-r-r-r* when alarmed; song is a series of *chirps*

## FOOD
Eats mainly grains and seeds; feeds chicks on insects; takes seeds, scraps and breadcrumbs from bird-tables

## BEHAVIOUR
Highly gregarious, garrulous birds travelling around in flocks for most of the year; frequent rowdy scuffles break out

**ENEMIES:** eaten by sparrowhawks, barn owls and cats; hit by cars

## BREEDING
**PAIRING UP:** from March to August; first clutch laid in April and May; usually rears at least 3, maybe 4 broods each year
**NESTING:** male selects site but both build a scruffy nest of straw and feathers under eaves, in holes or nest-boxes
**EGGS:** usually 3-7 white to grey-green eggs heavily speckled with grey or black
**INCUBATION:** both parents brood the eggs for 11-14 days
**YOUNG:** newly-hatched chicks bare; mouths lined in orange with pale yellow flanges; fed mostly on insects by both parents; fledged in 11-19 days but continue to beg for food from parents
**MOULT:** adults in summer; juvenile males acquire black bib in first autumn moult
**LIFE EXPECTANCY:** 8 years at most; average 3 years, with many dying young

## POPULATION IN BRITAIN
About 4.5 million breed each year; noisy roosts and flocks make the sparrow seem more common than it is; it may be in serious trouble – numbers have fallen by 75% in the last 25 years and more drastically in London in the last 10 years

## HABITAT
Anywhere there is human settlement, near to a good source of food

## NATURE WATCH
● A census taken in Kensington Gardens in 1925 recorded 2603 sparrows; a similar count in 1995 saw only 46.
● The use of cars and combine harvesters instead of horse-pulled carts has cheated the house sparrow of easy gleanings from stables and wheat fields at harvest time. Urban development is has also deprived them of nesting and roosting sites on farms. Garden-feeding has been their saving grace.

# The Jackdaw

## Distribution

*Jackdaws are common and widespread all over Britain and Ireland throughout the year, except in the northwest of Scotland. Their distribution is limited by the availability of sufficient suitable nesting sites to form a viable colony.*

*Flocks of young jackdaws disperse ito new locations in the autumn. As the weather cools, upland and northern birds drift south and west. Residents on the coasts are joined by jackdaws from Scandinavia and Holland from mid October to early November. The visitors stay for the winter, then start returning to their breeding sites in March. The jackdaw breeds across Europe, in North Africa, through Turkey and Russia as far east as Siberia.*

## NAMES
**SCIENTIFIC NAME:** *Corvus monedula*
**NICKNAMES:** Jack, Daw, Cawdaw

## IDENTIFICATION
**APPEARANCE:** male and female are very similar; both have slightly shimmery black plumage with paler grey 'shawls' around their necks and cheeks, strikingly pale eyes and short black beaks and legs; juvenile looks like a browner-black adult without the pale grey neck and with a paler beak and bluer eyes
**SIZE:** 33-34cm (13in) long
**WINGSPAN:** 67-74cm (26³/₄-29¹/₂in)
**WEIGHT:** 220-270g (7³/₄-9¹/₂oz)
**FLIGHT:** deep, fast and flappy; flock performs an amazing aerobatic display before roosting
**VOICE:** noisy, very chattery birds splitting the air with loud, harsh *tchaak tchaak* and *kyaw* calls, especially when going to roost; shreiky *karr-r-r* alarm cries

## FOOD
Consumes a great variety of foodstuffs – insects, snails, slugs, earthworms and small rodents – found mainly on the ground in pastures and grassland; vilified as a nest-robber, taking eggs and nestlings; visits bird-tables for scraps

## BEHAVIOUR
Highly sociable hole-nesters that form breeding colonies and overwinter in large flocks; intelligent, observant and bold
**ENEMIES:** foxes and other crows – colony members unite to send intruders packing

## BREEDING
**PAIRING UP:** often pairs for life; breeds from April to July; almost always rears just 1 brood a year
**NESTING:** mates build a large twiggy platform in a hole in a tree, among rocks or ruined buildings, or down a chimney; central cup is lined with grasses and hair and wool
**EGGS:** lays 4-6 greenish eggs with grey or brown splotches and splashes
**INCUBATION:** female starts sitting while laying the clutch; hatch in 17-18 days
**YOUNG:** hatchlings are scantily covered in grey down with purplish-pink lined mouths framed in pale yellow; fed by both parents, fledglings leave the nest in 30-35 days to join family flocks
**MOULT:** from July to September
**LIFE EXPECTANCY:** up to 7 years

## POPULATION IN BRITAIN
Up to 600,000 pairs breed each year and numbers are rising

☐ areas where the bird stays all year
☐ areas where the bird is a summer visitor
☐ areas where the bird is a winter visitor

## HABITAT
Seen feeding on grassland, nests and roosts in trees, sea-cliffs, quarries and rocky gorges, churches and ruined buildings, rooftops and chimneys

## NATURE WATCH
● For most of the year, jackdaws lives in large mixed flocks with rooks.
● For a fascinating insight into the social life of a jackdaw colony, it is well worth reading Chapter 11 of *King Solomon's Ring* by Konrad Lorenz.

# The Jay

## NAMES
**SCIENTIFIC NAME:** *Garrulus glandarius*
**NICKNAMES:** Blue Jay, Jay Pie

## IDENTIFICATION
**APPEARANCE:** males and females look alike, with pinkish-brown body plumage; cream-and-black streaked crown which is raised into crest; black tail and black, chestnut and white wings with bright blue-and-black patches; white rump clearly visible in flight; juveniles are a slightly duskier pink than their parents
**SIZE:** 34-35cm (13⅔-14in) long
**WINGSPAN:** 52-58cm (20⅞-23¼in)
**WEIGHT:** 140-190g (5-6oz)
**FLIGHT:** dodges into cover; often laboured over glades; direct when on migration
**VOICE:** vocal; typical strident *kraak-kraak* warning call; makes a mewing *peeoo*; makes a soft, musical gurgling sound in courtship; mimics other birds and noises

## FOOD
Varied tastes, including acorns, beechnuts, hazelnuts and sweet chestnuts, insects, small mammals, eggs and chicks; stores acorns in autumn; raids garden for peas and fruit or peanuts from bird-table

## BEHAVIOUR
Mistrustful of humans; issues raucous alarm calls but silent when breeding to avoid drawing attention to the nest; mates maintain lifelong pair-bonds
**ENEMIES:** other crows, tawny owls, stoats, squirrels and cats

## BREEDING
**PAIRING UP:** noisy tree-top courtship gatherings in late April and early May; rears only 1 brood a year
**NESTING:** the pair builds a platform of twigs bound with mud, lined with rootlets and horsehair, in tree or bush
**EGGS:** 5-6 green-blue eggs with light dusting of grey-brown freckles
**INCUBATION:** female does the incubating for 16-17 days
**YOUNG:** chicks bare on hatching with pink lining to the mouth; fed caterpillars and other insects at first by both parents, then acorns and nuts; fledge in 19-20 days; form into rowdy family parties for several months after fledging
**MOULT:** adults after the breeding season
**LIFE EXPECTANCY:** up to 18 years in captivity; many die in their first winter

## POPULATION IN BRITAIN
Roughly 170,000 breeding each year

## Distribution

*Jays are common and widespread in England and Wales, rarer in Scotland and absent from many upland areas, presumably due to a lack of trees.*

*The British jay is known as* Garrulus glandarius rufitergum *(meaning ruddy), to distinguish it from another sub-species,* G glandarius hibernicus, *which lives in Ireland. European jays are generally darker than British ones, although they have similar markings. Various races of jay are spread across Europe and Asia, to coniferous forest in Siberia and southeast Asian rainforests.*

*Occasionally, when the acorn crop fails in Europe, huge flocks of up to 3000 jays migrate from the continent to south and east England.*

☐ areas where the bird stays all year

## HABITAT
Lives in deciduous, coniferous and mixed woodlands, with an especial fondness for oak woods, and mature parkland

## NATURE WATCH
● Normally reluctant to venture far from the protection of trees in woodland, the jay is so fond of green peas and broad beans that it is unable to resist ransacking rows of pea and bean pods in vegetable gardens.
● Oddly enough, you stand a better chance of seeing jays in urban parks, as town-dwellers are less furtive than those living in country woodland.

# The Long-tailed Tit

## Distribution

*Although resident all over the British Isles, long-tailed tits are less common in hilly areas and in northern Scotland and the far west of Ireland. They are also found throughout Europe, except in northern Scandinavia, and eastwards as far as China and Japan. Only a few stragglers ever make it to North Africa.*

*Head patterns and the amount of pink and black in the plumage vary across its range. The pink* rosaceus *group lives in Britain and western Europe; the* caudatus *group from northern Europe has an all-white head.*

*Long-tailed tits rarely roam far from their family territory. White-headed Scandinavian long-tails are very rare visitors to these shores.*

☐ areas where the bird stays all year

## NAMES
**SCIENTIFIC NAME:** *Aegithalos caudatus*
**NICKNAMES:** at least 25 local names –
Bumbarrel, Mumruffin, Bottle Tom

## IDENTIFICATION
**APPEARANCE:** tiny, spherical body with a stubby beak and very long, narrow tail; plumage is mainly black and white with variable amounts of pink and grey on flanks and belly; sexes are similar; juveniles are darker with short tails
**SIZE:** 13-16cm (5-5³⁄₄in) long, of which the tail comprises 6-10cm (2¹⁄₂-4in)
**WINGSPAN:** 16-19cm (6¹⁄₃-7¹⁄₂in)
**WEIGHT:** 8g (¹⁄₃oz)
**FLIGHT:** erratic, whirring and bouncing
**VOICE:** brief *tsirrip* contact call; a soft high-pitched *sree-sree-sree* in flight when flock is on the move and from stragglers – their song in spring is a richer version of this

## FOOD
Consists of tiny insects and spiders on tree trunks and leaves; occasionally visits gardens for peanuts and fat

## BEHAVIOUR
Very gregarious, forming stable flocks based around the parents and offspring of the previous season, with related adult helpers; always on the move around the flock's territory
**ENEMIES:** nests raided by jays, magpies, squirrels and stoats; icy winters

## BREEDING
**PAIRING UP:** breeding starts earlier than for the true tits and lasts from March to June; rears 1 brood a year
**NESTING:** builds nest in thorny gorse, brambles or blackthorn or high up in the fork of a tree
**EGGS:** 8-12 white eggs with red spots
**INCUBATION:** female sits on her eggs for 12-18 days
**YOUNG:** downless on hatching; inside of the mouth is yellow with yellow flanges; both parents bring food but the female does most of the feeding; young fledge in 14-18 days with short tails
**MOULT:** adults and juveniles undergo a full moult in July; by October the young look exactly like adults with long tails
**LIFE EXPECTANCY:** 3-5 years; most die in their first winter, especially if it is frosty

## POPULATION IN BRITAIN
About 250,000 breeding each year; numbers are currently stable but can collapse in severe winters

## HABITAT
Frequents open lowland country, woodland and farmland with mature trees and hedges, parks and big gardens

## NATURE WATCH
● Thirty years ago, long-tailed tits rarely visited garden bird-tables. Now they are often seen hanging on to bird-feeders and nets of peanuts, particularly during the winter. Once a group has discovered garden freebies, visits soon become a habit, especially in cold snaps.
● Long-tailed tits rarely feed on the ground but will seek out suet rubbed into the crevices of the bark on tree trunks.

# The Magpie

## Distribution

*Magpies are common and widespread across England, Wales and Ireland but less frequent in Scotland, maybe because there are fewer trees in the Highlands.*

*Breeding magpies generally hang on to their territories all year round. Migration is unheard of. The magpie is found across most of the northern hemisphere, in Europe, as far south as North Africa, through central Asia to China and across the Bering Straits to Alaska and down the west coast of North America to California.*

*With the relaxation of persecution in recent years, magpies have become bolder and moved into the suburbs of towns and cities where they pose a threat to garden-nesting birds.*

☐ areas where the bird stays all year

## NAMES
**SCIENTIFIC NAME:** *Pica pica*
**NICKNAMES:** Madge, Maggie, Maggot, Pie, Chatterpie, Nanpie, Pianet

## IDENTIFICATION
**APPEARANCE:** the male is slightly larger than the female but otherwise they have the same striking iridescent black-and-white markings with a very long tail and strong beak; the white shoulder patches are particularly prominent in flight; the juveniles are also black and white but have shorter tails at first
**SIZE:** 44-46cm (17½-18½in) long, of which over half is tail
**WINGSPAN:** 52-60cm (20¾-24in)
**WEIGHT:** 200-250g (8-10oz)
**FLIGHT:** wings are short and flight is floaty, laboured and wavy but agile
**VOICE:** notoriously chattery, with harsh, football-rattle *chak-chak-chak* call; more intimate murmurings are softer

## FOOD
Hunts for insects – mainly beetles and grasshoppers – slugs, snails and spiders on the ground in summer; also takes eggs and nestlings from nests; switches to eating more fruit, nuts, acorns and berries in winter and visits bird-tables

## BEHAVIOUR
Sociable bird, usually seen in pairs but frequently in noisy flocks
**ENEMIES:** goshawks, buzzards and sparrowhawks; owls, squirrels, crows and jackdaws rob nests and steal food

## BREEDING
**PAIRING UP:** from mid-March to June; rears just 1 brood a year
**NESTING:** both male and female construct a large nest with a domed roof from mud and twigs, lined with hair and rootlets, usually high up in a tree or hedge
**EGGS:** lays 5-8 greenish-blue eggs heavily-mottled with ash and brown
**INCUBATION:** by female for 22-24 days
**YOUNG:** as the hatchlings are naked and helpless the male does most of the feeding at first while the female keeps them warm; later both parents feed the nestlings until they leave the nest after 27 days; fledglings receive 4-6 weeks after-nest care
**MOULT:** June to September; new flight and tail feathers grow in about 95 days
**LIFE EXPECTANCY:** 5-10 years for adults

## POPULATION IN BRITAIN
About 900,000 pairs breeding each year and numbers are rising

## HABITAT
Found on farmland, in hedges and along the fringes of open woodland, in urban parks and gardens

## NATURE WATCH
● The magpie has a jaunty way of flicking up and fanning out its long tail as it alights on a perch. On the ground, it immediately raises its tail feathers clear of the dirt and mud.
● The magpie is one of the more brightly marked members of the crow family. In other respects, it is a typical crow: gregarious, bold and intelligent.

# The Pied Wagtail

## Distribution

*One of the most widely distributed birds in Britain, the pied wagtail is a native British bird which also breeds in western France, Belgium and southern Norway. Either pied or white wagtails are found all over Europe and Turkey throughout the year, spreading to Scandinavia and Russia to breed.*

*Many pied wagtails stay in Britain for the winter, with those in the north moving south to milder areas. The rest congregate in autumn to migrate to the west coast of France and on to Spain and North Africa in October.*

*Pied wagtails are one of the first migratory birds to return to Britain in the spring to breed, arriving back as early as mid-February in mild years.*

☐ areas where the bird stays all year
☐ areas where the bird is a summer visitor
☐ areas where the bird is a winter visitor

## NAMES

**SCIENTIFIC NAME:** *Motacilla alba yarrellii*
**NICKNAMES:** Waggie, Quaketail, Washtail

## IDENTIFICATION

**APPEARANCE:** in spring the male's crown, back, throat and breastplate are very black and his cheeks and underparts are very white while the female is greyer; in autumn the male's back is greyer and his throat is white with a small crescent-shaped bib (gorget); both have black wing and tail feathers with white edges; juveniles are pale grey with olive-green tinge and shorter tail
**SIZE:** 16.5-18cm (6½-7in) long
**WINGSPAN:** 55-65cm (22-26in)
**WEIGHT:** 17-25g (½-1oz)
**FLIGHT:** direct and undulating
**VOICE:** loud *tchizzick* call as the adults take flight and during courtship

## FOOD

Chases flying insects on the ground; picks insect larvae from the earth; will come to the garden in the winter for scraps scattered on the ground

## BEHAVIOUR

Frenetically active when it is hunting for insects, dashing around, tail wagging to keep its balance; territorial during the breeding season and for feeding in the winter but roosts in large flocks during the winter; mobs predators
**ENEMIES:** sparrowhawks, little owls, cats and cars

## BREEDING

**PAIRING UP:** from mid-April to August; rears 2, maybe 3 broods a year
**NESTING:** female builds an untidy nest of twigs, leaves, moss and grass lined with hair, wool and feathers usually hidden in a crevice in walls, other old nests, by thick vegetation, machinery or open nest-boxes
**EGGS:** 5-6 greyish-white with grey spots
**INCUBATION:** female sits for 11-13 days
**YOUNG:** newly-hatched chicks are covered in grey down, with orange-yellow lining to mouth outlined in pale yellow flanges; fed by both parents, leave nest in about 14 days; then male teaches the ropes for three or four days
**MOULT:** full moult to winter plumage in late summer; partial moult in spring to reveal breeding colours
**LIFE EXPECTANCY:** 3-5 years

## POPULATION IN BRITAIN

About 430,000 breeding each year

## HABITAT

Found in watery places, beside rivers, streams, lakes and ponds and in open areas, on lawns, golf courses and cricket pitches, roofs and car parks

## NATURE WATCH

● The number of pied wagtails in Britain has dropped by nearly half since 1973, largely because there are fewer insects around as a result of cleaner farmyards and the increased use of insecticides on farmland and in gardens.

# The Robin

## Distribution

*The European robin is very familiar, common and wide ranging in Britain, except right up in the northwest tip of Scotland. It is also resident throughout Europe as far east as Turkey although, in summer, the robin's breeding range extends as far east as central Siberia. Robins never lives in the mountainous regions of northern Scandinavia and Russia or the Caucasus range in southern Russia.*

*In the winter, the resident population of robins in Britain – especially along the east coast – is joined by transitory migrants from Scandinavia. Most of the travellers simply pass through on their way south to warmer climes in southern Spain and North Africa.*

☐ areas where the bird stays all year
☐ areas where the bird is a summer visitor
☐ areas where the bird is a winter visitor

## NAMES
**SCIENTIFIC NAME:** *Erithacus rubecula*
**COMMON NAME:** European robin
**NICKNAMES:** Redbreast, Ruddock

## IDENTIFICATION
**APPEARANCE:** adult has an olive-brown back and wings separated by a grey band from distinctive orange breast, throat and forehead; pale buff flanks and white belly; sexes alike; juvenile has a brown back speckled with paler spots and speckled brown fronts with no sign of a red breast until after its first moult in late summer
**SIZE:** length 14cm (5½in)
**WEIGHT:** on average about 19.5g (⅔oz), equal to three 10p pieces
**VOICE:** the cock robin sings a cheerful high-pitched warbling song issued in short bursts almost all year long; hard *tic-tic-tic* warning cry to intruders and a metallic *tseeee* alarm call

## FOOD
Eats insects, spiders, woodlice and earthworms during the summer; in the winter it is more reliant on fruits, seeds and household scraps, fat and cheese put out on bird-tables to supplement its natural diet

## BEHAVIOUR
Defends a territory of up to 1.5 hectares (3½ acres) all year; males and females hold separate territories in winter
**ENEMIES:** cars, cats, other robins, birds of prey, cold weather and disease

## BREEDING
**PAIRING UP:** in December or January
**NESTING:** late March to June; raises 2-3 broods a year, depending on the weather and food supply; female builds a well-concealed cup-shaped nest from leaves, lined with hair and moss
**EGGS:** 3-6 white eggs with rusty red speckling
**INCUBATION:** female sits for 11-14 days
**YOUNG:** hatchlings covered in black down with a yellow lining to their mouths; fed by both parents, they leave the nest after 12-15 days
**MOULT:** for 5-6 weeks in late summer, early autumn, adult birds lose their old feathers and grow new ones
**LIFE EXPECTANCY:** up to 5 years; only a quarter of young robins survive until their first birthday; about two-thirds of adult birds die each year

## POPULATION IN BRITAIN
About 5 million pairs breed each year

## HABITAT
Favours areas of thick, low cover in hedges and woodland, churchyards, parks and gardens

## NATURE WATCH
● As a special treat buy your home-grown robins some mealworms – now available from pet shops and by mail order from birdfood suppliers.
● Robins use open-fronted nest-boxes. To encourage robins to nest in your garden, hide an old flowerpot in dense ivy or creeper on a wall or up a tree.

# The Siskin

## Distribution

*Siskins breed commonly but locally in coniferous woods and pine plantations. They used to be restricted to the Scottish pine forests each summer. But in the last century, with the planting of new pine plantations all over Britain, the siskin has started breeding in Wales, East Anglia and the West Country too.*

*Once breeding is over, siskins form into largish flocks and roam the countryside looking for seeds in pine, larch, alder and birch trees, on thistles and other weeds.*

*British residents are joined by thousands of northern European siskins for the winter. The siskin is spread out over much of eastern Europe, across Russia into China and Japan.*

☐ areas where the bird stays all year
☐ areas where the bird is a summer visitor
☐ areas where the bird is a winter visitor

## NAMES
**SCIENTIFIC NAME:** *Carduelis spinus*
**NICKNAMES:** Aberdevine, Barley Bird

## IDENTIFICATION
**APPEARANCE:** a yellow-green finch; all have pale, stubby beaks, broad yellow bars across black wings and a deeply forked tail; in his breeding plumage the male has a black cap and bib with a brilliant yellow breast and rump; the female is browner and streakier; juvenile looks like a dull copy of the female
**SIZE:** 12cm (4³/₄in) long
**WINGSPAN:** 20-23cm (8-9in)
**WEIGHT:** 12-18g (³/₈-¹/₃oz)
**FLIGHT:** light and bounding
**VOICE:** these musical little finches chatter away to one another in loud, shrill *tsooee* and *teeyu* calls; the song is a whistling trill which ends on a low buzz

## FOOD
Seen hanging from alder and birch catkins and spruce and larch cones in search of seeds; visits gardens with peanut-feeders; feeds chicks on caterpillars and aphids

## BEHAVIOUR
Sociable bird that forages in flocks throughout the year; frequently travels around with redpolls and goldfinches during the winter
**ENEMIES:** shortage of food, bad weather

## BREEDING
**PAIRING UP:** pairing starts before the winter flocks split up; the male performs an elaborate aerial display over the tree-tops; usually rears 2 broods a year
**NESTING:** both male and female weave a compact nest from fine twigs, grass, moss and lichen and line it with hair, plant down and a few feathers; usually sited well out along a branch, high up in a pine tree
**EGGS:** 3-5 bluish-white eggs with brown, purple and pink streaks
**INCUBATION:** female sits for 12-13 days, fed by the male
**YOUNG:** the hatchlings are covered in long blue-grey down; fed insects by both parents, they are fledged in 13-15 days
**MOULT:** adults after breeding; juveniles replace only their body feathers in late summer and autumn
**LIFE EXPECTANCY:** 2-3 years

## POPULATION IN BRITAIN
As many as 360,000 pairs breed each year; up to an extra 500,000 arrive from Scandinavia to overwinter here

## HABITAT
Based in coniferous woodland and pine plantations during the breeding season; more nomadic at other times; often found in alder and birch groves in winter

## NATURE WATCH
● Siskin numbers increased largely as the result of the planting of subsidised commercial pine plantations. Now most of the grants have been withdrawn, the numbers of siskins may fall again.
● Ornamental conifers and peanut-nets in gardens may be their saving grace.

# The Song Thrush

## Distribution

*Despite falling numbers, the song thrush is still a common bird over much of Britain. Although most stay put for the whole year, some northerly ones move south for the winter. Many Scottish thrushes overwinter in Ireland and England. There they are joined by other migrant song thrushes that spent the summer in northern Europe. Some of these visitors spend the whole winter in the UK; others are just passing through, on their way to overwinter in southern Europe, and return the following spring.*

*In late September or early October, some young birds from southern England also fly off to winter quarters around the Mediterranean, notably in Spain and North Africa.*

☐ areas where the bird stays all year
☐ areas where the bird is a summer visitor
☐ areas where the bird is a winter visitor

## NAMES
**SCIENTIFIC NAME:** *Turdus philomelos*
**NICKNAMES:** Throstle, Mavis, Throggie

## IDENTIFICATION
**APPEARANCE:** adults have warm brown upperparts, while the breast has a creamy yellow wash and is neatly flecked with arrowhead-shaped spots; underwings are pale orange; male and female look identical; the juvenile's back is streaked with buff
**SIZE:** smaller than a blackbird; 22-24cm (8½-9½in) long from beak to tail
**WINGSPAN:** 33-36cm (13-14in)
**WEIGHT:** 70-90g (2⅓-3oz)
**FLIGHT:** swift and direct, flitting
**VOICE:** famed for its loud, sweet song featuring constant repetition of short phrases; soft *tsip* call in flight; urgent, shrill *tchick tchick* alarm cry

## FOOD
Consumes slugs, snails, worms, insects and berries; renowned for cracking snail shells on an anvil stone or patio paving

## BEHAVIOUR
Perches in the open to sing in the early morning and evening; otherwise quite shy, preferring to stay hidden in the undergrowth and among the trees; hops or runs on the ground
**ENEMIES:** environmental changes, bad weather, pesticides and hunters

## BREEDING
**PAIRING UP:** in March and April; rears 2, and up to 3 broods each year
**NESTING:** female builds a strong bowl-shaped nest of grass, moss and twigs and plasters the inside with mud, dung or rotten wood and saliva; up to 7.5m (25ft) off the ground in a dense bush, hedge or tree
**EGGS:** 4-6 bright blue eggs lightly dusted with black speckles in each clutch
**INCUBATION:** female sits for 11-15 days
**YOUNG:** the chicks hatch helpless, with a covering of golden down and a bright yellow lining in their mouths; fed by both parents, they fledge in 12-16 days
**MOULT:** loses and replaces feathers after the breeding season
**LIFE EXPECTANCY:** up to 5 years; over half the young thrushes reared in one season die during their first year

## POPULATION IN BRITAIN
Up to 1 million breeding pairs remain after numbers declined alarmingly in the second half of the 20th century

## HABITAT
Favours woods and copses, gardens and parks with plenty of cover

## NATURE WATCH
● At first glance or when it is partially concealed in bushes, a song thrush can easily be mistaken for a mistle thrush, but there are key differences: the song thrush is browner and reveals a pale orange colour under its wings in flight, rather than the mistle thrush's white.
● The song thrush also sings far more beautifully than a mistle thrush.

# The Starling

## Distribution

*Starlings live all over Britain. Their distribution seems to be governed by the availability of grassland to forage on and holes for nesting.*

*The starlings visiting your garden in the winter are unlikely to be the same birds that dropped in over the summer. From the end of September to mid-November many British starlings move south to spend the winter in France and Spain. At the same time a much larger number arrive from Scandinavia.*

*The starling is found all over the world, thanks to homesick settlers who took them to Australia and New Zealand. In 1872 one man took all the birds in Shakespeare's plays to America with him where starlings are now very common.*

**NAMES**
**SCIENTIFIC NAME:** *Sturnus vulgaris*
**NICKNAMES:** Stare, Starnel

**IDENTIFICATION**
**APPEARANCE:** the male's breeding plumage is a glossy iridescent black while the female's is duller with more buffy specks; after an autumn moult all adults have pale freckles; beak is yellow in summer, black in winter; juveniles are pale greyish-brown, moulting into adult plumage in autumn
**SIZE:** 21cm (8½in) long
**WINGSPAN:** 37-42cm (14½-16½in)
**WEIGHT:** 75-90g (2⅝-3¼oz)
**FLIGHT:** triangular wings create a typically 'arrowhead' silhouette; beat in rapid bursts interspersed with open and closed-wing glides
**VOICE:** song is a medley of whistles, clicks, gurgles, rattles and squawks; main call is a grating *tcheerr*; a skillful mimic, often copying other sounds

**FOOD**
Forages on the ground for insects and earthworms in the summer; also catches flying insects on the wing; eats fruit, berries and seeds in autumn and winter; flocks raid bird-tables for scraps

**BEHAVIOUR**
Bold, bustling, extremely sociable bird which gathers in colossal communal roosts at dusk in autumn and winter
**ENEMIES:** sparrowhawks, bad weather

**BREEDING**
**PAIRING UP:** breeds from April to July; rears 1, often 2 broods a year
**NESTING:** male selects a suitable hole for the nest, in a tree, cliff or building, and constructs a ramshackle nest of straw and dried grass which the female later lines with wool and hair
**EGGS:** 4-6 pale blue eggs
**INCUBATION:** both parents take turns to sit on the eggs for 12-13 days
**YOUNG:** hatchlings are clad in black down with a yellow lining to their mouths and a paler outline to gape; both parents supply their family with insects; chicks are fledged in 20-22 days
**MOULT:** adults moult in July; youngsters are still moulting their brown juvenile plumage in early autumn
**LIFE EXPECTANCY:** up to 5 years

**POPULATION IN BRITAIN**
Roughly 1.5 million pairs breed each year; population is three times bigger in winter, swollen by Continental migrants

areas where the bird stays all year
areas where the bird is a summer visitor
areas where the bird is a winter visitor

**HABITAT**
Common everywhere there is some open grassland for foraging or gardens for raiding and holes for nesting

**NATURE WATCH**
● Starling numbers are declining rapidly, especially on farmland, due in part to the extensive use of insecticides. Today's population is only about a third of what it was in the 1970s.
● The caustic droppings of thousands of starlings can seriously damage or kill off the trees they roost in.

# The Tawny Owl

## Distribution

*The tawny owl is the most widespread and common owl in Britain. There are no tawnies on Ireland, the Isle of Man and Isle of Wight. Their absence from Ireland probably reflects the way that ice retreated after the last Ice Age. The Irish Sea separated Ireland from the mainland before it was warm enough for trees to grow. Tawnies are also resident throughout Europe.*

*Woodland is more important to their distribution than geography. Fewer are found in unwooded areas, such as Dartmoor and the Fens, regardless of topography. Usually a pair stays in its woodland territory year after year, while the young owls spread out in the same wood and create their own territories.*

### NAMES
**SCIENTIFIC NAME:** *Strix aluco*
**NICKNAME:** Wood, Brown or Ivy Owl

### IDENTIFICATION
**APPEARANCE:** sexes look alike, with warm mottled brown feathers on the upperparts and pale buff underside streaked with brown; classic flat facial discs with huge dark eyes and vicious beak; juveniles are very fluffy when they leave the nest
**SIZE:** 37-39cm (14½-15½in) long ; females are slightly larger than males
**WINGSPAN:** 94-104cm (37-41in)
**WEIGHT:** 330-590g (12-21oz)
**FLIGHT:** slow but manoeuvrable
**VOICE:** male sings a deep, far-sounding mixture of short and quavering hoots: *hoo-hooh, hooo, hoo-hoo-hoo, hooooo-o-o-o-o-o*; female responds with a sharp *ke-wick*; chicks beg for food with a hoarse hissing *shee-eep*

### FOOD
Hunts at night, mainly for mice, voles and shrews on the woodland floor; also eats small birds, frogs, beetles and earthworms; crushes the skulls before swallowing its prey whole, head first; disgorges pellets of indigestible remains

### BEHAVIOUR
Defends a woodland territory which established pairs share in the winter; hooting heard in autumn and winter
**ENEMIES:** other owls and larger birds of prey, traffic, pesticides and cold weather

### BREEDING
**PAIRING UP:** March to June; usually rears 1 clutch a year, but in lean times none
**NESTING:** generally nests in a tree-hole with no lining; sometimes uses a building, a magpie's old nest or an abandoned drey
**EGGS:** 2-5 roundish white eggs laid at two-day intervals
**INCUBATION:** female starts sitting from the moment she lays her first egg; each egg takes 28-30 days to hatch
**YOUNG:** chicks are covered in white down; male brings carcasses to the nest which the female tears up and feeds to the chicks at first; later food is left for the chicks to swallow whole; they fledge in 32-37 days while still fluffy grey
**MOULT:** takes several years to replace the main flight feathers in easy stages
**LIFE EXPECTANCY:** many die in their first winter; after that may live up to 10 years

### POPULATION IN BRITAIN
About 20,000 breed each year

■ areas where the bird stays all year

### HABITAT
Found in woodland, well-wooded parks and gardens

### NATURE WATCH
● Tawny owls are frequent road casualties: low-flying tawnies get hit by car aerials, which often break a wing – an injury that usually proves fatal.
● If you hear a great hullabaloo of squawking and shrieking from a flock of excited birds while you are walking through woodland, try and track down the source. The noisy mob of songbirds might just give away the location of a tawny owl roosting in a tree.

# The Woodpigeon

## NAMES
**SCIENTIFIC NAME:** *Columba palumbus*
**NICKNAMES:** Ring Dove, Cushat, Culver

## IDENTIFICATION
**APPEARANCE:** the largest pigeon, with a small blue-grey head on a stout grey body with a pink-purple breast which is brighter in spring and summer; there are patches of glossy green, purple and white on either side of the neck and a white band on the wing; male and female look identical; juvenile is duller with no white on its neck
**SIZE:** 40-42cm (16-16½in) long
**WINGSPAN:** 75-80cm (30-32in)
**WEIGHT:** 480-550g (17-20oz)
**FLIGHT:** strong and fast; the clattering of wings on take-off serves as an alarm
**VOICE:** coos a lot from February to September; song has five notes – *coo-coo, coo-coo, coo* – repeated frequently

## FOOD
Eats a mainly vegetarian diet of grains, seeds and berries; also nibbles on buds, shoots and leaves; occasionally adds a few insects, snails and earthworms to its diet; visits gardens for scraps and seeds

## BEHAVIOUR
A wily, wary bird in the countryside where it is regarded as a pest, but much bolder in parks and gardens in towns and cities; very sociable, forming large winter flocks
**ENEMIES:** people with shotguns, birds of prey, jays, magpies and grey squirrels

## BREEDING
**PAIRING UP:** pair up with a lot of billing and cooing early in spring, maybe for life; rears 2, often 3 broods a year
**NESTING:** the male collects fine twigs which the female uses to construct a flimsy platform on a branch high up in a tree or hedge
**EGGS:** lays 2 roundish glossy white eggs
**INCUBATION:** male and female share the incubating for 17-19 days
**YOUNG:** young pigeons are called squabs; the hatchlings have a few strands of yellow down and long, flattened beaks; they grow very quickly, fed for the first week or so on a nourishing 'pigeon's milk' produced in the crops of both parents, then weaned on to partially digested seeds; fledged in 29-35 days
**MOULT:** as soon as breeding is over
**LIFE EXPECTANCY:** up to 10 years

## POPULATION IN BRITAIN
There are up to 5 million by the end of the breeding season each year

## Distribution
*The woodpigeon is an abundant and widespread resident in woodland, hedgerows, fields, towns and gardens across the British Isles. In fact, it is seen everywhere except on the higher hills of Scotland where there are few suitable woodland habitats.*

*Woodpigeons breed throughout Europe during the summer, spreading as far north as central Scandinavia, east into Russia, southeast to the Middle East and around the Mediterranean as far south as northwest Africa.*

*British woodpigeons stay here for the winter, forming into large flocks. Their numbers are increased by an influx of migrants from northern Europe in October and November.*

☐ areas where the bird stays all year
☐ areas where the bird is a summer visitor
☐ areas where the bird is a winter visitor

## HABITAT
Generally roosts and nests in woodland but forages over open arable farmland, pastures, playing fields and lawns

## NATURE WATCH
● Sowing cereal crops in autumn and the planting of oilseed rape has worked in the woodpigeon's favour. Numbers have doubled in the last 25 years.
● Stock doves may travel around with flocks of woodpigeons – the stock dove is the smaller, darker, bluer-grey pigeon with two short black wing bars.

# The Wren

## Distribution

*Wrens are numerous and widespread throughout the British Isles. Generally individuals do not move far from their home range. Very cold weather may drive some wrens south, occasionally as far as mainland Europe. In late September, a few migrants from the north of Europe may pass through southern England; some may even stay until the following spring.*

*The wren's range extends over most of Europe as far east as Japan. It is also found across North America. After colonising remote islands, off northern Scotland for example, different races have evolved in isolation. All these island races are larger, with shorter, rounder wings than the mainland wrens.*

☐ areas where the bird stays all year
☐ areas where the bird is a summer visitor
☐ areas where the bird is a winter visitor

## NAMES
**SCIENTIFIC NAME:** *Troglodytes troglodytes*
**NICKNAMES:** Wran, Stumpy, Jenny Wren

## IDENTIFICATION
**APPEARANCE:** the male and female look the same, with a dumpy, pear-shaped body and short cocked tail; nutbrown on top with dark banding on wings and tail; buff underparts with banded flanks; long, slightly curved, pointed dark brown beak; juveniles look slightly less distinctly banded than adults
**SIZE:** 9-10cm (3½-4in) long, including 2.5cm (1in) tail
**WINGSPAN:** 13-17cm (5¼-6⅔in)
**WEIGHT:** 8-13g (¼-½oz)
**FLIGHT:** straight, low and whirring
**VOICE:** male rattles off his short, loud and repetitive song all year; *tserr-tserr* when annoyed; loud *tit-tit-tit* like winding up a clockwork toy if alarmed

## FOOD
Great pest controller, eating lots of spiders, centipedes, woodlice, earwigs, aphids, flies and caterpillars from the ground under hedges or in thickets and on trees, bushes and undergrowth; in frosty weather, may visit a bird-table to eat breadcrumbs and mealworms

## BEHAVIOUR
Although largely invisible, this plucky little bird is more than prepared to speak its mind and stand up for itself
**ENEMIES:** cold weather and cats

## BREEDING
**PAIRING UP:** breeding lasts from mid-April to July; females raise two broods on their own; males are polygamous and may father four broods with two hens
**NESTING:** male builds several well-concealed but unfinished ball-shaped nests (called cock's nests) using dried leaves, grass and moss; lets his mate choose her favourite, which she lines with feathers and hair
**EGGS:** 5-7 white eggs with reddish spots
**INCUBATION:** female sits for 14-15 days
**YOUNG:** newly-hatched chicks covered in grey down; mouths lined in yellow with paler yellow flanges; fed by mother alone; fledged in 15-17 days; father helps with after-nest care for 2 weeks
**MOULT:** adults in late summer; male stops singing while his new feathers grow
**LIFE EXPECTANCY:** 2-3 years at most (cold winters take a devastating toll)

## POPULATION IN BRITAIN
Over 8 million breeding each summer

## HABITAT
Common anywhere there is low cover in dense undergrowth – in woods, parks and gardens, hedgerows, shrubberies, brackeny hillsides and gorsy cliff-tops

## NATURE WATCH
● Watch patiently and you may see a wren land on a fence or post, bob about and flick its tail before hurrying off again.
● You may also be lucky enough to catch sight of one busily inspecting the trunk of a tree or hopping from plant to plant in a flowerbed, looking for insects.

# The Yellowhammer

## Distribution

*Yellowhammers are the commonest bunting in Britain, enjoying a patchy yet widespread distribution. Populations are concentrated in eastern Britain and the Midlands but they are rarely seen in London. They are far less common in the uplands of Wales, northern England and Scotland. In recent years there have been many fewer yellowhammers in Ireland, especially in the north.*

*The yellowhammer is present throughout the year; breeding birds flock in winter with little sign of emigration. Immigrants from northern Europe arrive on the east coast of Britain from the end of September until late November and leave again in March to mid-May.*

☐ areas where the bird stays all year
☐ areas where the bird is a summer visitor
☐ areas where the bird is a winter visitor

## NAMES
**SCIENTIFIC NAME:** *Emberiza citrinella*
**NICKNAMES:** Yellow Bunting, Yorling

## IDENTIFICATION
**APPEARANCE:** in spring the male's head, neck and underparts are bright yellow streaked with brownish red; his upperparts are rich reddish-brown with broad black streaks; females are duller and smudgier; all adults have chestnut rumps and longish tails with white outer feathers; juveniles are streakier with a tinge of yellow
**SIZE:** 16-16.5cm (6½in) long
**WINGSPAN:** 23-29.5cm (9¼-11¾in)
**WEIGHT:** 24-30g (¾-1oz)
**FLIGHT:** jerky and undulating
**VOICE:** song is a rush of short reedy notes and sounds like *a-little-bit-of-bread-and-no-cheese*; tinkly *tink*, *tweek* or *twink* contact calls; *twick*, *trit* or *tillip* flight calls

## FOOD
Eats seeds and grains, except when feeding its chicks mainly on insects

## BEHAVIOUR
The cock yellowhammer sings tirelessly from the tops of hedges and bushes throughout the summer; except during the breeding season, it is sociable and travels about in flocks, often with other seed-eaters
**ENEMIES:** agricultural changes, nest-robbers and severe winters

## BREEDING
**PAIRING UP:** from April to August; courtship involves flirtatious chases ending up with the two birds tumbling to the ground; male sings from song-post above the nest site; rears 2 or 3 broods a year
**NESTING:** female builds quite a large nest on or near the ground at the bottom of a hedge or bush or in a clump of grass or nettles; it is made of grass, straw and moss lined with horsehair
**EGGS:** lays 4-6 pale lilac eggs with strange purplish-brown squiggles all over
**INCUBATION:** female does most of the incubating for 12-14 days
**YOUNG:** hatchlings are scantily covered in grey down with pink lining to mouth; fed by both parents; leave nest after 14 days
**MOULT:** loses old feathers and grows new ones in the autumn
**LIFE EXPECTANCY:** up to 9 years

## POPULATION IN BRITAIN
Up to 700,000 pairs breed each year

## HABITAT
Frequents hedgerows, bushy heath, commons and scrubland

## NATURE WATCH
● Yellowhammers used to subsist on spilt grains in stubble fields in the winter. The switch from spring to autumn cereal-sowing has been bad news for them.
● The loss of hedgerows is also a problem for yellowhammers, as they rely on hedges to furnish nesting sites and elevated song-posts.

# INDEX